SHADOW
OF A
DOUBT

One case. One truth.
Everything on the line.

Written By

Cordell Parvin

ISBN:

Hardcover: 978-1-967828-35-7

Paperback: 978-1-967828-37-1

Published by:
Pine Book Writing
www.PineBookWriting.com
R-10225 Yonge St Suite #250, Richmond Hill, ON L4C 3B2,
Canada.

Printed in the United States of America

Prologue

His source was ten minutes late. In his line of work, that could mean death. Reyes pressed his back against the wet brick and surveyed the narrow alley behind the Blue Marlin Pub. Puddles collected in the uneven dips of the concrete, reflecting neon fragments from the bar's faded sign. The Blue Marlin was a run-down pub in South Dallas, frequented by off-duty cops and weary city workers. It was the perfect cover for what Reyes had to do.

His shoes squished on the wet pavement as he moved deeper into the alley. The air stank of stale beer and soggy cigarette butts. A cat lounged atop the dumpster, watching him with lazy indifference before slipping into the shadows.

A voice, barely audible over the ceaseless patter of rain, emerged from behind a stack of discarded wooden pallets. "You Reyes?" it asked.

"Yeah," Reyes replied quietly, his eyes scanning every shadow for potential onlookers. "You're late."

A figure stepped forward from the gloom. The man was partially hidden beneath the brim of a pulled-down baseball cap. Reyes guessed he was in his mid-forties, the man's eyes flicking between him and the alley's exits, adding tension to features already drawn tight. His clothes were deliberately plain, a choice Reyes recognized from past encounters with sources on the edge of revealing secrets that could destroy lives, including their own.

"Almost didn't come," the man admitted, hastily wiping rain from his face with a trembling hand. "They're watching. Morrison has people everywhere."

Reyes offered only a curt nod, knowing that sources always imagined eyes in the shadows. In matters involving men like Phillip Morrison, such fears were rarely unfounded. Morrison, the powerful oil tycoon, cast a long, sinister shadow over Dallas, his influence stretching from corporate boardrooms to city hall. Men like him collected politicians as if they were mere trading cards.

"You said you had something solid," Reyes pressed, impatience sharpening his tone. Standing in one place too long was a liability.

Glancing over his shoulder, the informant reached beneath his raincoat and pulled out a battered leather briefcase. Over the years, Reyes had seen older lawyers carrying critical documents in briefcases like this one. Once expensive-looking, the case now bore the marks of water damage and rough handling.

"Don't let anyone see these papers," he hissed, thrusting the case into Reyes's hands with a force that belied his anxious demeanor. "Morrison would kill you to keep this quiet. Do you understand?"

The briefcase was heavier than Reyes expected. The man looked genuinely terrified, a stark contrast to the feigned fear Reyes had often seen in others. His pupils widened, and his gaze flicked from shadow to shadow, never settling.

"What am I looking at?" Reyes asked. Keep him talking, he told himself. The more they talked, the more they leaked.

"Everything you need," the man replied in a voice lowered to a whisper. "Dates, locations, photographs. Morrison is not just a crook. He's in bed with the cartel. They order hits on anyone who crosses them."

A car passed by the alley's entrance, its headlights briefly illuminating the space between the buildings. The informant flinched and pressed himself against the wall.

"I've done my part," he murmured, already beginning to retreat. "If this gets traced back to me..."

"It won't," Reyes assured him, though both knew such promises were as fragile as the night's safety. "Did you make copies?"

He shook his head. "Too dangerous. That's all I got. Make it count."

Before Reyes could ask another question, the informant turned and swiftly moved toward the far end of the alley. His footsteps splashed in the puddles until the rain-drenched darkness swallowed him. Reyes was left alone, water trickling down his neck as he clutched a briefcase that now felt alarmingly like a ticking bomb.

Reyes stepped into a recessed doorway to get out of the rain and carefully opened the case. He found a thick manila folder inside, and beneath it, a USB drive was taped to the bottom. As he flipped open the folder, his pulse began to quicken.

The top document was a high-resolution photograph showing Morrison shaking hands with Carlos Delgado, a mid-level cartel member, whom Reyes recognized from DEA wanted posters. The photo was dated three months earlier, taken at a private airstrip where, in the blurry background, Morrison's private jet was barely discernible.

Reyes flipped through photo after photo, each one more revealing than the last. One showed Morrison dining with two known cartel associates, another captured him entering a warehouse with property records attached that tied the building to a shell corporation connected to his oil business. Every image was carefully labeled with names, dates, and locations. Reyes's journalistic instincts kicked in. This wasn't the story he had expected to tell, but if true, it had the markings of something more sinister.

Interspersed among the photographs were documents: bank statements detailing suspicious transfers, shipping manifests with discrepancies in cargo weights, and emails filled with coded language, each accompanied by helpful translations. The informant had been thorough, assembling a case that linked Morrison's legitimate business interests with cartel money laundering and smuggling operations.

The deeper he looked, the murkier the financial picture became. At first, he had suspected cartel pressure or extortion, the kind of quiet threats other U.S. oil companies had faced south of the border. But now, with the contents of the briefcase laid out before him, the story had shifted. This wasn't about a company being targeted. It looked more like cooperation. If what he was seeing held up, Morrison was a collaborator, tied to Mexican criminal networks that reached far beyond oil rigs and boardrooms.

As rain dripped from a leaky gutter above and landed on the folder, Reyes quickly closed it and returned the documents to the briefcase. Even in the cool night air, his hands were all clammy. He couldn't get over the idea of a top businessman in the city, who usually supported political campaigns and charity events, being connected to such violent people, or even why Morrison had decided to drill in Mexico in the first place.

Why Morrison made this deal didn't matter right now. What mattered was proving it and staying ahead of whoever might already be on his trail. Don Thompson had backed Reyes's investigations before, but this revelation would demand serious legal vetting. Pursuing Phillip Morrison meant bracing for an onslaught of lawyers and retribution that extended far beyond the courtroom. Men like Morrison did not accept defeat.

Zipping the briefcase into a large plastic bag, Reyes shielded it from the rain. He contemplated the dangerous knowledge he carried: publishing this story could ruin lives, while silence would let Morrison operate with impunity.

Reyes stepped toward the street, his footsteps merging with the unending rhythm of the rainfall. Far off, the city was humming along, unaware of the explosive hidden in his bag, a secret that could turn Dallas upside down.

The informant had risked everything. Now Reyes had to decide what to do with it. One carefully reported and fully substantiated story might finally do what years of law enforcement had failed to achieve: expose Phillip Morrison for the man he truly was.

Reyes emerged from the alley, his eyes scanning the street for any sign of surveillance. Finding none, he melted into the sparse late-night pedestrian traffic, a solitary figure hurrying home in the rain, burdened knowing that what he'd been given could bring down an empire.

#

Murder

He pulled his collar tighter against the relentless rain and quickened his pace, eager to reach a dry place. The satchel pressed into his side, reminding him what was inside. Ten years of instinct told him to find shelter where he could meticulously examine the documents his informant had provided.

Just a block away lay a street where taxis occasionally passed, promising discreet transportation to the sanctuary of his apartment. There, behind closed doors, he would spread the documents across his desk and begin constructing the story that would ultimately bring Phillip Morrison to ruin. The exhilarating prospect poured adrenaline through his veins, affirming the very reason he had taken up journalism.

Water dripped relentlessly from his hair into his eyes; he wiped it away with one hand while firmly gripping his satchel with the other. As he walked, the rhythmic clack of his shoes on the wet pavement echoed too loudly between the imposing buildings, a sound that betrayed his location. In that moment, he slowed, acutely aware that every hurried step was a beacon to anyone lurking in the shadows.

He paused, listening to the nocturnal symphony: the staccato patter of rain against metal dumpsters, the distant murmur of traffic, and the fading strains of music emanating from the Blue Marlin. Yet amid these sounds, something else seized his attention. His gaze swept over an alley where only water cascaded steadily toward storm drains.

Taking another step forward, he halted, struck by the unnerving sensation of being watched. He was quite familiar with this territory, recognizing it as the prelude to a narrative that would unsettle those in positions of power and authority. Sometimes, a quiet paranoia crept in like a whisper in the dark. He had learned to accept the challenge of telling fear from fact.

"Hello?" he called out, immediately regretting the breach of silence. In his line of work, professional journalists maintained their distance, observing, recording, and remaining unseen until their byline graced the front page. The rain was his only reply, its steady patter against pavement and metal filling the void.

Leaving the pause behind, he resumed walking at a faster pace, no longer troubled by the sound of his footsteps. He moved toward the streetlight, needing the cover of traffic and people nearby. His eyes strained to see, and he perceived a dark figure approaching, its presence too purposeful to be accidental or coincidental.

The figure straightened, emerging as a stark silhouette in the faint light filtering from the street. Of average height and athletic build, the stranger's face was concealed beneath a black ski mask, signaling that he was no random mugger but a professional operative. Even as his muscles tensed in readiness to run, the journalist's mind swiftly calculated the distance to safety against the probable pace of his pursuer. The outcome seemed grim.

"The briefcase," the figure stated, his voice unnervingly flat, as if deliberately masking its natural cadence. "Just give me what the man gave you, and we can avoid unpleasantness."

The journalist's fingers instinctively tightened around the satchel, his primal instincts flaring as he felt a sudden need to protect its contents. He hadn't seen everything inside, but he trusted what the informant had handed over would back up months of reporting.

"I don't know what you're talking about," he replied, stepping back cautiously. "I'm just a guy walking home from a bar."

The figure emitted a small, almost disappointed sound before a gloved right hand emerged from the shadows, revealing a silver-plated revolver. The barrel caught the faint glow of a distant streetlamp, its expensive appearance incongruous with the otherwise unremarkable figure. Despite the overwhelming fear, the journalist's sharp mind meticulously recorded each detail, from the gun's gleaming surface to the likely caliber .357. This was someone who left no trace.

"Last chance," the figure intoned, raising the revolver. "The documents."

In that fleeting, almost imperceptible moment, a torrent of thoughts, each as sharp and urgent as a breaking news headline, flooded the journalist's mind: should he run, should he fight, or should he surrender the satchel, the object of so much intrigue and danger? Yet none of these options held a promising future. The seconds stretched interminably between them.

"Who sent you?" he inquired, a desperate ploy to buy time, his eyes searching for an opening. "Morrison?"

The assailant raised the gun, its cold metal aimed squarely at his chest. The question was interrupted by the flash and crack of a gunshot, striking his shoulder. The force spun him partially around, and although the pain took a moment to register, it swiftly cascaded into a searing agony that nearly bowed his knees.

As he stumbled backward, his free hand frantically covered the fresh wound, hot blood welling between his fingers in stark contrast to the cold rain. He struggled to grasp the escalating violence, his mind reeling.

A second shot thundered into his chest, a deeper, more venomous pain that sapped his strength. His legs buckled, unready to support his weight, and he slid against a cold brick wall, leaving a crimson trail as he fell.

The assailant advanced with mechanical precision, the revolver unflinchingly tracking his descent. The journalist's pleas for answers and attempts at negotiation were met only by a wet, blood-sprayed cough that rasped into the rainy air, a stark and horrifying response.

Then came the third shot, a concussive blow to his temple, the world tilting around him. His cheek scraped harshly against the rough brick as gravity claimed him.

He hit the ground with brutal finality, his satchel tumbling from his grasp. Upon impact, the clasp broke, releasing a flood of evidence and the results of years of meticulous work that cascaded across the wet, glistening pavement. Water seeped into the manila folder, diluting the crimson splatter that stained it while photographs of Morrison curled at the edges under the relentless assault of rain, his once-assured smile marred by streaks of blood.

Watching in despair, he saw his vision narrow, the world becoming a dim tunnel of blurry light and shadows, as each piece of evidence and fragment of his legacy dissolved into red-tinted streams carried away by rainwater.

Through his dimming eyes, he observed the assailant kneeling to gather the scattered papers. With deliberate, methodical precision, the gloved hands collected each photograph, bank statement, and annotated email, reassembling them into order before slipping the folder back into the satchel.

An instinctive movement to reach for his phone, to summon help or record one last fact, proved futile. Blood pooling under his head mixed with the rainwater, a grim sign that his life was ending tragically, his body failing him.

As he looked back, he regretted missing the meeting with Don and not keeping his promises to call his parents in Austin or reassure the woman seeking more commitment than he could give. In that dark, rain-soaked alley, everything he had worked for was gone in seconds.

The assailant rose and placed the briefcase next to Reyes' body. In the dim haze of encroaching darkness, the revolver was raised one final time. Though the journalist wished to close his eyes and escape the pain, he had neither the strength nor the control.

The ending shot, subtle and conclusive, marked the end of a story never to be written. The assailant stepped over the lifeless body with calm, deliberate movements. As the echo of his footsteps merged with the sound of the rain and a heartbeat slowing to silence, the distinction between sound and oblivion faded.

The last thing he saw was the neon shimmer of the Blue Marlin's sign reflected in a shallow pool of rain and blood. Red and blue light rippled across the pavement before everything went dark.

Chapter One

Two years in Washington had left Gabriela with an impressive collection of accolades, yet a persistent hollowness had settled within her. The overcast gray sky outside her office windows mirrored the dimming of the initial fire that had propelled her into politics. What had once felt like an office brimming with potential now seemed more like a repository of good intentions swallowed by the grinding gears of the capital.

She'd arrived in Washington with a clear vision: to build a lasting career as a powerful voice for change, fueled by the same fierce determination that had driven her in the courtroom. But the endless compromises, the partisan gridlock, and the slow, often imperceptible pace of progress had chipped away at that idealism, leaving behind a sense of opportunities lost and dreams deferred. Gabriela lingered on the seal of Congress, then placed the final certificate into her briefcase.

Towering windows framed the Washington skyline, the monuments and domes shrouded in a blanket of winter clouds. She'd spent countless hours fixed on that view, drafting legislation that committees would later gut or partisan squabbles would bury.

Her hands worked with practiced precision. She wrapped each item with care and placed it in the sleek, black leather briefcase that had once carried briefs and motions instead of congressional mementos. The tactile routine steadied her mind, silencing the second-guessing that had shadowed her for months.

She lifted a framed photograph of Congressman Moreno and herself at their first campaign stop in McAllen, remembering how he'd persuaded her to run for his seat in Congress when he decided to retire. His arm was draped around her shoulders, both of them squinting into the Texas sun, their smiles wide with the certainty of the untested.

"You have fire, Gabriela," he'd told her that day. "Washington needs your voice."

Gabriela wrapped the frame in tissue paper, wondering if her voice had ever been heard over the cackling of career politicians and the whispers of lobbyists. Perhaps it had been naive to think one freshman representative could make a difference in a system designed to reward longevity over principle.

Next came her leather-bound notebook, its edges worn soft from constant handling. Gabriela flipped through pages filled with her handwriting. It was neat at first, then messier as sessions wore on. Notes on border policy, healthcare reform, and educational initiatives. Lists of promises she'd made to herself and her constituents. Diagrams of coalition-building strategies that had evaporated like morning dew under the heat of partisan sunlight.

She'd written her acceptance speech in this notebook, scratching out and rewriting phrases until they sang with the rhythm of possibility. She remembered practicing in front of her bathroom mirror, the echo of her voice against tile a poor rehearsal for the roar of the crowd on election night.

A series of polished plaques came next, including her recognition from the Hispanic Chamber of Commerce, the Texas Women in Politics Association, and the National Education Alliance. Gabriela traced the engraved letters of her name, remembering the rubber chicken dinners and perfunctory applause. She had thought the awards were meaningful at the time, tangible proof that she was making an impact. Now, they stood as participation trophies for a game where the rules kept changing.

With measured motions, she silenced the clatter of papers, sorting through the desk's remaining contents. Policy briefs on immigration reform that had died in committee. Letters from constituents seeking help navigating byzantine federal agencies, thanks for small victories, disappointment when she couldn't deliver on promises that had seemed so achievable on the campaign trail.

Gabriela ran her fingers along the surface of a vintage push-pin map of Texas that hung beside her desk. She had placed red pins in every Rio Grande Valley town she'd visited during her campaign. She'd kept adding pins during her term, tracking field office openings, town halls, and district visits. The map was densely populated with these markers of connection, each representing faces and names and stories she'd carried with her to Washington.

She slid the map from the wall with a steady hand, rolling it into a tight cylinder. This, at least, had been real, it included the connections she'd made with the people she represented. Everything else was a compromise and concession that led nowhere meaningful.

She paused to glance at the framed photo still sitting on the corner of her desk. It had been taken on her parents' porch in Harlingen. Her mother stood proudly behind a table full of homemade tamales, wearing the same apron she always wore at Christmas. Her father smiled beside her, arms around her two brothers and their families. Gabriela stood in the center, mid-laugh, with her niece on her shoulders. That afternoon had been filled with family, laughter, and her father's stories from the courtroom. It reminded her of what mattered most.

Leaving Congress didn't mean walking away from purpose. It meant returning to the roots that shaped her. In that house, she wasn't Congresswoman Sanchez. She was just Gabriela, daughter of Roberto and Alita, part of something bigger than ambition.

The top drawer of her desk contained the usual office supplies, including pens bearing the congressional seal, notepads, paper clips, and rubber bands. She swept them into a box without ceremony. The middle drawer held more personal items with a bottle of Advil that had seen heavy use during budget negotiations, a compact mirror, and a spare pair of earrings for unexpected press conferences.

The bottom drawer was where she kept the things that mattered most. There were family photos, including one of her parents on the day they became U.S. citizens, their faces shining with pride; a handwritten note from her favorite Notre Dame Law School professor after she won her first major case in the Rio Grande Valley; a smooth river stone from the banks of the Rio Grande that she'd carried for luck since childhood.

She placed these items into her purse rather than the briefcase. They weren't part of Congresswoman Sanchez. They belonged to Gabriela.

As she emptied each drawer, memories surfaced. The late-night strategy sessions dissolved into ordering takeout and swapping courtroom war stories with her staff. The crushing defeat when her bill to reform immigration detention policies died without even reaching the floor for a vote. All that work. All those late nights drafting, lobbying... for nothing. The unexpected alliance with a conservative colleague on criminal justice reform had given her a fleeting taste of what bipartisanship could accomplish.

She'd come to Washington burning with purpose, determined to be a voice for those who'd been systematically silenced. She'd left Notre Dame law with a similar fire, but in the courtroom, she'd found ways to channel that energy into tangible results. In Congress, the victories were rarer and more symbolic, the defeats numerous and soul-crushing. The truth was, this wasn't the path she had imagined for her legal career.

Her eyes fell on the leather briefcase, now filled with the physical artifacts of her congressional career. It was the same briefcase her father had given her when she finished law school. The worn leather felt like an old friend, reminding her of the rush of standing before a judge, the chess match of cross-examination, and the sweet satisfaction of winning in court. That was where she belonged. Not in endless meetings and pointless debates.

Chuck Green called in the spring of 2024, just when she needed it most. By that point, Gabriela's disillusionment with Washington politics had reached its peak. She couldn't do this anymore. "The firm needs you, Gabriela," he'd said, his voice warm with genuine re-election affection beneath its usual gravitas. "Dallas needs you. Don't run for. Come back home to Parker & McEvoy."

Home. The word didn't bring to mind her D.C. apartment or even her childhood house in the Valley, but her office at Parker & McEvoy, her steady assistant Lucia, and the courtroom tension she had come to expect. On that day in early spring, Gabriela announced she would not run for re-election in November.

She removed her congressional pin from her lapel and placed it in a small velvet box. She'd worn it every day as a symbol of her responsibility, a reminder of the trust placed in her by her constituents. Now, it felt like a weight being lifted.

The decision not to run for re-election had been difficult. She had run to serve her hometown community, but she had accomplished nothing that made a difference in their lives.

She glanced at the clock. Her driver would be waiting downstairs to take her to the airport. Her furniture and most of her clothes had already been shipped to her condo in Dallas. All that remained was to close this door and open another.

Standing in the center of the empty office, she permitted herself one final moment of reflection. The room seemed smaller now, the ceiling lower, the walls closer. Or perhaps she had grown.

She flicked off the lights and pulled the door shut behind her, the latch clicking with quiet finality. The nameplates would be changed by morning, and the space prepared for Victor Herrera would take her place in the next session.

As she walked down the marble-floored corridor toward the elevator, her heels echoing in the emptiness, she felt the first stirrings of something she hadn't experienced in months. The halls of Congress had taught her valuable lessons about power and persuasion, about the art of the possible and the price of principles.

Gabriela exited the marble-floored corridor of the congressional building. Outside, the security guard, a Vietnam veteran with a permanent squint and a penchant for weather predictions, nodded in silent acknowledgment of her departure. The late afternoon air carried a bite that penetrated her wool coat, Washington's parting gift.

"Heading back to Texas, Congresswoman?" he asked, his voice gravelly from decades of cigarettes and outdoor shifts.

"Former Congresswoman," she corrected him while smiling. "And yes. Back to Dallas."

He nodded, his eyes crinkling at the corners. "They've got better weather there. And better barbecue."

Gabriela smiled, appreciating his simple assessment. Washington was a complex city, but sometimes it came down to weather and food. "You're not wrong about that."

Gabriela's driver's limo waited at the curb, its sleek black exterior gleaming even under the dull winter sky. John had been her driver from her first day in Congress. She slid into the back seat, the butter-soft leather greeting her like an old friend. The interior smelled of subtle citrus and cedarwood. During her time in Washington, John drove her to the airport and drove her around the city in inclement weather.

The car's engine purred to life, and John eased away from the curb, merging into the early evening traffic departing Capitol Hill. As they navigated the streets, the city offered fleeting glimpses of its vibrant tapestry: a young staffer in a rumpled suit clutching a coffee cup, an older woman walking impeccably groomed poodles, and tourists huddled around a map, debating their next destination.

Driving along Independence Avenue, they passed the Supreme Court building. Its imposing facade once inspired reverence in her; now, she viewed it through a lawyer's discerning eyes. It was a place where legal theories were tested and constitutional principles upheld or challenged, swayed by prevailing philosophies.

She'd argued before the Texas Supreme Court twice but never before the nine justices in Washington. That ambition had been set aside when she ventured into politics. Now, as they drove past the building, she allowed herself to resurrect that dream. Perhaps someday, she'd stand at that podium, her voice resonating within that hallowed chamber.

Crossing the Potomac River via the 14th Street Bridge, the Washington Monument came into view, its obelisk reaching toward the cloud-laden sky. Gabriela recalled attending a Fourth of July celebration there during her first summer in Congress. She'd mingled with colleagues, exchanging pleasantries and seeking support for a healthcare amendment she championed, all while fireworks illuminated the night sky.

As they continued onto the George Washington Memorial Parkway, the Jefferson Memorial appeared, its dome reflecting off the Tidal Basin's serene waters. The journey to Ronald Reagan Washington National Airport was brief, but each landmark they passed stirred memories and reflections, marking the intersection of her past aspirations and future ambitions.

Her mind drifted to memories of particularly heated congressional debates. There had been a border security bill in her first year that had devolved into thinly veiled racial invective. She'd stood at her desk on the House floor, gripping its edge until her knuckles whitened, delivering a speech that had later been described as "scorching" by the Washington Post. The momentary satisfaction of speaking truth to power had faded when the final bill passed anyway, its most draconian provisions intact.

Then, there had been the education funding battle, where she'd successfully secured additional resources for schools in underserved communities, only to watch as implementation guidelines rendered those resources inaccessible to the very students they were meant to help. The regulatory maze had proven as challenging as the legislative one.

She'd maintained her composure in public, reserving frustrations for private moments like when she was pounding the treadmill in the congressional gym at midnight or sipping tequila alone while drafting futile amendments.

John, her driver for the past two years, pulled up to the curb. The drive to Reagan National Airport had been swift and familiar.

A few hours later, Gabriela collected her luggage at DFW's Terminal C and stepped outside into the bright Texas sun, awaiting her favorite Dallas driver.

She'd departed as a rising star in Dallas courtrooms, carrying the hopes of constituents eager for change. Now, she returned as... what, exactly? A former congresswoman? A once-again attorney? A political has-been or a legal comeback story? The narrative remained to be written.

As she waited outside the terminal, her cell phone vibrated. She took the phone out of her purse and saw the caller ID on the screen: "Chuck Green" glowed in bold letters.

Her pulse quickened. Chuck rarely called directly. He preferred to have his assistant set up calls in advance, allowing him to prepare and ensuring that his time was used efficiently. A direct call when she'd just landed at DFW suggested urgency, Gabriela had not expected.

She touched her phone. "Chuck. This is a surprise."

"Gabriela." His voice filled the car, as resonant and authoritative as she remembered. Chuck Green had a voice made for the courtroom. It was clear enough to carry to the back row, warm enough to put juries at ease, and steady enough to unnerve even seasoned opposing counsel. "Where are you?"

"I just landed at DFW, and I'm waiting to be picked up."

"Good, good." There was a brief pause, the sound of papers rustling. "Listen, I know you just got back, but we need to talk as soon as possible. There's a case—a big one—and we need you on it."

She felt a flicker of irritation. She'd just left Washington four hours ago, hadn't even had time to get back to her North Dallas condo and unpack her suitcase, and already Chuck was trying to pull her into a major case. But the irritation was tempered by curiosity and, if she was honest with herself, a spark of interest.

"What kind of case?" She asked, keeping her tone neutral.

"Murder." The word hung in the air, stark and unadorned. "The rich oilman Phillip Morrison is accused of murdering the journalist Ethan Reyes. I'll tell you all about it when we can meet in person."

#

Gabriela failed to see her driver, who had stopped at the curb. "Murder? Phillip Morrison? It's going to be a media circus."

"It already is," Chuck confirmed. "Which is precisely why we need you, Gabriela. You handled the Duval case and kept him out of prison despite overwhelming public opinion against him. Morrison is one of Duval's best friends, and he needs that same kind of representation."

The Hope Riley case had been her last major trial before running for Congress. She'd mounted a successful defense, but taking on her defense during COVID and waiting a year before the Dallas courts reopened had drained her. The year-long delay and pressure to win had driven her to give in to Congressman Moreno and go back to The Valley and run for Congress.

"Chuck," she said, measuring her words, "I just arrived in Dallas. I haven't been in a courtroom for over two years. I'm not sure I'm prepared to jump into another high-profile case right now." Even as she said it, Gabriela recognized the halfhearted nature of her objection.

"Gabriela, we need you on this case that could redefine everything," Chuck's voice took on the persuasive cadence she'd heard him use with reluctant witnesses and hesitant clients. "This isn't just another rich man in trouble. There are political implications, media manipulation, and possibly even corruption in the prosecutor's office. It's exactly the kind of complex situation where your skills shine brightest."

"What's the timeline?" Gabriela asked, neither accepting nor rejecting the opportunity yet.

"We need to move quickly on building a defense strategy."

"The evidence against him?" She continued her cross-examination of Chuck.

"Circumstantial but compelling. They found Reyes's blood in Morrison's car. Cell phone data places Morrison near the murder scene. And Reyes had been working on a series of articles about Morrison's business dealings with shady characters."

Chuck's bare outline of the case presented the kind of challenging facts that would require every bit of her strategic thinking and courtroom skills. The kind that would consume her days and nights for months to come. The kind that would thrust her back into the spotlight she'd ostensibly left behind in Washington.

"Let me get settled first," she said. "I'll meet with you when I get settled in my Dallas home."

"Tomorrow?" Chuck pressed. "The Morrison family is getting anxious. They specifically requested you."

She suppressed a sigh. "Fine. Tomorrow morning. Calloway Office Building at nine?"

"Perfect." The relief in Chuck's voice was unmistakable. "And Gabriela, it's good to have you back. The firm hasn't been the same without you."

She knew that the firm had done well without her, but she appreciated Chuck's thought. After they disconnected, Gabriela rode home in silence, already thinking about the Morrison case.

The next morning, she drove downtown. Dallas had changed during her absence. There were new glass towers punctuating the skyline, their surfaces reflecting the gray sky in fractured patterns. Yet the city's peculiar blend of Southern hospitality and naked ambition, old Texas money mingling with new technological wealth, and conservative tradition coexisting with progressive pockets remained.

She turned onto Field Street, heading towards Ross Avenue, muscle memory guiding her through traffic patterns that had shifted slightly during her absence. The Calloway Office building rose before her, fifty-six stories of steel and smoked glass housing some of the most prestigious law firms, financial institutions, and corporate headquarters in the Southwest. Parker & McEvoy occupied the fiftieth through the fifty-sixth floors.

Turning from Field Street into the parking garage, she rolled down her window and pressed her palm against the scanner, half-expecting rejection. Instead, it beeped cheerfully, and the barrier arm rose in welcome. Apparently, Chuck had ensured her biometrics had been kept active despite her two-year absence.

She descended into the cool dimness of the garage and navigated past rows of luxury vehicles—BMWs, Mercedes, and Lexuses predominantly, with the occasional Ferrari or Porsche announcing a partner who prioritized flash over practicality.

Gabriela's assigned space on Level 3, Section E, waited for her like a faithful retainer. The painted white lines and her name stenciled in block letters—G. SANCHEZ—seemed to welcome her back to the fold. She eased her car between the lines and cut the engine, sitting for a moment in the sudden silence.

She gathered her briefcase and purse, checked her appearance in the rearview mirror, and stepped out of the car. The concrete floor of the garage still bore the same faint oil stains near the elevator that she remembered from before. Some things, at least, were constant.

The parking garage elevator was empty when it arrived, its interior lined with brushed steel that reflected her image in distorted fragments. She pressed the button for the main lobby, and the doors slid closed with a pneumatic sigh. The elevator rose swiftly, numbers illuminating in sequence, carrying her toward the surface world again.

The main lobby of the Calloway building showcased Texas prosperity with soaring ceilings, marble floors veined with gold, and a massive sculpture of abstract bronze forms that suggested either corporate ascendance or ecological disaster, depending on one's perspective. Security guards in tailored uniforms monitored the entrance points with professional vigilance, their earpieces occasionally crackling with coded communications.

Her heels clicking against the marble with metronomic precision, she crossed the polished expanse toward the elevators. The sound echoed in the cavernous space, announcing her presence to anyone who cared to listen. A few heads turned to look at her, recognizing another of their species, perhaps, or simply people responding to the confident cadence of her stride.

The elevator that would take me to the Parker & McEvoy offices required a key card for access. She withdrew the one Chuck had couriered to her condo the previous day and swiped it through the reader. Another beep of recognition.

The elevator rose smoothly, the rich mahogany walls and gleaming brass fixtures designed to instill a sense of quiet power. It was a moving vault, a space where legal battles were fought and won.

As the elevator rose, so did her awareness of returning to professional heights she had temporarily abandoned. Each floor represented another layer of the legal ecosystem of Dallas, with mid-sized firms on the lower levels, then boutique specialists, then finally the rarefied air of one of the top-tier law firms in Dallas.

When the doors opened on the fifty-sixth floor, Gabriela stepped directly into the reception area of Parker & McEvoy. The space was designed to impress without intimidating, with warm wood tones softening the modern lines of the furniture, carefully selected artwork by Texas artists adorning walls painted in neutral tones, and fresh floral arrangements providing bursts of controlled natural beauty.

The reception desk itself was a massive slab of polished black granite, behind which sat Diane Bradley. Diane had been the firm's receptionist for nearly thirty years, outlasting managing partners, market downturns, and dramatic changes in office technology. Her silver hair was styled in the same elegant bob she'd worn since Gabriela had first joined the firm as an associate, and her pearls, rumored to be an appreciation gift from a grateful client, gleamed against her cream-colored blouse.

Diane glanced up from her computer screen, her professional smile freezing momentarily before blooming into genuine delight. She rose from her chair with surprising grace for a woman in her sixties and came around the desk, arms outstretched.

"Gabriela!" she exclaimed, enfolding her in an affectionate embrace that smelled of Chanel No. 5 and peppermint tea. "You're back!"

Gabriela returned the hug, surprised by how much this simple welcome affected her. In Washington, greetings had been strategic with handshakes calibrated to convey just the right amount of dominance or deference, embraces performed for the benefit of cameras or constituents. Diane's unvarnished pleasure at seeing her again was refreshingly sincere.

"It's good to see you, Diane," Gabriela said, meaning it. "The reception area hasn't changed much."

"Oh, there have been changes," she replied, stepping back to appraise her with a critical eye. "But the bones are the same. You look good. Washington didn't wear you down too much."

"I escaped before it could finish the job," Gabriela said with a dry smile.

Diane laughed, a warm sound that seemed to ripple across the reception area. "Smart woman. Politics ages people faster than law, and that's saying something." She glanced at the large clock mounted on the wall behind her desk. "Chuck's been asking about you all morning. He's in a meeting now, but wanted to know the minute you arrived."

"I'll find him," Gabriela assured her, glancing down the familiar corridor that led to the partners' offices. "First, I want to see if my office is still standing."

"Chuck made sure no one touched it," Diane confided, lowering her voice slightly. "Said you'd be back someday. Looks like he was right."

Gabriela raised an eyebrow. "He usually is, though don't tell him I said that."

Diane ran her fingers across her lips like a zipper and smiled. "Your secret's safe with me. Welcome back, Gabriela." Gabriela nodded, taking in the familiar rhythm of the office. It had been more than two years since she left Parker & McEvoy for Congress, but little had changed. Now she was back in the city where she'd built her name, ready to step into the fight again.

As she moved past the reception desk toward the corridor beyond, she caught sight of her reflection in a decorative mirror: a woman in a perfectly tailored charcoal suit, her dark hair framing sharp features, her posture radiating the quiet confidence of someone who knew exactly where she belonged.

Gabriela had initially envisioned a lasting career in Congress, but her time in Washington turned out to be nothing more than a necessary detour. However, it was within the polished corridors of Parker & McEvoy and Dallas courtrooms that Gabriela Sanchez truly came alive.

She headed down the corridor, her footsteps muffled by the plush carpeting that had cost more than her first year's rent in law school. The corridor stretched before her, lined with glass-walled conference rooms named after Texas landmarks, including the Alamo, Cadillac Ranch, Big Bend, River Walk, and Stock Yards. Behind each transparent barrier, lawyers hunched over documents or gestured emphatically to clients, their mouths forming words she couldn't hear. The silenced drama of legal negotiation played out like a pantomime, reminding her of congressional committee rooms where the real decisions happened before the cameras ever rolled.

When she came around the bend in the corridor that would lead to the partners' wing, a tall figure appeared, blocking her path. Chuck Green stood like a sentinel at the end of the hallway, his silver hair freshly cut, his navy suit impeccable against the cream-colored walls. At sixty-two, he remained the firm's most intimidating presence through the quiet confidence that radiated from him.

"Gabriela," he said, extending his hand. "Punctual as always."

She took his hand, noting how he'd positioned himself to greet her before she could reach her office. It was Chuck's way of making a subtle assertion of control that she might not have recognized before her time navigating congressional power dynamics. "Chuck. Diane told me you've been waiting for me."

"She's right. Thank you for agreeing to meet with Morrison and take on his defense."

Gabriela's eyebrows arched, wanting to let him see her surprise at his presumption. She hadn't agreed to anything yet, merely to a meeting with Chuck. But he had always operated this way, treating the desired outcome as a foregone conclusion. It was a negotiation tactic she'd adopted herself in countless courtrooms and congressional hearings: speak of what you want as if it's already decided, and often, people will fall in line with your narrative.

Before she could respond, other partners emerged from their offices, drawn by the sound of their voices or perhaps alerted by Diane's efficient communications system. They surrounded Gabriela with welcoming smiles and eager handshakes, a reception committee for the returning attorney.

Elena Woodward, head of the corporate division, air-kissed Gabriela's cheek and whispered, "We've missed having one more woman in the partners' meetings."

David Childers, whose mastery of tax law had saved countless clients from IRS entanglements, pumped her hand enthusiastically. "We've missed hearing your stories while you were gone."

The welcoming circle parted as Jack Wainwright emerged from his office, shorter than Chuck but wider in the shoulders, with a red tie that was askew, matching the perpetual dishevelment that belied his sharp legal mind. As the firm's managing partner, Wainwright tracked billable hours and collections and judged attorneys solely by the revenue they generated.

"The prodigal daughter returns," Jack said, smiling in a way that didn't quite reach his pale blue eyes. "Those of us who handle finances are particularly glad. You brought in a ton of new business."

"Glad to know I was missed for my personality," Gabriela replied with a thin smile. The comment was delivered lightly, but she felt a familiar tension coiling at the base of her spine. Wainwright had been the one who had criticized her pro-bono work, arguing that time spent on indigent clients was time stolen from paying ones. He'd called it "bleeding heart nonsense" during a heated partners' meeting.

But Gabriela's history with Wainwright stretched back further than that disagreement. On her first day at the firm, fresh from a clerkship with the Texas Supreme Court, he had encountered her in the file room and assumed because she was Hispanic that she was part of the cleaning staff. "The desk in 714 needs attention," he'd said without looking up from his phone. "Coffee stains."

She'd stared at him for a beat before replying, "I'll be sure to mention that to the actual cleaning staff when I see them. I'm Gabriela Sanchez, the new associate in litigation."

His face had flushed red beneath his perpetually sunburned complexion, but he'd never apologized. Over the years, as she'd risen through the ranks to become the youngest partner in the firm's history, Wainwright had maintained a careful professional courtesy that never quite masked his underlying resentment.

"Your personality is an added bonus," Wainwright said now, his smile fixed in place. "But let's not pretend the bottom line isn't important. Your congressional connections should prove lucrative."

She felt her face cool, blood draining from her cheeks as it always did when anger took hold. In Washington, she'd learned to harness this physiological response, using the ice in her veins to deliver devastating rebuttals while opponents lost their composure. "I didn't cultivate relationships in Congress to monetize them, Jack. I was there to serve my constituents."

"Of course," he backpedaled, though his expression suggested he considered her answer naive. "I meant the expertise you've gained. Regulatory knowledge. Legislative insights. Valuable perspectives for our clients."

Chuck stepped forward, smoothly inserting himself between them like a veteran referee separating boxers between rounds. "Jack's point, however clumsily made, is that your experience enriches what we can offer clients. Speaking of which, your office is ready. Same one as before. We kept partners at bay who were circling it like vultures."

The tension in the air dissipated somewhat, replaced by nervous chuckles from the assembled partners. Everyone knew the prime corner offices were coveted prizes in the law firm ecosystem, and hers, with its views of both downtown Dallas and the Trinity River corridor, was particularly desirable real estate.

"Appreciate that," Gabriela said, genuine gratitude coloring her tone. Chuck's decision to preserve her space spoke volumes about both his faith in her return and her standing within the firm hierarchy. Some bridges, at least, remained unburned.

"Your office has been maintained exactly as you left it," Chuck continued. "Though I believe Lucia may have updated your law library with relevant volumes from the past two years."

The mention of Lucia, Gabriela's trusty assistant, her right hand, the person who had kept her professional life running smoothly for nearly a decade, brought a genuine smile to her face. "I should go find her."

"She's been counting down the days," Chuck said, a rare warmth softening his usually stoic features. "We all have, in our way."

Gabriela nodded. Chuck's public welcome had just repositioned her near the top of the Parker & McEvoy hierarchy, regardless of her two-year absence.

As she continued down the hallway, her former partners watched, each aware that her return would disrupt the firm's delicate balance. In Washington, she'd been one voice among many, subject to party priorities and leadership directives. Here, she had built a reputation as a tough litigator, and one favored by Chuck Green. The question now was whether she was ready to leap back into the spotlight with a case as potentially explosive as Morrison's or ease her way back into the practice of law through less high-profile work.

Soon, she saw Lucia Martinez at the desk outside her old office. Her dark hair was pulled back in a neat bun, and reading glasses perched on her nose. Lucia had been her right hand through countless cases, ensuring no detail was overlooked and no deadline missed. Gabriela frequently joked that clients tolerated her but loved Lucia; she was Gabriela's secret weapon.

She had asked Lucia to join her in Washington, but her family was in Dallas. They stayed in touch for a while, but their calls became less frequent. Other partners likely tried to poach her, yet here she remained, guarding Gabriela's office as faithfully as ever.

When she looked up, with eyes brightening, she removed her glasses, stood, and hurried around the desk, arms extended.

"¡Por fin regresas!" Lucia exclaimed, embracing Gabriela. She pulled back, studying Gabriela's face with maternal scrutiny. "¿Cómo estás?"

"Estoy bien, Lucia. Te he extrañado," Gabriela replied, smiling genuinely for the first time since entering the building. With Lucia, there was no need for the political masks she'd worn in Washington or the professional veneer maintained with her partners. She had seen Gabriela at her best and worst, staying up with her during trial preparations and handing her tissues after rare defeats.

"Yo también, mija. I haven't been the same since you left," she said, the endearment slipping out naturally despite our professional relationship. After a decade together, Lucia had become a trusted confidante and protective aunt.

"Let's hope Congress didn't soften me up too much," Gabriela said, glancing toward her closed office door, waiting for her return to open.

Lucia chuckled, her voice carrying the same musical cadence as her speech. "Your time representing the Rio Grande Valley only sharpened your claws, I think." She mimicked a catlike swipe. "I've been following your speeches." She kissed her fingertips. "You made Representative Whitmore look like an intern in that border security address."

Gabriela felt a flush of pride. The border security debate had been heated, with conservative senators pushing for measures that would militarize the region where she'd grown up. Her speech opposing the bill had gone viral in political circles, though the legislation ultimately passed with minor amendments.

"And gave me an appreciation of how much I missed the courtroom," Gabriela admitted. The congressional floor had its drama and importance, but it lacked the immediate impact of courtroom victories or losses.

"Well, you're back where you belong." Lucia switched to English, a habit they'd developed over the years, blending languages as seamlessly as their professional rhythms. In an environment where Spanish could be seen as unprofessional by some clients, they used Spanish for personal matters and English for business, often blurring the lines naturally.

She handed Gabriela her calendar for the week. "What's this block on Thursday labeled 'P. G. initial'?"

Lucia's expression remained professionally blank, though her eyes held amusement. "That would be the Phillip Morrison matter Mr. Green mentioned. He was quite insistent about reserving the time."

Gabriela shook her head, unsurprised but slightly irritated by Chuck's presumption. "He's already scheduled me to take the case before I've agreed to it?"

"He may have expressed a high degree of confidence in your eventual decision," Lucia replied diplomatically.

Their eyes met in shared understanding. Chuck Green hadn't become chair of the litigation department at Dallas's most prestigious law firm without an ability to predict outcomes and position resources where they'd have the greatest impact. He'd already decided that Gabriela would take Morrison's case and had begun arranging the firm's machinery to support that decision.

"I see my office is still intact," Gabriela said, changing the subject as she gestured toward the closed door.

"Exactly as you left it," Lucia confirmed. "Though I've added fresh yellow roses."

The thoughtful touch was typical of Lucia, remembering Gabriela's preference for Texas's state flower. Their relationship existed in that perfect balance, a professional partnership enhanced by genuine affection.

"Thank you." The words were simple but heartfelt. During her time in Washington, Gabriela had gone through a string of staff assistants, most using their congressional experience as a stepping stone to lobbying or law school. None came close to Lucia's blend of efficiency, discretion, and loyalty.

"De nada." She made a shooing motion toward Gabriela's office door. "Go. Reacquaint yourself. I've held all calls for the next hour so you can settle in." She paused, then added, her tone teasing, "Unless you'd rather have Mr. Green brief you on the Morrison case right away?"

Gabriela gave her a narrow look. "You too? Is everyone in this firm determined to push me into this case before I've even reviewed the basics?"

"Not everyone," Lucia replied, her expression suddenly serious. "Jack Wainwright suggested you might want to 'ease back in' with some small, less important cases' until you 'readjust to the real world.'" Her perfect mimicry of Wainwright's condescending tone made it clear what she thought of his suggestion.

"Did he now?" Gabriela felt that familiar cooling in her cheeks, the anger response that had served her well in contentious negotiations. "And what did you tell him?"

Lucia's smile was sweet but carried a sharp edge. "I told him I'd pass along his concern right after I updated the calendar on your computer with the Morrison case preparation as Mr. Green requested."

Gabriela laughed, the sound startling in its genuineness after days of careful political chuckles and diplomatic smiles. "Remind me to approve your raise request, whatever it is."

"Already on your desk," she replied, turning back to her computer with efficient grace. "Along with the Morrison case file. For your consideration only, of course."

Of course. Gabriela shook her head, still smiling, as she reached for the door to her office. Lucia had always anticipated, not just what she needed, but what she would ultimately decide, often before she knew herself.

Gabriela sat in her office on the 56th floor, the city skyline stretching out behind her. She leaned back in her chair, staring at the file on her desk. Phillip Morrison's name was printed in bold at the top. Her phone buzzed, and her father's name lit up the screen. She hesitated before picking it up.

"Hey, Papa."

"Welcome back to Texas, Mija. I only wish you had come home and rejoined me."

Gabriela laughed. "Papa, they wanted me back here, and I still have a home here."

"I know. I know. But your mother and I miss you. What do they have in store for you?"

"Chuck Green wants me to defend Phillip Morrison."

"Mija, Green wants you to defend Morrison?"

"That's the plan. Green said that Sparks Duval recommended me, and Morrison took up his recommendation."

"Chuck Green thinks Morrison's worth the risk?"

"He thinks there's a strong defense, and Morrison insists he's innocent."

"Of course he does. I've been around long enough to know how a man looks when he's hiding something. Sometimes, it's not the words—it's the confidence. Some men are so sure of themselves that they believe their own lies."

Gabriela pressed her lips together, fighting the instinct to argue.

"I know how to judge credibility, Papa. I've handled rich clients like this before."

"Just be careful. You've built a career on winning tough cases, but some clients will do anything to convince you they are the victim. If you take this case, make sure you're not putting your reputation on the line for a man who doesn't deserve it."

"I'll make sure. I trust my instincts to make the right decision."

"I know you do. Just remember that instincts can be wrong when your heart gets involved. Make sure you're seeing clearly."

Gabriela didn't respond right away. She knew her father was only trying to protect her, but his warning hit harder than she wanted to admit.

"Whatever you decide, I'm behind you. Just wanted to remind you to look beyond what he's saying and see the whole picture."

"I will. Thanks, Papa."

As she hung up, she couldn't help but feel the doubt creeping in. Chuck was sure Morrison was telling the truth, and she had to trust that. But the conversation left her uneasy. Maybe she needed to take a closer look at the case before committing.

She glanced down again at her phone and saw a calendar reminder: "Morrison, Phillip - Case Overview - Tomorrow, 9:00 AM."

#

The next morning, Gabriela paused outside Stella's Coffee Shop, a cornerstone of Dallas's legal community where judges and attorneys socialized. Inside, the aroma of fresh coffee and pastries filled the air. She spotted Chuck Green, Dallas's most sought-after trial attorney, seated in a corner. He beckoned her over, his demeanor blending urgency with reassurance. Gabriela wondered why someone of his stature wanted her to defend Phillip Morrison. It must be extraordinarily lucrative, complex, or risky to the firm's reputation, or perhaps all three.

"Gabriela," Chuck said, rising when he saw her. His voice carried the gravitas that had swayed countless juries, embodying a balance of authority and warmth. "Like I've told you, Phillip

Morrison, the oil tycoon, has been accused of murdering Ethan Reyes. I believe you've encountered Reyes during your political tenure."

"I know Reyes," Gabriela said. "He covered the Sparks Duval trial."

"He was investigating some of Morrison's less savory business connections. The prosecution is arguing that Morrison killed him to prevent publication of a damning exposé."

"Morrison is currently in every headline in Texas and has made the national news," Chuck added.

"The stakes couldn't be higher, Gabriela. This trial has become the media's latest feeding frenzy. Everyone's watching."

From her experience defending Duval, Gabriela could imagine the frenzied reporters, the flashing cameras, and the court steps besieged by the curious and the opinionated. The thought alone was overwhelming, but she remained composed, her gaze steady.

"You told me they found Reyes's blood in Morrison's car. Blood in the car and cell phone data... compelling but not definitive. What kind of unsavory characters are we talking about?"

He glanced around the café before continuing, though his caution seemed more theatrical than warranted. "Reyes has always been a thorn in Morrison's side. He's been digging into some of Morrison's less savory connections, including rumors of cartels and under-the-table deals. Ethan's a bulldog; he wouldn't let go. He was ready to do a series of articles on Morrison, and that's why they're pinning Reyes's murder on him."

"The prosecution claims Morrison killed Reyes to stop the exposé?" Gabriela asked, her brow furrowing. *Pinning it on him... that sounds like Chuck already has doubts.*

"Exactly," Chuck said, leaning closer still, his voice a confidential whisper amidst the surrounding din. "Ethan's work was about to expose something big. Too big. I believe someone wanted to silence both Reyes and Morrison, and the perfect way to do it was to kill Reyes and frame Morrison for the murder."

Gabriela considered this. "Frame Morrison? Why would someone want to do that? And who has the power to pull that off?"

Chuck Green leaned back, a contemplative look in his eyes. "It's perplexing," he admitted. "However, there have been instances where affluent individuals become entangled with cartels, often through money laundering schemes. For example, the Sinaloa Cartel has collaborated with external parties to launder drug proceeds." He paused, then added, "We need to investigate further to understand Morrison's potential involvement."

"So, you think it's possible Morrison is involved with the cartels, and someone else is framing him for Reyes's murder related to that?" Gabriela clarified, wanting to ensure she understood Chuck's line of thinking.

"That's one possibility we need to explore," Chuck replied. "Morrison's business dealings span multiple industries and borders. He's made enemies among competitors, politicians, environmental activists, and possibly even organized crime figures. Determining who had the means and motive to frame him for murder will be a significant part of the defense strategy."

"Why do you want the firm to defend him? You've made it sound like winning the case will be challenging."

"Look, Gabriela, there was a moment when Morrison first approached us where I seriously questioned the wisdom of taking this on. The potential damage to Parker & McEvoy's reputation if we lost a high-profile case like this with a client accused of murder... that could have lingered for years, despite the hefty fees. But the potential upside? A successful defense in a case this big? It's the kind of win that forges careers and keeps the firm very comfortable, attracting even more of Dallas's elite."

"And you want me to spearhead this defense," Gabriela said, making it a statement rather than a question. "Why me instead of you, Chuck? I'd think Morrison would want you to defend him."

"Sparks Duval told Morrison that you would be the best lawyer to defend him. So, when Morrison learned you were coming back, he asked for you to be his lawyer."

He was referring to the Duval case. A public relations firm advised Duval that he had chosen me to defend him because I was Latina. They thought jurors would relate better to me than Chuck. They also went against my advice and persuaded Sparks Duval to testify. That was a disaster. Thankfully, I caught the federal prosecutor in misconduct that ultimately led to Sparks being found not guilty.

"I'll need to review the full case file," Gabriela said, neither accepting nor refusing the case outright. "And I want to meet with Morrison personally before making any decision."

Chuck's smile was subtle but unmistakable. "Of course. The file is being delivered to your office as we speak. There are some cases, Gabriela, where… well, some things are better left unsaid."

What was he saying that was best left unsaid?

"And I've arranged for you to meet Morrison tomorrow morning in our offices."

Gabriela's eyebrows shot up. "You've arranged? Chuck, I haven't even said I'll take the case. I haven't reviewed the full file."

She was irritated. This was classic Chuck, steamrolling over any potential objections.

Chuck merely shrugged, his expression unperturbed. "Preparation isn't presumption, Gabriela. Morrison is anxious, and frankly, so is the firm. Getting you in front of him quickly shows him we're serious. Besides," he leaned forward slightly, a persuasive glint in his eyes, "seeing him face-to-face will give you a much better sense of the situation than any file ever could. You'll know in five minutes whether you can work with him."

He had a point, she conceded internally, the lawyer in her recognizing the strategic advantage of meeting Morrison sooner rather than later. Yet, the familiar prickle of Chuck's presumption still rankled. It was a tactic he'd always employed, and two years navigating the political backrooms of Washington had only sharpened her sensitivity to such maneuvers. A faint coolness edged her tone as she finished her latte and rose.

"Tomorrow morning, then. Nine o'clock at Calloway." Her gaze held his for a moment, a silent reminder of her awareness. "And Chuck," she added, her voice firm, "next time, try asking rather than setting the stage. My time in Washington taught me to recognize a setup a mile away."

The question wasn't really whether Gabriela would defend Phillip Morrison. The real question was what defending him might cost her, professionally and personally. After two years in Washington's political trenches, she was acutely aware of how quickly public opinion could turn, how thoroughly one's principles could be misrepresented by opponents, and how permanently certain associations could taint one's reputation.

She slid behind the wheel of her car, and her phone chimed with a text message from Lucia: "File delivered. 600+ pages. Coffee ready when you arrive."

Six hundred pages of police reports, witness statements, forensic analyses, and background information on both Morrison and Reyes. A case that would consume her waking hours and test her rusty trial skills.

After parking her car in the parking garage and taking the elevator to the atrium, Gabriela walked toward the elevator bank for the upper floors, her mind already on the upcoming meeting with Morrison.

#

Chapter Two

The Cadillac Ranch Conference Room was Gabriela's favorite. The twenty-foot cherry wood table dominated the space, surrounded by fourteen high-backed leather chairs, each positioned with mathematical precision. Tasteful oil paintings of Texas landscapes lined the walls, interrupted only by a burnished plaque listing the firm's founding partners. A discreet sideboard held a crystal decanter of water and perfectly aligned tumblers, catching the light like diamond facets. The room smelled of lemon polish and power.

This was where Gabriela had been promoted to partner at Parker & McEvoy and where she'd interviewed countless witnesses and clients. Lucia had booked it for her to meet Phillip Morrison.

She settled into one of the leather chairs, the scent of the polished wood and fine leather a familiar comfort. She adjusted the lapel of her charcoal suit, tailored to perfection, the red stitching just bold enough to remind people she noticed details others missed. She placed her briefcase on the chair to her right, not the table, a habit developed from years of needing clear sightlines to witnesses. Extracting her slim silver MacBook Air and a leather-bound notebook, she arranged them with geometric precision before her.

Ten minutes later, Diane's voice buzzed through the intercom. "Mr. Morrison has arrived."

At nine o'clock, the door opened. Phillip Morrison entered. He was slightly taller than six feet, with the confident stride of a man accustomed to people stepping aside for him, Gabriela noted. His suit and watch fit the role of a wealthy Dallas businessman. His smile was too smooth, like he'd used it one too many times to close deals.

Gabriela rose. "Mr. Morrison," she said, extending her hand. "Gabriela Sanchez."

"Ms. Sanchez," Morrison replied, his handshake firm but not aggressive. "I've heard much about you from Sparks Duval, and I saw you in court when you defended him."

"Mr. Morrison, Chuck Green has told me a great deal about you. He's out of the office," a lie, "otherwise he'd be sitting in with us."

Phillip Morrison sat across from Gabriela. He gave her a quick nod, then looked down at the table like he was more interested in what it cost than why he was there. She noted the subtle shift in his shoulders, a tightening as if bracing against an invisible blow.

Under his ruddy complexion, Gabriela caught a pale cast. His hand hovered over the water glass, then pulled away. A bead of sweat slid down his temple, even though the room was cool.

Gabriela's hands were above the keyboard of her open MacBook Air, studying Morrison's every move. Her screen was pristine except for a single, stark question displayed in a large, bold font: "Why?"

There was tension between them. It was clear that Morrison didn't like the reason that had brought him to Parker & McEvoy, and Gabriela didn't like Morrison and was certain jurors would not.

"Mr. Morrison," Gabriela began, "you are aware that the charges you're facing are severe. Your gun was found at the crime scene. And there's video footage. It may be grainy, but it's clear enough to raise questions. Someone who looks like you was at the scene when Ethan Reyes was shot."

Her gaze held his, unwavering, as she laid out the stark reality of his predicament. She brought her weight forward, resting her hands flat on the table, her posture exuding confidence and control.

Phillip Morrison tried to compose himself, but his jaw clenched, and his fingers tapped an uneven rhythm on the conference room table.

"I know what this looks like, but you have to understand. I didn't kill Reyes."

His voice strained, cracking the polished image he'd worked to project. His styled hair now disheveled, his earlier swagger replaced by a look of uncertainty.

She leaned in. She stared into his eyes, trying to determine if he was concealing something. Tell me everything from the beginning."

Morrison's shoulders relaxed marginally, and he took a deep breath before beginning his account.

Morrison shifted in his seat, the creak of expensive leather betraying his discomfort. "Reyes had planned to write a story detailing what the cartel had done to our company when we started drilling in Mexico," he stated, avoiding Gabriela's probing stare. *So, that was the narrative he was pushing,* Gabriela thought, observing his reaction.

"He previously had a vendetta against me, always accusing me of shady business practices. But I swear, Gabriela, this time he planned to write what the cartel had done to me and my company. I had no reason to murder or harm Reyes.

"Mr. Morrison, help me understand what makes you think Reyes was writing about what the cartel had done to you and your company and not that you were colluding with the cartel. The evidence the police found in the briefcase is damning, to say the least."

"I admit," Morrison continued, "there were interactions with certain individuals, but they were strictly business-related and within legal boundaries. The so-called evidence in the briefcase was fabricated."

Gabriela nodded, making notes. "I appreciate your candor, Mr. Morrison. To build a strong defense, it's crucial that we address these allegations directly. Let's work together to clarify these misunderstandings."

Morrison met her gaze, a flicker of hope in his eyes. "Thank you, Ms. Sanchez. I trust your expertise to navigate this."

"Did he now?" Gabriela didn't believe him. She was skeptical as she unfolded a set of documents. "Because the documents Reyes received the night of his death make it appear he planned to write that you have connections with a Mexican cartel." She stared once again, waiting for his explanation.

"I told you before those are baseless rumors, and that's not what he planned to write," Morrison retorted, but there was a falter in his conviction.

"Baseless?" Gabriela echoed. "Help me understand. There is evidence in the briefcase of uncovered wire transfers and intercepted communications. How can I show this evidence is baseless?" She tapped a finger on the papers, the sound punctuating her words.

"I told you none of it is true. For now, you'll have to take my word for it."

"Okay, let's turn to the night Reyes was killed. Your account of events doesn't align, Mr. Morrison. You claim you weren't anywhere nearby, but phone records place you within two blocks of the shooting just minutes before it happened.

"Those can be explained." Morrison started, but she pressed him, her questions sharp and unwavering, giving him no room to deflect or evade.

"Okay, help me out. Explain them," she said.

She watched with folded arms as Morrison struggled to help her understand. His bravado had faded, cornered by the evidence against him. Gabriela's sharp questioning had led them here.

"Look," Morrison said, "there's more to this than you know."

"Tell me. I need to know to defend you," Gabriela said.

Morrison clasped and unclasped his hands. Gabriela noted a slight twitch at the corner of his eye as he prepared to deflect her next question.

"Mr. Morrison, we need to discuss the firearm," Gabriela stated, pressing him. "Ballistics matched it to the bullets found at the crime scene."

He leaned back, attempting a careless shrug. "That gun was stolen from my collection weeks ago. I reported it, you can check." His words came out rushed, an uneven rhythm betraying his anxiety.

"Stolen?" Gabriela raised an eyebrow. "And when did you report it stolen? My investigator told me you reported it stolen three weeks before the shooting. The government will say that's quite a coincidence. How do we respond to that?"

"It's true. I only found it missing two days before the shooting." Morrison replied. "Look, if you don't believe me, maybe I need to find another lawyer."

"Mr. Morrison, it's not a matter of whether I believe you. It only matters if I can convince a jury. That's why I'm asking you these questions."

"Okay, I understand."

"What about the video footage? The figure resembles your build, the way you walk."

"Grainy footage proves nothing. It's not me," he cut in before she could finish.

Gabriela leaned forward, hands flat on the table. "It's not just the footage, Mr. Morrison. Witnesses place a man matching your description near the scene."

“Unreliable testimony,” he dismissed her with a wave, but the gesture lacked conviction.

“Is it?” she pressed. “Because when coupled with the evidence stacking up against you, these ‘unreliable’ accounts start painting a very reliable picture.”

Morrison swallowed hard, his Adam’s apple bobbing. It was clear he wanted to escape the room, the scrutiny, the relentless probing into the facets of his story that didn’t quite align. But Gabriela wasn’t one to relent, not when winning in court hung in the balance.

“Let’s talk about Reyes,” she continued, undeterred by his discomfort. “His research indicates a pattern of contact between you and certain... influential individuals south of the border.”

“Pure speculation,” Morrison responded, yet the color drained from his face.

“Speculation grounded in financial records and encrypted messages,” Gabriela corrected him. “Should we go through them line by line?”

She tilted forward across the table, her gaze steady. “Help me understand your perspective,” she urged.

Morrison hesitated, then sighed. “There are details I’ve withheld,” he admitted.

“I need complete honesty to defend you effectively,” Gabriela emphasized.

After a pause, Morrison began his account. Gabriela listened intently, analyzing his words.

When he finished, Morrison leaned back, tension evident. “Gabriela, influential parties are invested in this trial’s outcome,” he cautioned.

“I’m focused solely on the evidence and your defense,” Gabriela replied firmly.

Morrison nodded, recognizing her unwavering commitment.

“Remember,” Gabriela added, “complete transparency is essential. What you share stays between us.”

“Understood,” Morrison agreed, appreciating her dedication.

Gabriela stood, gathering her notes. “I’ll take your case, but we must navigate these challenges together. I need to review this file and compile my own notes. I will begin that this evening.”

As she left, Gabriela’s focus sharpened. The stakes were high, and she was ready for the fight. She’d dissect the evidence, piece by piece, until she could put together what really happened.

Chapter Three

The Morrison case files were spread across the conference room where Gabriela Sanchez was busy at work. She'd arrived early, before dawn, the office still dark around her except for the lights in the conference room. Her coffee had gone cold, forgotten as she absorbed the details of what the media had portrayed as 'an open-and-shut case.'

She scanned the evidence, looking for alternative conclusions to what the prosecution would present. Their case was pretty straightforward. Her defense would be more complex. She rubbed her temples and reached for her coffee, grimacing as the now cold beverage touched her lips. The Parker & McEvoy offices wouldn't come alive for another hour at least. She preferred these quiet moments when she could think without the constant hum of noise during business hours.

The morning newspaper sat folded at the corner of her desk, Morrison's face staring up from below the fold. "Oil Tycoon Charged in Journalist's Murder," the headline screamed. Gabriela flipped it face down. The media had already tried and convicted him.

She turned back to the police report. Ethan Reyes, an investigative journalist known for uncovering corporate corruption, found dead in a South Dallas alley with two bullets to the chest and one bullet to the head. She reviewed the evidence again, the gun and the footage forming a compelling narrative. The draft article was the lynchpin. The prosecution claimed it proved motive beyond doubt.

Their case was straightforward: Morrison had silenced a journalist who threatened to expose his illegal business dealings.

Her fingers drummed against the cool aluminum of her MacBook Air. Too clean. The phrase echoed in her mind. Morrison was arrogant, calculating, and ruthless in business. But he wasn't stupid. And this crime, if he had committed it, was stupid.

The Morrison case would be her first major trial since coming back. If she won, it would cement her reputation once again as one of the best defense attorneys in Texas. If she lost...

She shook her head. She couldn't afford to think that way.

She scrolled through the list on her screen, each name a potential ally in the fight. She needed a team, one with diverse expertise. The firm had plenty of talented attorneys, but this case required more than just legal minds. She needed investigators who could dig where the police hadn't bothered to look. Experts who could challenge the forensic evidence. Someone who knew Reyes's world of investigative journalism.

She opened a new document, and the cursor blinked at the top.

Marissa Ortega – Reyes' assistant. She could either help or hurt Morrison's case.

Detective Samuel Hayes – Retired Dallas PD, now a private investigator. Meticulous, thorough. Green had worked with him on three previous cases, all wins.

Dr. Eliza Fleming – Forensic pathologist who'd previously contradicted the Dallas Medical Examiner's findings in a well-known case.

Marcus Patel – Digital forensics specialist. If there was anything on Reyes's computer that the police had missed, he'd find it.

Gabriela paused, her fingers hovering over the keyboard. An understanding of cartel operations was essential, but such contacts weren't typically found in law firm directories. That connection would have to wait. The door to her office opened without a knock, and Chuck Green entered, carrying two fresh coffees.

"Six a.m. and already deep in the trenches," he said, placing one of the coffees on her desk. "Some things never change."

"Old habits," Gabriela replied, accepting the coffee with a grateful nod. "Why are you here so early?"

"Because knowing you, I figured you'd be here early. I guess I hadn't figured that you had been here all night." He settled into the chair across from her desk. "What do you think so far?"

"It's winnable," she said, with more confidence than she felt.

"I hope you're right, but Morrison's fingerprints are on the murder weapon." Green picked up one of the files. "And the security footage—"

"Shows someone of his general height and build wearing a hat and coat that obscures their face," Gabriela interrupted. "And his fingerprints on his own gun aren't exactly shocking."

"The press has already convicted him."

"You've won plenty of cases when the press had convicted your client before the trial."

"I brought you back because you're one of the finest legal minds who has ever worked with me. And because this place hasn't been the same without you." A rare softness crept into his eyes. "I'm counting on you to win this one."

Her eyes held his. "If I believed he was guilty, I would have told you I didn't want to take the case. I'm certain there's reasonable doubt." She picked up the list she'd been working on. "I'm putting together a team. The best people I know for a case like this."

He paused at the door. "Gabriela? Just remember, I have great confidence in you to find a way to win. You'll find things others would miss."

The evidence against Morrison was strong, but evidence could be misleading. Context could be missing. And even powerful people could be framed.

Her phone buzzed with a calendar reminder. Time to start making calls. Time to assemble a team that could untangle what promised to be one of the most complex cases of her career.

She picked up her phone and hovered over Marissa Ortega's name before making the call. She needed someone who knew the inner workings of Morrison's world.

Two hours later, Gabriela sat in the café, which buzzed with lunchtime chatter. She had chosen this place deliberately. It was in uptown, far enough from the courthouse and business district to avoid running into anyone connected to the case, but public enough that Marissa Ortega wouldn't feel trapped.

She'd arrived fifteen minutes early to secure the corner table, her back to the wall, giving her a clear view of both entrances. Old courtroom tactics were applied everywhere: control your environment whenever possible.

The door burst open, sending a shaft of midday light across the wooden floor. Marissa Ortega entered, pausing to scan the room with the wary eyes of someone who'd learned the hard way to be vigilant. She was younger than Gabriela expected, her navy dress and jacket exuding professionalism.

Gabriela raised her hand in a subtle greeting, watching as Marissa navigated between tables, clutching her purse. "Ms. Sanchez," Marissa said when she reached the table while extending her hand. Her grip was firm. "Thank you for suggesting somewhere... discreet."

"Please, call me Gabriela. Thank you for agreeing to meet."

Marissa sat, placing her purse in her lap rather than on the floor or table. She was keeping her belongings close, Gabriela noted. A server approached, and Marissa ordered an herbal tea.

"I can't stay long," Marissa murmured once the server left. Gabriela noted Marissa's fidgeting with a silver bracelet, a classic sign of anxiety. *Was she nervous, or hiding something?* "And I'm not sure I should be here at all."

"I appreciate the risk you're taking," Gabriela replied, keeping her voice low and steady. "How are things at Morrison Enterprises since Phillip's arrest?"

Marissa's mouth tightened. "Chaos. The board called an emergency meeting. The interim CEO has me organizing damage control with the PR team. Everyone's walking on eggshells, watching what they say." She glanced toward the door. "If anyone knew I was meeting with you..."

"This conversation stays between us," Gabriela assured her. "I'm not asking you to betray any confidences. I'm asking you to help your boss."

"By helping the man who might have killed Ethan Reyes?" A flash of real anger broke through Marissa's careful façade.

Gabriela tilted her head. "You knew Reyes?"

The server returned with Marissa's tea, creating a momentary pause in the conversation. Marissa's hands trembled slightly as she added honey to her cup.

"Everyone in Dallas business circles knew of him," Marissa said after the server left. "His exposés took down three executives over the last five years."

"Was he investigating Morrison Enterprises?"

She looked up, then away. "I can't discuss ongoing company matters."

"Marissa," Gabriela leaned forward, lowering her voice, "I'm not asking as an attorney right now. I'm asking as someone trying to understand what happened. Was Phillip Morrison under investigation by Ethan Reyes?"

"I assume so. Mr. Reyes called the office four times during the last couple of weeks before Reyes was murdered."

"Did he ever explain what he was working on?"

"Not directly," Marissa replied. "The first time, Mr. Morrison wasn't in. I offered to take a message, and Reyes just said he was investigating Morrison's energy operations in Mexico."

"Did he mention organized crime? Cartels?"

"No. But I'd seen the company's wire transfers to Mexican accounts I didn't recognize. The timing lined up. I assumed Reyes was writing an exposé about Morrison being involved in something dirty south of the border.

"Did Morrison meet with him?" Gabriela asked.

"Once." Marissa stopped, swallowing hard. "Three days before Mr. Reyes was found dead."

Gabriela's expression remained unchanged. "How did Morrison seem after that meeting?"

"He was calm. Too calm." Marissa took a sip of her tea. "In the past, when someone threatened the company's reputation, he got angry, called in his legal team, and plotted counterstrategies. This time, he just said, 'It's being handled, and changed the subject."

Gabriela's pulse picked up. She pictured the witnesses, the cameras, the pressure building.

"Marissa, I believe in attorney-client privilege and the right to a fair trial. That's the foundation of our justice system." Gabriela spoke calmly but with passion. However, defending those I believe committed murder is far more difficult.

"You don't think he did it?" Marissa's eyebrows shot up. Her eyes widened.

"The evidence is too neat. It doesn't fit a man who built an empire through meticulous planning and foresight. The prosecution's narrative asks us to believe he suddenly became careless enough to use his own registered weapon and leave it where it could be easily found."

Marissa started. "But the security footage—"

"Shows someone of Morrison's build entering Reyes's building. The face isn't clear."

"His fingerprints were on the gun."

"His registered gun," Gabriela emphasized. "Which means his fingerprints should be on it. The question is how it got from his possession to the murder scene."

Marissa's fingers froze on her bracelet. "You think someone set him up."

"I think it's a possibility that deserves investigation." Gabriela reached into her briefcase and pulled out a thin folder. "These are the inconsistencies I've identified in the prosecution's timeline."

There was a thirty-minute gap where Morrison's location was unknown, but that wasn't sufficient time to carry out the murder and get rid of the weapon, considering the traffic conditions that evening.

Marissa took the folder with evident reluctance but opened it, her eyes scanning the neatly organized timeline. "Why are you showing me this?"

"Because you know Morrison's habits and his routines. You manage his schedule, his communications, and probably aspects of his personal life. You could help identify where he might have been during that window."

"And if that place turns out to be Ethan Reyes's apartment building?"

"Then I'll have done my job by ensuring all evidence was properly considered." Gabriela met Marissa's gaze directly. "I'm not asking you to lie or fabricate an alibi. I'm asking you to help ensure that the truth comes out."

Marissa closed the folder, her expression troubled. "Even if I wanted to help, the company has instructed all employees not to discuss anything related to Mr. Morrison or the case. I could lose my job."

"You'll likely be subpoenaed by the prosecution, which would put you in the position of potentially testifying against him."

"They haven't contacted me yet."

"They will," Gabriela asserted. "You're too valuable a witness to ignore. Wouldn't you rather work with the defense, where attorney-client privilege can offer some protection for our discussions?"

Marissa's tea sat cooling, forgotten. "What exactly would you want from me?"

"Information about Morrison's habits, his potential enemies, and anyone who might have had access to his gun. Access to his private calendar and communications, with his permission. And your insights. Since you've worked closely with him for years, you know things about him that wouldn't appear in any official record."

"And what would I get in return?"

"Legal protection to the extent I can provide it. And the knowledge that you helped ensure justice was properly served, regardless of the outcome."

Marissa stared at her tea, the internal struggle visible on her face. "He's not always a good man," she said finally. "But I never thought he was a murderer."

"Has he talked with you since his arrest?"

A small nod. "He asked me to secure certain documents. Business matters that needed attention." Her voice lowered further. "And he asked me to trust you if you reached out."

That was unexpected. Gabriela kept her surprise from showing. "He told you I'd contact you?"

"He said you might. That if you did, I should listen." Marissa's eyes came up, searching Gabriela's face. "He said you were 'one of the few people who could see through the smoke.'"

The phrase struck Gabriela as unusual for Morrison, whose speech patterns she'd studied from recorded interviews. Either he'd been coaching Marissa, or there was more complexity to the man than his public persona suggested.

"Will you help us, Marissa? Not just for Morrison, but for the truth?"

Marissa glanced toward the window, watching pedestrians pass by, people with lives untouched by trials, headlines, or questions with no good answers.

When she turned back, her features sharpened with resolve.

"I'll help, but with conditions. I won't lie. I won't fabricate evidence. And if I discover something that convinces me he's guilty, I won't hide it."

Those were exactly the conditions I expected from someone I wanted on my team. "Welcome aboard," Gabriela said, extending her hand.

Chapter Four

By mid-February, the investigation into Ethan Reyes's murder had pulled Gabriela into unexpected corners of Dallas, including Jeffson Boulevard. The office building belonged to another era, its brick facade a testament to a time when Dallas was still finding its identity. Gabriela passed through the doorway on the third floor, where a frosted glass panel announced "Hayes Investigations" in chipped gold lettering.

Detective Samuel Hayes sat behind a desk that had seen better decades, his attention fixed on a stack of photographs spread before him. He didn't look up when she entered, though the slight pause in his movements confirmed he'd registered her presence.

"Detective Hayes?" Gabriela began, her voice steady and professional.

He glanced up then, his weathered face revealing a lifetime of experiences. Hayes moved with deliberate slowness, a slight stiffness in his gait that hinted at old injuries.

"Ms. Sanchez," he acknowledged, setting the photographs aside. "Chuck Green spoke highly of you."

"Likewise," Gabriela replied, settling into the chair across from him without waiting for an invitation. "He mentioned you might assist with a challenging case."

Hayes leaned back, his chair protesting with a creak. "Green rarely sends clients my way unless the stakes are high. What's the situation?"

Gabriela noticed steaming hot coffee in a well-worn Dallas PD mug at his elbow, a familiar sight that spoke to his years on the force. Despite its modest size, the room showed Hayes' meticulous attention to detail.

"It's a high-profile case involving Phillip Morrison," she said. "The media's having a field day, and the evidence is...complex."

Hayes raised an eyebrow a bit. "Morrison, as in the Texas oil tycoon? I've heard whispers about his dealings. What's he caught up in now?"

"He's been charged with the murder of Ethan Reyes. The prosecution's case is built on circumstantial evidence."

Gabriela leaned forward, her expression resolute. "Mr. Hayes, the case against Morrison hinges on several critical pieces of evidence: a firearm registered to him found at the scene, grainy surveillance footage, and alleged connections to organized crime."

Hayes nodded, acknowledging the gravity of the situation. “That’s substantial, if it’s all true. How do you propose we tackle this?”

“We need to dissect each element with meticulous care,” Gabriela asserted. “Starting with the firearm: it was discovered in a dumpster three blocks from the scene, wiped clean except for Morrison’s prints on the grip and magazine. No prints on the bullets, casings, or trigger.”

Hayes narrowed his eyes. “Selective wiping suggests someone intended to implicate him while erasing their own traces.”

“Precisely,” Gabriela agreed. “Next, the surveillance footage shows a figure matching Morrison’s build entering the alley at 8:47 PM. The individual’s face is obscured, and they avoid looking directly at any cameras.”

“Could be anyone, or so they want us to think,” Hayes mused. “And the alleged cartel connections?”

“Based on intercepted communications and financial records, the prosecution claims Morrison was involved in money laundering,” Gabriela explained. “However, these connections are tenuous and lack direct evidence.”

Hayes leaned back, contemplating the information. "So, your strategy is to challenge the credibility and interpretation of each evidence piece."

"Exactly," Gabriela affirmed. "I need to uncover the truth wherever it leads."

Hayes nodded, and Gabriela knew what he was thinking.

"If that truth is that Morrison killed Reyes, I'll use it to negotiate the best plea deal I can," she said. "But if, as I believe, someone else pulled that trigger, they're walking free while an innocent man faces life in prison."

Hayes stood, moving to the window that overlooked a less glamorous section of Dallas. For a long moment, he stared out at the city that had defined his career, his back to Gabriela as he considered her proposal. *Too many loose ends. Too many convenient coincidences.*

"The cartel angle complicates things," he noted. "If Morrison really does have those connections, anyone digging too deep could find themselves in dangerous territory."

"Are you concerned about cartel retaliation or about discovering your former colleagues were right?"

He turned, a flash of irritation crossing his face. "I'm concerned about walking into a hornets' nest without knowing which way the stingers are pointing. If Morrison is connected to the cartel and I start undermining the case against him, I could be doing their dirty work. If he's not, and someone else is, I could be putting targets on both our backs."

Gabriela nodded, acknowledging the legitimate concern. "Fair point. But wouldn't you rather know which scenario we're dealing with?"

"What makes you so sure he's innocent?" Hayes asked, returning to his seat. "Your gut? Or has Morrison convinced you with his charming denial?"

"Three things don't add up," Gabriela counted on her fingers. "First, the timeline. The prosecution places Morrison in the alley at 8:47 PM. His last confirmed location before that was his office, where he was seen leaving at 8:15. His next confirmed location was a charity gala at 9:30, where multiple witnesses spoke with him. Given Dallas traffic that night, the timing is extremely tight."

"Tight but not impossible," Hayes noted.

"Second, the gun." She continued. "Morrison reported it stolen from his home safe three weeks before the murder. The police report was filed, but conveniently disappeared from the system."

This caught Hayes's attention. "That wasn't in the discovery documents."

"Because the prosecution doesn't have it. My associate found it buried in county records yesterday. The original report never made it into the digital system."

His expression darkened. "That's not a clerical error. That's deliberate suppression."

"Third," Gabriela pressed her advantage, "Reyes was investigating several other high-profile targets besides Morrison. His notes mention at least two other executives and a state senator. Yet the prosecution has focused exclusively on Morrison."

Hayes picked up a pen and began to write on a notepad, his movements were quick and precise. "What do you need from me specifically?"

"A thorough review of the crime scene and evidence collection. Interviews with witnesses, the police may have rushed through. And..." she hesitated, "access to your contacts in places where Parker & McEvoy's investigators can't go."

Hayes set down his pen. "You're asking me to work my street sources. People who talk to me because I've built twenty years of trust."

"I'm asking you to use every tool at your disposal to find the truth." She leaned forward. "If Morrison murdered Reyes, I need to know. If he didn't, it would be helpful to know who did."

Their eyes met across the desk, a moment of professional assessment between two people who had seen enough of the justice system to know its imperfections.

"My fee has gone up since the last time I worked with Chuck," Hayes added.

"Morrison can afford it."

"I work independently. I don't answer to Parker & McEvoy, and I don't share my sources. My reports go directly to you, and you decide what to do with them."

"Agreed."

Hayes extended his hand across the desk. "Then, I'm in, Counselor. But let's be clear: I'm not doing this for Morrison. I'm doing it because Chuck asked me, and if Dallas PD rushed this case, they need to be held accountable."

They shook hands, a current of shared purpose passing between them despite their different motivations.

"I'll need everything you have," Hayes said, returning to business. "Police reports, witness statements, photographs, the coroner's findings. And I want to talk to Morrison myself."

"I'll have the files delivered this afternoon," Gabriela said, rising from her chair. "Morrison is currently out on bail, but I can arrange a meeting at our office."

"Good." Hayes stood as well. "And Gabriela? Watch yourself. If someone was sophisticated enough to frame Morrison this effectively, they won't appreciate you unpicking their handiwork."

She paused at the door. Gabriela locked eyes with him. "Are you concerned for my safety, Detective Hayes?"

"Just stating facts," Hayes said, his voice flat.

Gabriela smirked while meeting his gaze. "Then it's fortunate I've enlisted Dallas's most observant watchdog to keep an eye out."

As she left the office, a small, almost imperceptible smile played on her lips. Hayes would be thorough, uncompromising, and honest, which was exactly what this case needed. With Marissa Ortega providing insider knowledge and Hayes bringing investigative expertise, her team was taking shape.

She needed to combine their perspectives to unravel the complex web of evidence and motive.

#

Chapter Five

Two weeks later, her mind sharp from an early morning workout at Cooper Aerobics and the crime scene still fresh in her thoughts, Gabriela surveyed the panoramic view of downtown Dallas from the Calloway building's conference room. The city's sprawl spoke volumes of the power held within those walls. She stood at the head of the polished mahogany table, watching as her hastily assembled team filed in.

Marissa Ortega entered first, clutching a leather portfolio to her chest like armor. Samuel Hayes arrived next, his weathered face impassive as he nodded to Gabriela. He carried a battered messenger bag that had seen more crime scenes than most detectives, its worn leather a testament to years of meticulous investigation.

He picked a seat close to the door, a habit born of wanting a clear path to exit.

Dr. Eliza Chen followed, her posture as precise as her reputation for forensic detail. The pathologist's silk scarf provided the room's only splash of color, a defiant crimson against her otherwise monochromatic outfit. She carried an iPad loaded with autopsy reports and crime scene photographs.

The final arrival was Marcus Patel, a digital forensics specialist, who entered with the casual confidence of someone more comfortable with computers than people. His rumpled blazer over a faded tech company T-shirt marked him as the least conventional member of the team, but his reputation for extracting data from the most protected systems made him invaluable.

Gabriela closed the door and activated the privacy glass with a touch to a panel on the wall. The windows turned opaque, shutting out the Dallas skyline and creating an island of focus.

With a clear tone, she started, "Thank you all for coming on such short notice. Some of you know each other; others are meeting for the first time. What unites you is that each of you brings the expertise we need to construct a viable defense for Phillip Morrison."

She pressed a button, and the wall screen illuminated with a photograph of Ethan Reyes, taken during an interview, his intense green eyes seemingly staring into the room.

"Ethan Reyes, investigative journalist, was found dead two months ago, one bullet to the right shoulder, one to the chest, and one to the head. Phillip Morrison has been charged with his murder, the prosecution claiming he killed Reyes to prevent an article linking Morrison Enterprises to cartel money laundering. Key evidence includes: Morrison's registered Glock 19, found near the scene with his prints on the grip and magazine but nowhere else; grainy footage showing someone of his build near Reyes at the estimated time of death, though the face is obscured; and a tight timeline, placing Morrison between his office and a charity gala with just enough time to commit the crime."

Gabriela turned off the screen and faced the team. "That's what we're up against. The DA is calling it an open-and-shut case. I believe it's anything but."

Hayes leaned forward, arms crossed on the table. "Let's start with the obvious question: do we think he's innocent, or are we just looking for reasonable doubt?"

The question hung in the air. Marissa fidgeted, her gaze darting between Hayes and Gabriela, a visible tension in her shoulders. Dr. Chen, in contrast, remained a study in professional detachment, her expression betraying nothing, though her fingers entered text on her iPad, a subtle sign of her focused analysis.

"I've met with Morrison twice since his arrest," Gabriela replied. "He maintains his innocence. Says he was being set up."

"They all say that," Hayes countered, his expression neutral.

"What matters for our purposes," Gabriela continued, "is that there are significant problems with the prosecution's case. Problems that suggest either sloppy police work or deliberate manipulation of evidence."

"Or a wealthy client who's good at lying," Marcus Patel interjected, glancing at Dr. Chen with clear skepticism toward her forensic focus.. "I looked into Reyes's digital footprint before coming here. He was methodical and backed up everything in triplicate. If he had dirt on Morrison, it would be documented."

"That's exactly why we need you," Gabriela acknowledged. "We need to know what was on Reyes's devices beyond what the prosecution has shared."

Dr. Chen cleared her throat. "I've reviewed the medical examiner's report. Time of death is estimated between 8:30 and 9:15 PM, based on body temperature and lividity. The shots hitting his right shoulder, chest, and temple suggest either luck or training on the part of the one who fired them."

"Morrison has no military or law enforcement background," Marissa offered, speaking for the first time. "He does own several firearms and belongs to a shooting club, but I've never known him to carry a weapon personally."

"Tell us about the gun," Gabriela prompted. "The one used in the murder."

"It was kept in a safe at his home," Marissa said. "He rarely accessed it. I was surprised when he reported it missing last month."

Hayes's head snapped up. "You were aware of the theft report?"

Marissa nodded. "I helped him file it. The police seemed... uninterested. Said it was probably misplaced."

"That report conveniently disappeared from the system," Gabriela added. "We found it buried in county records."

"That's not a coincidence," Hayes stated flatly. "Someone wanted that gun to be linked to Morrison when it turned up at a crime scene."

Marcus frowned. "So we're saying someone stole his gun, saved it for weeks, then used it to kill Reyes and frame Morrison? That's premeditated on a whole new level."

"It also suggests inside knowledge," Gabriela noted. "Someone who knew Morrison's routines had access to his home and car, and understood how to manipulate evidence."

A heavy silence fell over the room as the implications sank in.

"What about the cartel connection?" Dr. Chen asked. "Is there any truth to Reyes's allegations?"

All eyes turned to Marissa, who looked down at her hands before answering.

"Morrison Enterprises has legitimate business interests in Mexico. When Mexico opened up its energy industry to outside investors. Morrison was one of the first to take advantage of the opportunity. I've never seen evidence of anything illegal, but..." she hesitated. "There are meetings Mr. Morrison takes alone. Transactions that go through separate channels. Areas where even I don't have full visibility."

When Marissa hesitated, Hayes leaned forward, his gaze sharp, a silent pressure for her to reveal more. Marcus shifted in his seat, a flicker of impatience crossing his face as if he considered this line of questioning a distraction from the hard data. "Could he be laundering money?" He pressed.

"I'm not sure how someone launders money. So, I have no idea," Marissa replied. "But, even if he is, he'd never murder anyone. He's ruthless in business, yes, but calculating. He neutralizes threats through legal channels—lawsuits, counter-narratives, and financial pressure. Not... murder."

Gabriela nodded, appreciating Marissa's candor. "Let's talk about the timeline. Hayes, you've reviewed the prosecution's sequence of events?"

The detective pulled a notebook from his bag. "It's tight. If Morrison left his office at 8:15, drove to where Reyes was walking, arrived at 8:47 as the footage shows, committed the murder, disposed of the weapon, then made it to the gala by 9:30... everything would have had to go perfectly. No traffic delays, no complications at the scene."

"Dallas traffic on a Thursday evening?" Marcus scoffed. "I've missed dinner reservations driving shorter distances."

Gabriela noted that Morrison, when this point was raised, had remained oddly unconcerned as if the timing presented no issue at all. She launched into the timeline analysis, her tone measured. "Reyes left the Blue Marlin at approximately 8:30 PM. He was found dead in the alleyway at 9:30 PM. It was raining, and he was on foot."

As Gabriela laid out the timeline, Dr. Chen raised an eyebrow, a subtle indication that she had a different perspective on the time of death estimations, a point she chose to hold back for the moment.

Gabriela leaned forward, her gaze intense. "It strikes me as incredibly convenient for Morrison that Reyes happened to be walking alone in a specific alley, in the rain, at that precise hour. How could Morrison have predicted such an unpredictable choice without prior knowledge or surveillance?" She let the question hang in the air.

Hayes rubbed his chin thoughtfully. "It's unlikely. Unless Morrison had someone tailing Reyes or had access to his plans, he couldn't have predicted Reyes's movements with such precision."

Gabriela interjected, "And there's no evidence suggesting that Reyes's routine was predictable. His decision to walk seemed spontaneous. This unpredictability undermines the prosecution's narrative. It suggests that someone else, perhaps with closer surveillance on Reyes, orchestrated this."

Hayes leaned back, arms crossed. "We need to explore who had the means and motive to monitor Reyes so closely. That could lead us to the real perpetrator."

Gabriela's eyes narrowed with determination. "Let's dig into Reyes's recent contacts, his stories in progress, and any threats he might have received. Someone wanted him silenced and had the resources to track his every move."

"Could he have had help?" Dr. Chen suggested. "Someone to dispose of the weapon while he established his alibi at the gala?"

"If so, we need to identify that person," Gabriela replied. "Marissa, who in Morrison's inner circle might be loyal enough to assist in something like this?"

Marissa considered the question carefully. "There's his head of security, Mitch McCoy. Former military, completely devoted to

Morrison. And his younger brother, James, though he was supposedly in Houston that week."

Hayes scribbled a note, his eyes flicking towards Marcus, a silent question passing between them, a hint of his own reservations about relying solely on digital evidence. "I'll look into both."

"What about Reyes's other investigations?" Gabriela redirected. "Marcus, can you access his work files to see who else he was targeting?"

The digital specialist grinned for the first time. "Already started. His cloud storage has decent security, but nothing I can't work around. A preliminary scan shows he was investigating Stephen Penbrooke. And trust me, that's not good news."

"Penbrooke?" Gabriela's voice tightened. "He's a powerful guy with resources to eliminate a threat and to frame someone else. He tried to bribe me last year, when I was in Congress, and made it clear I'd regret crossing him. He's always been a snake, always involved in shady dealings."

"That's an understatement," Hayes observed, his eyes narrowing. "He's got friends in high places, and crossing him could be dangerous. Reyes was digging into some seriously dirty financial transactions, shell companies, offshore accounts... the kind of thing that makes powerful men very nervous."

"And nervous men make mistakes," Gabriela added. "We need to investigate potential connections between these individuals and Morrison. Any business rivalries, political disagreements, or personal grudges. Especially any links to Penbrooke's operations."

Dr. Chen tapped her iPad. "I'd like to re-examine the autopsy findings, particularly the angle of the three gunshot wounds. The height and position of the shooter might tell us more than the ME included in the report."

Forensic Review (Dr. Chen):

Assess Environmental Impact: Evaluate how the rain may have affected the crime scene, potentially compromising or eliminating evidence that could have been collected under different conditions.

Alternative Evidence Sources: Focus on evidence less likely to be affected by weather, such as bullet trajectories or the condition of the victim's clothing.

Field Investigation (Hayes):

Witness Canvassing: Given the public nature of an alley, there may be individuals who witnessed the crime or observed suspicious activity. Re-interviewing residents or passersby who were in the vicinity could yield new leads.

Surveillance Footage: Search for security cameras from nearby establishments or traffic cameras that might have captured relevant footage, considering the alley's proximity to other buildings.

Digital Investigation (Marcus):

Mobile Device Analysis: Investigate the victim's and potential suspects' cell phone records to establish their locations and movements on the night of the murder.

Social Media Activity: Review Reyes's social media for any posts or messages indicating his whereabouts or plans that evening.

As the team dispersed, Marcus lingered, his eyes fixed on Hayes. 'You still playing old-school, Detective?' he asked, a hint of disdain in his voice. Hayes met his gaze, his expression unreadable. "Some things don't change," he replied, a clear sign that their methods, and perhaps their personalities, were at odds.

"Old-school gets results," Hayes continued, his gaze unwavering. "Especially when the new tricks haven't found the bodies yet."

When he was the only one left with Gabriela, Hayes spoke once again, "You know we might not like what we find," he said quietly. "Rich men with secrets rarely emerge from scrutiny unscathed."

"Secrets have a way of surfacing, regardless of how deeply they're buried. It's better to confront them now than to find out what they are in the middle of the trial."

After Hayes departed, Gabriela remained alone in the conference room, staring at the whiteboard with its neat categories and assignments. Expertise, resources, and determination filled the room. What they didn't have was time.

She pulled out her phone and dialed Morrison's direct number. Regardless of her team's findings, she needed her client's complete honesty to defend him effectively.

The system would determine his guilt or innocence, her role was to provide the best defense possible based on all available facts.

As the call connected, she steeled herself for what promised to be a difficult conversation.

Chapter Six

March brought a brief respite from the relentless pace of the investigation, a chance for Gabriela to return to the quiet warmth of the Rio Grande Valley. Her mother's birthday, a celebration of family, and the familiar comfort of home filled the weekend with the scent of traditional dishes and the joyful clamor of her nieces' laughter. It was a world away from the sterile hum of her Dallas office, a reminder of the life she had left behind.

But duty called, and the Monday morning after her mother's birthday arrived, a stark contrast to the lingering warmth of the weekend. Gabriela entered her office, the sterile hum a stark reminder of the work that awaited her. Evidence boxes from the prosecution dominated the center of her workspace. She'd already contacted the lobby guard with her team's names. Now she waited for their arrival.

A knock at the door broke her concentration. Hayes entered without waiting for a response, carrying a cardboard box marked "EVIDENCE - COPIES" in bold red letters.

"You look like hell, Counselor," he observed, setting the box on the conference table.

"Professional hazard," Gabriela replied, gathering her notes. "The others coming?"

"Dr. Chen is parking. Marcus sent a message that he's running late, but he has 'interesting findings,' whatever that means."

Marissa arrived next, immaculately dressed despite the late hour, carrying a tablet and several folders. "I brought Morrison's calendar for the past three months," she said, "and the visitor logs from his office building."

Dr. Chen came in last, a little flustered, carrying her bag and a bunch of big photos. "The medical examiner was reluctant to share his original photographs," she said, laying the images on the table, "but a former colleague owed me a favor."

Gabriela cleared space on her desk, transferring the prosecution's files to make room for their own materials. "Let's start with the physical evidence," she said. "Dr. Chen, what did you find?"

The pathologist arranged the autopsy photos in a precise sequence. "One gunshot wound to the shoulder, one to the chest, and one to his head. The first bullet entered here." She pointed to the right shoulder, "Not immediately fatal. The second shot," her finger moved lower, "hit the heart. Death would have followed within minutes. The third wound hit his temple."

"Consistent with the official report," Hayes added.

"Yes, but look at the angles." Dr. Chen overlaid a transparent diagram on the photographs. "Two of the three shots traveled at a slight upward angle, consistent with a shooter who was shorter than the victim."

"Reyes was six feet," Gabriela recalled from the case file.

"And Morrison is six-two," Gabriela added. "If he fired the shots, the trajectory would likely angle downward, not upward."

Dr. Chen produced another photograph. "Reyes was walking when he was shot, based on how the blood dispersed. The shooter was positioned here," she indicated a spot on a rough diagram of the alley, "firing upward."

"So, we're looking for a shorter killer," Gabriela mused.

"Not necessarily." Dr. Chen's precise tone betrayed no emotion. "The shooter could have been crouching or firing from a lower position. But it's an inconsistency worth noting."

The door swung open, and Marcus hurried in, his laptop already open in his hands. "Sorry, I'm late," he said, finding a place at the table. "I was chasing a digital trail that kept splitting, one lead turning into five more."

"What did you find?" Gabriela questioned.

"First, the security footage." Marcus connected his laptop to the room's display screen. "I enhanced the images of the person walking in the alley."

The grainy footage appeared on screen, now clearer though still far from perfect. A figure in a dark coat and hat walked in the alley.

"Watch the gait," Marcus instructed, playing the clip at half speed. "See how the man favors his right leg? It's almost imperceptible, but it's there."

"Morrison has no limp or injury," Marissa confirmed.

"More interesting is what I found on Reyes's laptop," Marcus continued, his fingers flying across the keyboard as he switched to a different file, the glow of the screen reflecting in his intent gaze. "The article about Morrison and cartel connections was created two days before the murder, according to the file information. But the metadata shows it was modified after Reyes's estimated time of death."

A heavy silence descended upon the conference room. Gabriela felt a chill crawl up her spine. The implications of this were enormous. Hayes leaned forward, his brow furrowed, while Marissa gasped softly. Dr. Chen, ever analytical, tilted her head, her gaze fixed on the screen.

"Someone accessed his computer after he was killed?" Gabriela pressed, her voice sharp with urgency. This changes everything. This isn't just about Morrison; someone else is actively manipulating the narrative.

"Exactly," Marcus confirmed, pointing to the screen. "And they did more than just open it. Look here." He pulled up a side-by-side comparison, the two versions of the article starkly different. "The original draft mentioned corporate irregularities and suspicious Mexican business partners, vague stuff. But these explicit cartel allegations, the detailed accounts of Morrison's supposed meetings... these only appear in the version the police found." He zoomed in on specific paragraphs, highlighting the additions.

Hayes whistled low, a long, drawn-out sound that spoke volumes. "That's not just framing Morrison. Someone manufactured evidence after the fact. This is deliberate."

"It gets better," Marcus added, a grim satisfaction in his tone. "I traced the IP address that accessed the laptop that night. It was routed through multiple VPNs, slick work. But I followed the breadcrumbs. It bounced through servers in three different countries before landing in a high-end residential building downtown."

"Can you identify the specific unit?" Gabriela inquired, her mind already racing through possibilities. Who in a high-end building would have the technical skills and the motive to do this?

"Not yet. Working on it," Marcus replied, his fingers were already dancing across the keyboard again.

Gabriela faced Hayes. "What about the murder weapon? Any updates there?"

The detective pulled several documents from his box. "Ballistics confirmed it was the gun used in the shooting. Morrison's prints are exactly where they should be if he handled it normally. But as we noted, no prints on the trigger or bullets."

"Suggesting someone wearing gloves fired it," Gabriela concluded.

"Or wiped it selectively," Hayes added. "I spoke with Morrison's home security company. Their system shows the alarm being deactivated with a valid code on the night the gun was allegedly stolen, but no forced entry."

"Who has access codes?" Gabriela prompted Marissa.

She frowned. "Morrison himself, his brother James, his head of security, Mitch McCoy, and me, for emergencies. The cleaning service has a temporary code that changes weekly."

"So, our suspect pool includes anyone who could have obtained one of those codes," Hayes suggested.

"What about the timeline?" Gabriela shifted focus, sensing they were circling an important point.

Marissa opened her tablet, displaying a detailed schedule. "Morrison left his office at 8:15 PM. The security cameras in the parking garage confirm this. His driver had the night off—Morrison wanted to drive himself to the gala."

"Which is unusual?" Gabriela suggested.

"Very. He almost always uses his driver, especially for evening events where alcohol might be served."

"Convenient change of routine that night," Hayes added.

"The gala was at the Crescent Hotel," Marissa continued. "Valet records show his car arriving at 9:27 PM. Multiple witnesses place him inside by 9:35 PM, speaking with the mayor."

Gabriela spread a map of Dallas on the table. "If the shooter encountered Reyes in the alley at 8:47 PM, and the murder took place shortly after, that gives us a very tight window. Morrison would have had to commit the murder, dispose of the weapon three blocks away, then drive across downtown Dallas at rush hour to reach the gala."

"And arrive looking immaculate and unruffled," Marissa added. "I've seen Mr. Morrison after rushed trips across town. He always needs a moment to compose himself, straighten his tie, check his appearance."

As Marissa detailed Morrison's movements, Hayes's gaze lingered on her, a flicker of doubt in his eyes, as if questioning her complete objectivity.

"Witnesses at the gala described him as 'relaxed' and 'engaged in conversation,'" Gabriela read from her files. "Not the demeanor of someone who just committed murder."

Dr. Chen, who had been silently examining the autopsy photos, spoke up. "There's another inconsistency in the medical evidence. Reyes had minor cuts and bruises on his hands consistent with a struggle."

"Meaning?" Hayes prompted.

"If there was a struggle, there should be trace evidence—the attacker's skin cells, fibers, hair—transferred to the victim. The medical examiner found nothing matching Morrison under Reyes's fingernails or on his clothing."

"The prosecution will say he wore gloves and protective clothing," Gabriela pointed out.

"Which further complicates the timeline," Hayes countered. "Now, he would have needed to change clothes between the murder and the gala."

Marcus, who had been typing furiously during this exchange, looked up. "I've been checking traffic camera footage from that evening. Morrison's black Mercedes S-Class doesn't appear on any cameras along the most direct route between the alley where Reyes was murdered and the Crescent Hotel."

As Marcus confirmed the absence of the traffic camera footage, Dr. Chen nodded, a silent confirmation of their combined progress. "Alternative routes?" Gabriela wanted to know.

"Checking those now, but it's strange. If he made that trip, he should have been captured on at least one traffic camera."

Marissa hesitated, then spoke. "There's something else. Morrison received a call at 7:30 that evening, just before he left the office. He took it in private, but when he emerged, he told me to clear his schedule for the next morning. He seemed... disturbed."

"Did he say who called?" Hayes asked.

"No, but I checked his phone records. The call came from a burner phone."

Gabriela felt a chill along her spine. Each piece of evidence they examined seemed to create more questions than answers.

Inconsistencies in the Prosecution's Case:

1. The bullet trajectory suggested a shorter shooter.
2. There was no Morrison DNA from the victim's defensive wounds.
3. The timeline was extremely tight, possibly impossible.
4. Reyes's article was modified after his death.
5. The gun was reported stolen three weeks before the murder.
6. Security footage showed a person with a slight limp.
7. Morrison's car was not on the traffic cameras.
8. Lack of evidence showed Morrison knew Reyes's location on the night of the murder.

She turned back to the team. "This is more than enough to establish reasonable doubt, but I want to go further. I want to identify the actual killer."

"You think Morrison is being deliberately framed?" Dr. Chen asked.

"Based on what we've uncovered, the idea that he was framed is becoming increasingly plausible," Gabriela replied. "And if so, whoever did this had resources, inside knowledge, and a compelling motive."

Hayes rubbed his jaw. "We need to look closely at the other targets of Reyes's investigations. Any of them could have decided to solve two problems at once by eliminating Reyes and implicating a rival."

"I'll dig deeper into the senator and the other executives," Marcus promised.

"And I need to speak with Morrison again," Gabriela said. "These findings raise new questions he needs to answer."

"Like, why he decided to drive himself that night?" Hayes suggested.

"And who might have had access to his gun and security codes," Marissa added.

"We also need independent experts," Gabriela decided. "Dr. Chen, can you recommend a ballistics specialist not affiliated with Dallas PD? And a forensic technician to re-examine the crime scene evidence?"

"I have several colleagues who would be suitable," the pathologist confirmed.

As the meeting stretched into the late hours, Gabriela sensed a shared purpose was developing. The initial skepticism had transformed into a focused determination, a collective resolve to unravel the truth. With each inconsistency they uncovered, the prosecution's seemingly airtight case crumbled, fueling their shared determination to expose the truth.

But even as they identified these weaknesses, Gabriela remained troubled by a nagging question: if Morrison was innocent, why had someone gone to such elaborate lengths to frame him? The answer might lie in the cartel connections, or in business rivalries, or in something they hadn't yet discovered.

Whatever the truth, she was now certain they weren't just building a defense strategy anymore. They were hunting for a killer who had orchestrated an elaborate frame-up. And that made their task both more complicated and more dangerous.

As the team packed up their materials, the detective nodded, picking up on Gabriela's concern. Whoever did this is sophisticated. We can't afford to be careless. Someone had already committed one murder and gone to extraordinary lengths to pin it on Morrison. If that person felt threatened by their investigation, they might not hesitate to eliminate new obstacles.

The hunt for truth had just become a high-stakes game with lethal consequences.

#

Chapter Seven

With the trial of Phillip Morrison looming in June and two months into her trial investigation and preparation, Gabriela navigated the winding driveway of his Highland Park estate. The mansion loomed ahead, a testament to modern architecture with its sleek lines and expansive glass facades reflecting the waning Texas sun.

Near the entrance, a private security guard stepped forward, his posture straight and professional. He scrutinized her identification briefly before nodding, his earpiece murmuring as he communicated her arrival.

Inside, a formally dressed gentleman greeted her at the grand double doors, ushering her into a cool marble foyer. He led her through a series of hallways, the contemporary art on the walls and the subtle lighting suggesting a carefully curated image. He finally opened the mahogany doors to Morrison's study.

The study was lined with floor-to-ceiling shelves of leather-bound books. Gabriela doubted anyone had opened one in years. A massive oak desk gleamed under focused lighting, a clear symbol of authority. Panoramic windows offered a view of manicured gardens in the fading light. Morrison stood by these windows, a silhouette against the golden hues. The scent of expensive wood and perhaps a hint of liquor hung in the air.

He turned as Gabriela entered, a glass of amber liquid in his hand, catching the light. His silver-streaked hair was precisely styled, and his tailored suit spoke of understated affluence. He raised the glass in a brief acknowledgment.

"Ms. Sanchez," he began, his voice smooth, a note of weariness beneath the surface, "I appreciate you meeting me here."

Gabriela offered a professional smile, her demeanor poised and attentive. "Mr. Morrison, meeting here made more sense than my office."

Morrison gestured to a pair of leather armchairs positioned before a low-burning fireplace. "Please, have a seat. Can I offer you a drink?"

"No, thank you," Gabriela replied, settling into the chair opposite him. She placed her briefcase beside her, extracting a notepad and pen with practiced efficiency.

Morrison lowered himself into the adjacent chair, his movements deliberate. He took another sip, the aroma of aged oak and caramel subtly permeating the air. "I assume you've reviewed the case files?"

Gabriela gave a curt nod, her expression remaining serious. "I have. There are several points I'd like to clarify with you, particularly concerning your whereabouts on the night in question and any potential connections to the victim."

Morrison's jaw tightened, the irritation there and gone in a flash. His left fingers tapped against the arm of the chair while his right hand swirled the bourbon, his eyes following the liquid as though it offered calm he could not find. Gabriela caught the rhythm, subtle but steady, a nervous tic he seemed unaware of.

"I assure you once again, Ms. Sanchez, I had no involvement in Mr. Reyes's death. This entire situation is a fabrication."

Gabriela met his gaze steadily. "Then let's work together to uncover the truth."

Gabriela removed several documents from her briefcase, arranging them precisely on the small table between them. "We've identified several inconsistencies in the prosecution's case. The timeline of your movements that evening is particularly problematic."

"Problematic, how?" He leaned forward slightly.

"The prosecution places you near the alley behind the Blue Marlin Pub at 8:47 PM, based on security footage of someone entering the area. You arrived at the charity gala at 9:27 PM. That would give you just forty minutes to commit murder, get rid of the weapon, and drive across downtown Dallas during evening traffic. That's not much time to pull all that off."

Morrison acknowledged with a nod. "As I told the police, I was never near that alley. I drove directly from my office to the gala."

"Your car doesn't appear on any traffic cameras along that route, and it wouldn't take forty minutes to get from your office to the gala."

Something changed in Morrison's posture. "I took side streets. The main roads are always congested at that hour."

"Coincidentally avoiding every traffic camera in the area?" Gabriela kept her tone neutral.

"Not intentionally." His voice was carefully measured, though Gabriela detected a trace of his growing irritation. "I specifically remember taking Elm Street and then cutting over."

Gabriela switched tactics. "Let's discuss your gun. The one found at the scene."

"Stolen from my safe three weeks before the murder," Morrison stated flatly. "As I reported to the police."

"A report that mysteriously disappeared from their system."

Morrison pressed his fingers to his temple. "What are you suggesting?"

"That someone went to extraordinary lengths to frame you, Mr. Morrison. Someone with access to your home, knowledge of your movements, and a sophisticated understanding of how to manipulate evidence." She paused. "Or that you're lying to me."

Their gazes met, a silent battle of wills waged across the desk. Gabriela had faced hostile witnesses, corrupt politicians, and criminals, but Morrison's calculating gaze was different.

"I'm not lying," he stated, his voice low and deliberate. "But there are... complexities," he paused, the word hanging in the air, "to my situation that I've been reluctant to share. Until now."

"This is no time for hesitation. If I'm going to defend you, I need complete transparency," Gabriela said. "I grew up near the border. I've seen how complicated things can get. Legal, political, and personal lines often overlap. My father spent his career handling cases where influence and loyalty sometimes carried more weight than the law. In Mexico, legitimate business can easily brush up against the wrong people. Sometimes it's not about intent. It's about who you're seen with, where you sit, or whose favor you unknowingly gain. If you crossed paths with anyone like that, I need to know now."

Morrison rose and walked to the window that overlooked his immaculate gardens.

"True, my business dealings in Mexico are legal but... complex," Morrison began. "Operating in regions where fuel theft is rampant, we've had to implement stringent security measures. While we've never knowingly engaged in money laundering or drug trafficking, we've had to navigate a landscape where organized crime groups attempt to infiltrate legitimate operations."

"Did Ethan Reyes discover these arrangements?"

A shadow crossed Morrison's face. "He was asking questions, yes. Called my office repeatedly in the weeks before his death."

"And you met with him," Gabriela pressed. "Three days before he was killed."

Morrison's surprise was brief but evident. "Marissa told you."

"She's helping us build your defense. What happened at that meeting?"

He settled back into his chair, a picture of composed ease, though the subtle shift of his posture betrayed a heightened awareness. "Reyes had bank transfers, shell company structures, meeting records, and other documents. Nothing explicitly illegal, but arranged in a way that suggested impropriety. He wanted a comment before publishing."

"And your response?"

"I told him he was misinterpreting legitimate business operations. I offered to have my CFO walk him through the transactions." Morrison's hand drifted to his bourbon glass. "He declined."

"Was that the extent of your interaction?"

Morrison hesitated for a microsecond, just long enough to notice. Then he responded, as if choosing each word carefully. "No. I also contacted his editor and reminded him that publishing unsubstantiated allegations could lead to a defamation suit. It's standard procedure."

"Did you threaten Reyes directly?"

"Of course not." Morrison's tone hardened. "I've been in business for thirty years. I know how to handle journalists without resorting to threats or violence."

Gabriela studied him, her senses heightened, searching for the subtle tells of deception, specifically a shift in his gaze, a tremor in his voice, anything that would betray the facade of composure. "The night before Reyes was killed, you received a call that upset you.

You canceled meetings and isolated yourself in your office. Can you explain what you did?"

Morrison's surprise was evident. "You've been thorough," he acknowledged. "The call was from Carlos Delgado, my primary contact in Monterrey. He informed me that certain groups were displeased with my decision to scale back operations in their areas."

As Morrison spoke of the call from Carlos Delgado, Gabriela noted the way his fingers tightened around the bourbon glass, a small, involuntary movement that spoke volumes.

"Are we talking about organized crime groups?" Gabriela inquired.

"He didn't specify," Morrison replied, his expression tense. "He merely mentioned there could be 'consequences' and advised caution."

Gabriela noted the almost theatrical way he delivered the word 'consequences,' as if he were reciting a line from a script.

"And your response, Mr. Morrison?" Gabriela asked, her voice sharp.

Morrison looked down at his hands, his voice subdued. "I told him, 'Not like this. There are other ways.' I was referring to negotiations, redirecting investments, and finding a compromise. I never imagined they'd go as far as framing me for murder."

Gabriela absorbed this information, weighing the possibilities. Either Morrison was being truthful, or he was an exceptionally skilled deceiver.

"I need names," she replied after a moment. "Anyone who might have had a motive to harm you or Reyes. Individuals with the means and reasons to orchestrate this setup."

Morrison hesitated briefly, then opened a drawer and retrieved a small notebook, which he handed to her. His movements were fluid, as if he had been waiting for this moment.

"Daniel Alvarez," he stated. "A former business partner. I bought out his share of our joint venture three years ago after discovering he was embezzling funds. He has connections in Mexico that I wasn't fully aware of when we began our partnership."

Gabriela opened the notebook, finding detailed records of Morrison's interactions with Alvarez, including dates, transactions, and locations. *Too* meticulous, she thought, a nagging suspicion forming. A convenient scapegoat wrapped in a bow of documentation.

"You kept detailed records on a former partner?" she asked, raising an eyebrow.

Morrison met her gaze. “In our line of work, it’s prudent to document everything. You never know when it might become relevant. Alvarez threatened me when I forced him out. He threatened me. Told me I’d regret crossing him. Then he disappeared back to Mexico, and I’ve not seen or heard from him since. ”

“And you think he could be behind this?”

“He has the motive, the connections, and the knowledge of my business to make it work.” Morrison tapped the notebook. “The last page has his known associates, including several in Dallas who could have carried out the actual murder.”

Gabriela closed the notebook and returned it to her briefcase. “I’ll have my team look into him. In the meantime, I need you to write down everyone who has access to your home, your safe, and your security codes. And I mean everyone. Family, staff, security personnel, even one-time visitors.”.

Morrison confirmed with a nod. “I’ll get it to you.”

As she prepared to leave, Gabriela studied Morrison. He seemed lost in thought, eyes fixed on something beyond the grand windows. He was silent as though he was thinking about what to say. Morrison turned to her, his face showing rare vulnerability.

“Ms. Sanchez,” he pleaded, his voice cutting through the air with a note of urgency, “I need to know if you believe I’m innocent.”

Gabriela paused at the door. "What I believe doesn't matter. My job is to ensure you receive a fair trial based on all available evidence."

"That's a lawyer's answer," he said, a hint of steel returning to his voice. "I'm asking for your personal assessment, Ms. Sanchez. Off the record."

She sensed he was testing whether she believed him. It wasn't the first time a defendant had asked that question, but it was strange that he ended with "off the record." *Why say that unless he was used to managing a narrative?*

She turned to face him fully. "I believe the evidence suggests you're being framed. Whether that means you're innocent is still an open question."

"Fair enough. But know this: I didn't kill Ethan Reyes. And when you find who did, you'll understand why this frame-up is about much more than one dead journalist."

Walking to her car, Gabriela processed the conversation, parsing truth from potential manipulation. Morrison had given her Daniel Alvarez as the new lead, wrapped in a neat package with supporting documentation. It was exactly what they needed.

This led her to question whether it was too good to be true.

As she drove away from Morrison's estate, she thought about what to do about Alvarez. She pulled to the shoulder, left the engine running, and called Hayes.

"Hayes," she said, her voice low and direct, "Morrison gave me a name: Daniel Alvarez. He claims Alvarez is a former business partner with a grudge. He even provided a notebook filled with 'evidence' against him."

"Sounds convenient," Hayes replied, showing his skepticism. "What's the catch?"

"That's what I need you to find out," Gabriela said. "I need everything you can dig up on Daniel Alvarez. Focus on his current whereabouts and activities in the last month. And Hayes?"

"Yeah?"

"Approach this with extreme skepticism. It feels too… perfect. Like a narrative, he was prepared to deliver. I want to know if this man is a real threat or just a distraction."

"Got it. I'm on it." Hayes replied.

#

Chapter Eight

Marissa Ortega sat in her living room calmly watching television when a sudden buzz of her phone against the coffee table jolted her. An unfamiliar number flashed on the screen, followed by a text. Marissa froze, staring at the stark message.

"I know who killed the journalist. I know why Morrison is being set up. Cannot speak safely by phone. Need guaranteed safety before the meeting. Reply if interested."

Marissa's breath hitched. Her gaze remained locked on the stark words. She placed her thumb over the delete icon, a tempting escape. To erase it felt like a return to solid ground. Her agreement to aid Ms. Sanchez had already felt like venturing into uncharted territory. This anonymous contact, arriving so late, felt like a descent into a shadowy realm.

But a stubborn seed of possibility took root. What if this held the truth? What if this unknown sender possessed genuine knowledge of Ethan Reyes's demise and the accusations against her employer?

She sank onto the sofa, her hand a tight clamp around her phone. Her mind raced, dissecting the message. The direct address of

"Morrison," not "your boss" or "the accused," troubled her. The mention of a setup resonated with the doubts Ms. Sanchez had raised about the evidence. This idea, a deliberate manipulation, was not public knowledge, a theory whispered only in their confidential exchanges. And the message had bypassed all professional channels, landing directly on her private number.

Someone knew my involvement, she thought, drawing a deep breath.

Her finger hovered over Gabriela's contact. Calling her was not just logical. It was necessary. Gabriela had the legal judgment to assess the situation, to weigh the danger against the potential for a breakthrough. She would know whether to ignore it, report it, or treat it as the lead they had been waiting for.

Yet, her hands were shaking. What if this was not a witness? What if it were a probe seeking to identify those aiding Morrison? Or worse, what if it was a lure from someone connected to Reyes's killer, now aware of her assistance? She shivered at the thought of the potential consequences.

She moved to the window, her gaze sweeping the quiet street. No unusual vehicles, no figures lurking in the shadows. Only the familiar stillness of a late weeknight.

A deep breath steadied her hand as she tapped Gabriela's number.

The attorney's voice, though sleep-tinged, sharpened instantly on the third ring. "Marissa? What is it?"

"I'm not sure," Marissa replied, her voice low with a tremor. "I just received a text from an unknown number. Claiming knowledge of Reyes's killer and Morrison's setup."

A brief silence hung between them, amplifying Marissa's anxiety. Then, Gabriela's calm authority cut through it. "Are you home?"

"Yes."

"Stay there. Do not reply to the text. I'm coming there now."

Twenty minutes passed, each one slower than the last. When the doorbell rang, Marissa jumped. Gabriela stood outside in sneakers and workout clothes, her hair pulled back. She hadn't come from court. She'd come the moment she got the call.

"Any other messages?" Gabriela asked immediately, her eyes sharp.

"No. Nothing else." Marissa led her to the living room, her phone displaying the stark text.

Gabriela read it twice, her brow furrowed in thought. "How many have this number?"

"Family, close friends, Mr. Morrison, a few executives." Marissa twisted her bracelet, a nervous habit taking hold. "It's private."

"Has your phone left your possession recently? Left on your desk at work?"

Marissa considered. "No. Company policy mandates we secure them."

Gabriela nodded. "The wording… 'set up'… it aligns with our discussions."

"Or they are part of it," Marissa murmured, a dark thought.

"Possible." Gabriela sat, gesturing for Marissa to join her. "Who knows you're involved and has this information?"

"Someone at Morrison Enterprises?" Marissa suggested. "Afraid to come forward directly?"

"Could be." Gabriela tapped her knee in deep thought. "Or someone tied to the cartels with inside knowledge. The protection request suggests fear of reprisal."

Marissa felt a coldness spread. "Cartels… that's dangerous territory."

"This entire situation carries risk," Gabriela stated plainly. "Questioning the official story puts us in the line of fire. Is this potential lead worth that increased danger?"

Gabriela made a call. "Hayes? Apologies for the hour. I need a secure phone, untraceable, for messages. How soon?" A pause. "Good. Marissa Ortega's apartment. Texting the address."

Ending the call, she said, "We respond cautiously. Verify their knowledge before any meeting."

"A trap?" Marissa's voice wavered.

"Caution is paramount." Gabriela's tone was firm. "Hayes brings a burner. We use that. Verification questions only an insider knows."

Marissa nodded, her worry evident. "Protection? We aren't law enforcement."

"We have options. Witness protection program if they're willing to testify. Relocation assistance. And Morrison certainly has the resources to ensure someone's safety if their information proves valuable." Gabriela studied Marissa. "You're having doubts."

Marissa looked at her hands. "This is… bigger than I imagined. I thought I'd help with schedules and business details. Not..." she gestured to the phone, "this."

“You can withdraw,” Gabriela offered. “No one would blame you.”

Marissa raised her gaze, a new resolve hardening her eyes. “I believed in Morrison’s work. If the company’s compromised, if he’s involved in something illegal, I need to know. If he’s innocent, he deserves a real defense.” She straightened. “I’m still in.”

Gabriela nodded. “Good. When Hayes arrives, we’ll craft a verification request. Something specific, not public.”

“Like what?” Marissa wondered.

“Details about the murder weapon, forensics… something only an insider would know.”

The doorbell rang. Hayes entered, a curt nod, and a small package.

“Untraceable,” he said, handing Gabriela the phone. “I’ve added some security features, including encryption and remote wipe capability if needed.”

“Thanks.” Gabriela showed the message to Hayes.

He read it, his face unreadable. “Carefully worded. Professional. Not random.”

“Recommendation?” Gabriela asked.

"Extreme caution. Public places, multiple exits, backup nearby." He looked at Marissa. "Understand that once you engage, there's no easy way to disengage."

Marissa swallowed, nodding.

Gabriela typed: "Interested. Need verification. Describe the murder weapon." Showed Hayes, who approved.

They waited. Five minutes. Ten.

The phone chimed.

"Silver-plated .357 Magnum. Custom grip. Morrison's initials."

Hayes and Gabriela exchanged glances.

"Not public knowledge," Hayes observed, a frown creasing his brow.

"Inside access or at the scene," Gabriela concluded.

"Or the killer," Marissa whispered, the thought chilling.

"We meet him," Gabriela decided. "Precautions." She typed: "Verification accepted. Protection needed? Information you have?"

Reply: "Safe passage south. Money for a new life. Killer's name, proof of setup, cartel link. The lawyer only, no police."

Hayes shook his head. "Demanding a lot on faith."

"Could break the case," Gabriela countered.

"Or get you killed," Marissa breathed.

Gabriela considered. "We discuss arrangements in person. Public location. Tomorrow night."

Immediate reply: "Warehouse district. Midnight. Building 17 Commerce. Alone, but someone can watch. No police, no deal."

Gabriela looked at Hayes. "Secluded but public," he noted, his expression dark. "Informant protocol."

"So, we go?" Marissa asked.

"We go," Gabriela confirmed. "Hayes watches. Contingency plan."

Marissa nodded, pale but resolute. "What do you need from me?"

"Nothing tonight. Tomorrow, I'd like you to quietly look into which of Morrison's associates might have connections to the cartels. Someone who could be our anonymous tipster."

As Hayes and Gabriela left, Marissa walked them to the door. "Be careful."

"Always," Gabriela replied, her confidence a thin veil. The text had changed everything.

Descending the stairs, the silence held a shared understanding. They were no longer just defending Morrison. They were walking into danger.

Hayes's presence made her feel less vulnerable. "I'll make sure we're covered from every angle," he affirmed, his mind already strategizing. But the risk was clear: one wrong step…

Chapter Nine

At 5:00 AM, Gabriela entered the Cooper Aerobics Center, put her work clothes in a locker, and headed outside for her run. As she ran, her breath hitched, not entirely from the exertion. Each rustle of leaves sounded like a footstep, and her pulse hammered against her ribs. The rhythmic pounding of her feet on the outdoor track and the cold bite of the iron weights forced her mind into sharp focus, each movement a counterpoint to the swirling doubts about the Morrison case.

By 6:30, the hot shower washed away physical exertion, leaving her mind clear and ready. Yet beneath the surface, a flicker of doubt remained. She thought of the informant's vague message. No name, no voice, just a promise of truth in the shadows.

While getting dressed, Gabriela glanced at the screen on her phone. One missed call from Hayes. Voicemail. "*Hey. Checked on Daniel Alvarez. He's not your guy. Been off the grid in Mexico, no current connection to anything here. If Morrison's trying to send us down a rabbit hole, he picked a quiet one.*"

Forty-five minutes later, Gabriela sat in her office and opened her laptop, creating a new document titled 'Morrison Case: Key Points.' She methodically listed 'Known Facts' and 'Critical Inquiries.' Reyes's investigation, the stolen gun, the altered evidence, and Morrison's claimed frame-up by Alvarez. The informant held potential answers, but the risk of the meeting loomed large.

As she sat at her desk, engrossed in typing out her thoughts, she became aware of a slight discomfort in her body. Her fingers, gliding over the keyboard, felt cold to the touch, a stark contrast to the warmth of the room. With each keystroke, she noticed tension creeping into her shoulders, causing them to hunch up unconsciously. Realizing this, she took a moment to consciously relax her shoulders, allowing them to drop back down to their natural position.

She glanced at the clock, the ticking seconds sounding like a countdown. She wondered if this meeting would be the moment the case turned deadly. If Morrison had lied to her, and she missed it, she wasn't just risking her reputation. She was helping a murderer walk free.

"Hola, mi amiga," Hayes greeted, his voice rough, his eyes red-rimmed.

"Still butchering the Spanish, I see," Gabriela replied, a faint smile tugging at her lips.

"Well, someone abandoned my lessons," he shot back, the playful accusation masking genuine concern.

"Touché," she conceded, her tone lightening. "So, what's the latest?"

"I just got off the phone with a contact who knows that warehouse district. Building 17 is an old textile factory, partially renovated but currently unoccupied. One main entrance on Commerce, a service entrance in the back, and a loading bay on the east side. Plenty of places for someone to hide, but also multiple exit routes."

"Surveillance cameras?"

"None functioning. The development project stalled when the investor pulled out last year." Hayes paused. "I've scouted more dangerous locations, but not many. We need a better safety protocol than me…just watching from a distance."

"What do you suggest?"

"Wire. Tracking device. And a panic button that signals me to move in."

"Won't they check for those?"

"Probably," Hayes admitted. "But we can be creative about placement. And having something is better than nothing."

Gabriela considered this. "Alright. What about backup? Should we bring Marcus?"

"Too inexperienced for this kind of situation. I have a former colleague. His name is Ron Ramirez. Twenty years on the force, the last ten in narcotics. He knows cartel operations and can be discreet."

"Can you trust him?"

"With my life. Have, several times."

"Call him," Gabriela decided. "But make it clear that this stays between us. No department involvement, no reports."

"Already stipulated. We're meeting at noon to review the layout and security positions."

The informant's knowledge and Morrison's gun strongly suggested inside information. If legitimate, this person could be the key to unraveling the entire case. If not, they could be leading her into an elaborate trap.

She called Marissa.

"Did I wake you?" she asked when Marissa answered.

"No, I've been up for hours. Couldn't sleep." Marissa's voice carried the strain of their shared predicament. "I've been looking into Morrison's associates with Mexican connections, like you asked."

"And?"

"Two names stand out. James Morrison, Phillip's brother, oversees their Mexican drilling operations and makes monthly trips to Monterrey. And Carlos Delgado. Morrison has told me that Delgado was their primary business partner in Mexico, whose name appears in a DEA report from 2018, though no charges were filed."

"Either of them in Dallas now?"

"Neither of them. James is supposedly in Houston but hasn't checked in with the office in three days, which is unusual. And Delgado is still in Mexico."

Gabriela absorbed this information. "Has anyone at the company shown unusual interest in your activities since you started helping us?"

"Not overtly, but..." Marissa hesitated. "Yesterday, I found someone had accessed my computer while I was at lunch. The system logs showed files related to Morrison's schedule had been viewed."

"Do you know who?"

"No. It was done using admin credentials."

Another variable in an already complex equation. "Be careful at the office today. Don't do any research on company computers, and watch for anyone taking special interest in your movements."

"You're scaring me, Ms. Sanchez…"

"Good. A healthy dose of paranoia is appropriate right now." Gabriela softened her tone. "Just stay alert until after tonight's meeting. Hopefully, our informant will give us what we need, and we can take a more official approach going forward."

After ending the call, Gabriela spent the next hours reviewing case materials and preparing for potential scenarios at the warehouse. She created a list of questions designed to extract maximum information while revealing minimum details about their investigation. She recalled recent reports detailing violent incidents in the warehouse district, including assaults and robberies, underscoring the area's high crime rate. She studied maps of the warehouse district, identifying escape routes and potential hazards.

At three o'clock, Hayes arrived with his equipment.

"Miniature transmitter," he explained, showing her a device smaller than a dime. "Range of half a mile, battery life of eight hours. We'll conceal it in your bra."

"My bra?"

"Yeah, it's the least likely place they'll check if they pat you down."

He showed her how to use the panic button on a tiny device that looked like a hair clip and explained the procedure they would follow if she required extraction.

"I'll be positioned here," Hayes indicated on the warehouse map, "with a line of sight to the main entrance. I'll also cover the rear exit. I'll be armed and wearing a tactical vest."

"And if the informant spooks?"

"Then, we get you out safely and regroup. No information is worth your life." Hayes's expression was deadly serious. "These cartel-connected individuals don't play by any rules you learned in law school or Congress. If something feels wrong, you use that panic button, no questions asked."

Hayes's words stayed with her. 'No information is worth your life.' She wondered if he was preparing her for the worst.

Gabriela nodded. The danger of what she was preparing to do was now very real. "I've faced difficult situations before, Hayes."

"Political opponents and hostile witnesses don't typically carry automatic weapons and dispose of bodies in acid," he countered bluntly. "This is a different territory."

The afternoon passed with further preparations. Hayes left to meet with his colleague and make final arrangements at the warehouse site. Gabriela changed into dark jeans, a black blouse, and a jacket with inner pockets for the secure phone and other necessities. Nothing that would restrict movement if she needed to run.

As evening approached, she called Chuck Green.

"Just checking in," she said, keeping her tone casual. "Any developments I should know about?"

"Nothing urgent," he replied. "How's the Morrison case progressing?"

"We're pursuing several promising leads." She deliberately kept it vague. "I may be unreachable tonight. I'm following up on something."

There was a pause on the line. During the silence, she could hear her own heartbeat. She reminded herself to breathe.

"Gabriela, you're not doing anything reckless, are you?"

"Define reckless."

"Don't be cute. I know that tone. You're about to do something I would advise against."

She smiled despite herself. After their time together in the firm, Green could read her even through a phone call.

"I'm being careful," she assured him. "But this case requires unorthodox approaches."

"Just remember, Gabriela, no case is worth your safety. Morrison included."

"Noted."

After hanging up, Gabriela sat in the deepening twilight of her home, mentally preparing for what lay ahead. She pressed two fingers to her wrist. Her pulse raced. Sweat rolled down her temple.

In law school, they taught that an attorney's primary duty was zealous representation of their client within the bounds of the law. They didn't mention midnight meetings with cartel informants or the flutter of fear that now resided in her chest.

Her phone chimed with a text from Hayes: "Equipment ready. Will pick you up at 11:15."

She sent a simple acknowledgment, then closed her eyes, focusing on her breathing. In her years as a trial attorney, she'd learned that fear could be managed and channeled into heightened awareness. Tonight, that skill would be tested in ways the courtroom had never demanded.

She scanned her condo, ensuring everything was in its place. She wanted no loose ends, no distractions. As darkness settled over Dallas, Gabriela Sanchez prepared to step beyond the familiar boundaries of legal practice and into territory where the stakes were no longer measured in verdicts and appeals but in whether her client walked out the front door with her or left through the side door on the way to prison.

#

Chapter Ten

The warehouses stood abandoned, their hollow shells casting long shadows under the dim streetlights. Gabriela zipped her coat against the biting chill, the wind whipping at the fabric. She slipped her cell phone into her pocket, noting the poor reception in this desolate area.

She breathed out hard, the cold air making her eyes sting. She questioned her decision to trust the informant. A flickering streetlight illuminated the dumpster's designated meeting point. She headed toward it, navigating the slick ground marred by oil stains and scattered debris.

Hayes, stationed on a rooftop overlooking the area, adjusted his scope to maintain a clear view of Gabriela. His years away from active duty made him wary, but his commitment to her safety was unwavering. He checked out the surroundings, noting potential threats and ensuring no unexpected visitors approached the meeting site.

Gabriela reached the dumpster, positioning herself with a clear line of sight to her car, where her nine-millimeter rested in the glovebox. A precaution she now regretted not keeping closer. She adjusted her stance, the concealed holster a reminder of the night's stakes. The distant hum of the city contrasted with the oppressive silence of the warehouse district, amplifying her awareness of every sound.

Hayes's experienced eyes caught a subtle movement. A figure emerged cautiously from behind a forklift. He tightened his grip on his rifle, ready to intervene at the first sign of trouble. The informant's nervous demeanor was evident even from a distance, his hands buried deep in his jacket pockets, shoulders hunched against the cold, or perhaps his conscience.

Gabriela's voice cut through the silence, firm yet measured. "That's far enough." The informant halted, glancing around as if expecting shadows to come alive. He gestured toward the dumpster, suggesting they move to a more concealed spot. Gabriela hesitated, then nodded, ensuring she remained within Hayes's line of sight.

From his rooftop perch, Hayes's scope swept the shadows, each flicker of movement drawing his attention. He noted the wind's direction, the play of light on metal, the subtle shifts that betrayed hidden threats. The wind clawed at his coat, a constant, whispering threat. He could feel the cold seeping into his bones, but his focus on Gabriela and the informant remained laser-sharp. He held his breath, listening for any sound beyond the wind.

Behind the dumpster, the informant's voice trembled as he spoke. "Did you get the files?"

Gabriela nodded. “I did. But I need names, dates, and more concrete evidence.”

He shifted nervously, eyes darting to the shadows. “It’s bigger than you think. They’re everywhere. I need protection.”

Before Gabriela could respond, a hollow boom echoed through the district, sharp and sudden. The informant’s breath hitched, a ragged gasp in the cold air. It had to be a gunshot. Had to be someone closing in. Gabriela grabbed the informant by his collar and pulled him further into the shadows. “Where is it?” she asked. “Where’s the rest?”

His breath sputtered. “It’s not safe,” he said. “They’re gonna know.” His nerves were shot, worse than hers. But he was right about one thing. They couldn’t talk there. She cut him loose, thinking about keeping Parker & McEvoy’s firm name out of the paper. More importantly, she thought about keeping her name out of the obituaries. She could see the headlines: Former Rep and Key Witness Found Dead in Warehouses.

“I can’t stay,” he repeated, his voice almost a whisper, as though the shadows themselves were listening in. She watched with conflicted resolve as he turned away and disappeared into the maze of warehouses, footsteps echoing through the empty alleys. Her instincts urged her to follow, to press him until she had all she needed, but logic reminded her of the plan. She was bait, after all, and if they were closing in, she'd better move fast. She touched the concealed transmitter, a silent signal to Hayes that the meeting had concluded. She exhaled a shaky breath, the cold air stinging her lungs. Each footstep crunched on the debris, amplified in the silence. She held her breath between steps, listening.

Hayes remained on the rooftop, shifting to keep Gabriela in view. From his vantage point, he saw her weaving between buildings, every line of her body tense with wary speed. She was moving too fast for comfort, which meant something had gone wrong. He swept the warehouses with his scope, finger hovering over the trigger, his military instincts alive with the expectation of conflict. No movement. No one is pursuing. Just the fading footfalls of the informant and Gabriela's distant silhouette.

He didn't relax or let his guard down. He wouldn't until Gabriela was safely inside her vehicle. Only then would he start to leave. The gunshot still echoed in his ears, louder than it had any right to be.

He disappeared down a fire escape, leaving no trace behind except the chill where he had been. They'd meet in her office the next morning if they both made it out.

No one followed. Maybe the shot was meant to scare them off. Maybe it was a warning. Or maybe it was just some kid fucking around with a piece of junk. At moments like this, paranoia came as easily as breathing.

She accelerated through the narrow streets of the warehouse district, lights flashing by in a blur. The adrenaline gave Gabriela focus, her thoughts sharp and jagged. The meeting had gone sideways fast, ending with a warning, a threat. She glanced in the rearview mirror. No one seemed to be following, but she knew they could be anywhere, watching, waiting. The danger didn't frighten her. It made her more determined.

The informant's nervous eyes, the distant sirens, the interrupted meeting. Setup. He was holding back. His final warning still echoed in her ears. They had just begun to uncover real information when it all went wrong. He had given her enough to pique her interest but not enough to act on.

Was he playing them? Or was he truly terrified? She could not tell. Her instincts told her he was holding back, playing both sides, or worse. She relived the moment of panic when their meeting was interrupted, and his final warning, vague and chilling, resonated in her mind.

Her thoughts shifted to the flash drive. She knew it was a risk. It might be nothing, a ploy to throw them off. It could be a trap. Yet, the urgency in the informant's voice convinced her to take it, and that act alone meant they were getting close to something. The information could lead them right into a well-laid ambush, but it could also be the breakthrough they needed. Doubts gnawed at her, but she refused to second-guess herself. They would know soon enough if it was genuine.

Gabriela navigated the maze of streets and approached the tollway. Her mind leapt from one possibility to the next, trying to piece together who might have sent the man and who would benefit from disrupting the meeting. There were too many variables, and all of them were dangerous. She had a list of potential enemies, but nothing concrete enough to narrow it down. All she knew for certain was that they were now on alert, and so was she.

Risk had always been part of her career, but this felt different. The stakes were higher, and the lines blurred between her professional obligations and personal convictions. The failed meeting only strengthened her resolve. Her principles wouldn't allow her to back down. Gabriela had been in tough spots before, but nothing with this level of complexity and threat. The investigation touched on more than just legal battles. It was a test of how far she was willing to go.

Her focus turned to Hayes and the meeting they had planned in the morning in her office. Their careful preparation for a scenario like this reassured her. They'd developed contingencies, anticipating moves and countermoves. She replayed the details, making mental notes on what to address first. Hayes would have insights she hadn't considered. The flash drive needed immediate attention, and they would approach it with caution. Gabriela's experience told her that timing was critical. Every moment counted.

As she merged onto the Dallas North Tollway, the reality of the situation hit her in waves. The road stretched out ahead, and with it, the enormity of what they faced. She felt alive, invigorated by the pursuit. There was no turning back now. The stakes, the risks, and the uncertainties pushed her forward, fueling her drive. With each passing mile, the distance from the warehouse faded, replaced by the urgency of the task ahead. She was in control, and her determination to see it through was absolute.

The morning sun filtered through the blinds of Gabriela's office, casting soft patterns on the polished wooden floor. Gabriela sat behind her desk, her fingers drumming an irregular rhythm on the mahogany surface, her thoughts miles away, replaying the events of the previous night.

A soft knock at the door pulled her from her reverie. Before she could respond, the door creaked open, and Lucia, followed by Hayes, stepped in, his presence as commanding as ever. Dressed in a crisp shirt and tailored trousers, he exuded an air of readiness, though the faint shadows under his eyes hinted at shared sleeplessness.

"Morning," Gabriela greeted, attempting a semblance of normalcy.

"Morning," Hayes replied, closing the door behind him. He took a seat opposite her, placing a slim folder on the desk between them. "You okay?"

Gabriela offered a tight smile. "I've been better. It went wrong fast," Gabriela began, dropping her bag next to a chair. She sat and leaned forward, tension evident in every movement.

"What happened?" Hayes asked, gaze sharp and unwavering.

"The informant was nervous, almost too nervous. Like he knew what was coming," she said, her voice measured and controlled.

"He warned you?"

"Yes. But not before giving us this." She took the flash drive from her pocket and placed it on the table between them. "The meeting got interrupted. Felt like a setup."

Hayes frowned, picking up the drive and turning it over in his fingers. "Police?"

"Or something else. There was no time to figure it out."

They paused, letting the uncertainty sink in. The air in the room was thin, charged with the gravity of their situation.

"You think it's genuine?" Hayes finally asked.

"I don't know. But it could be our only lead."

Hayes placed the flash drive back on the table and crossed his arms. "If it's real, it could blow this wide open. But if it's not..."

Gabriela nodded, understanding the implications. "We have to try. We can't ignore the chance."

"And what about the chance that they're watching us now? That they're one step ahead?"

"We knew the risks. We planned for this. We need to keep moving," Gabriela said, her voice steady with determination.

Hayes leaned back, considering her words. His mind was already sorting through possibilities, forming a strategy. "You said he warned you. What exactly did he say?"

Gabriela's gaze drifted for a moment, recalling the scene in vivid detail. "He said things were bigger than we thought. That we were close but didn't know how close."

"And you think he was holding back?"

"Yes," she replied, the conviction in her voice clear. "Either he's afraid, or he's playing us. But I think he's more scared of them than he is of us."

Hayes tapped a pencil against his notebook, a rhythmic sound in the otherwise silent room. “We need to analyze this drive, but carefully. If it’s a setup, we can’t walk right into it.”

“And if it’s not?” Gabriela asked, pressing the point.

“Then we need to move quickly before they have a chance to regroup. Either way, we act fast.”

She stood, pacing the small space, her mind racing with thoughts of their next move. “The interruption seemed deliberate. Like they wanted to scare us off.”

“Then we don’t give them what they want,” Hayes said, his tone resolute.

They both understood the gravity of their decision. The risks were enormous, but so were the potential rewards. Gabriela’s instincts told her to push forward, and Hayes’ logical approach balanced her determination with caution.

“We need to stay ahead,” Gabriela said, stopping to face him.

“Agreed. We operate as if they’re watching and cover all angles,” Hayes replied, his focus unwavering.

They had started this investigation knowing it would be difficult, but the failed meeting confirmed their fears about the complexity and danger. Still, neither was willing to back down. The flash drive was a gamble, but one they had to take.

As they prepared to analyze the data, a sense of urgency permeated everything. They were on the edge of something monumental, and both were acutely aware that this was just the beginning. They resolved to push forward, fully committed to seeing it through, no matter where it led.

Chapter Eleven

The flash drive clicked into the laptop. Gabriela watched as the screen came to life. They leaned in, shoulders nearly touching. Hayes typed rapidly, and the files popped up, row after row, until Gabriela lost count. There had to be hundreds of them. He opened the first. They scanned page after page of account numbers, business transactions, and payouts. Her head spun. This would take days to untangle. But with each file, the shape of it became a little clearer.

"So far, this was just scratching the surface," Hayes said, not looking up from the screen.

Gabriela leaned back, letting him work through the information. The room felt claustrophobic, closing in around her as the magnitude of what they were uncovering settled in. Hayes opened another file. Her eyes traced a familiar pattern. A shell company linked to another, hidden within multiple contracts and filings. It all looked legitimate until you dug deep enough.

Hayes scrolled through more transactions. Gabriela lost herself in thought. The last time she sat across from Hayes like this, everything unraveled in ways she couldn't control. She looked at the data on the screen, then at him. "Whoever set this up covered their tracks well."

"Not well enough." Hayes moved to the next file. "I wonder how long they thought this would stay hidden."

They uncovered several powerful and influential individuals tied to the conspiracy, including detailed financial records linked directly to Stephen Penbrooke. Gabriela stopped him when a name flashed by. A name she knew well. She gestured for him to go back. There it was. Stephen Penbrooke.

"Penbrooke?" Gabriela's voice was sharp, a mix of recognition and disgust. "I should have known he'd be involved. That snake lobbied me for months on that energy bill. He's always trying to line his pockets. And now, it seems, he's lining them with blood money."

"What is it?" Hayes asked, his eyes still on the screen.

Gabriela paused, her mind racing. "He met with me when I was in Congress. He's a real snake, always been involved in shady dealings. He tried to bribe me to vote for an energy bill, and when I refused, he made it clear I'd regret it."

Hayes looked up from the screen, his expression serious. "This changes everything."

She nodded. "The only surprise was that he wasn't more careful."

Gabriela looked at the list. There was a former governor, a federal judge, and an ambassador. Most of them she had only met in passing. A few were close enough that she wondered if any of this was her fault. If somehow she knew and ignored it. She was back in it, as she knew she would be, despite everything.

"This implicates your entire network," Hayes said. "How deep do you think it goes?"

"Deeper than either of us wants," Gabriela said, standing up with stiff legs. She paced, trying to grasp the implications of what they had just uncovered. If these names were tied to the conspiracy, it could reach beyond the people she knew directly. Beyond Washington and into areas she had no experience with. There could be dangerous people involved. People who did not make threats idly. "This changes nothing," she said. "If anything, we have to push harder now."

Hayes closed the laptop. "You're sure? You realize how personal this just got."

The only thing she realized was that there was no turning back now. "We should cross-reference this with public records and build a stronger picture before we move forward."

"And what about people who might help?"

She considered her contacts. Some were allies. Others were enemies. Many had been both. There were favors owed and grudges unresolved. Her reputation, already damaged, wouldn't survive another mistake, especially if she picked the wrong person.

"Someone from financial crimes," she said. "A former colleague. Someone I trust. Someone clean."

Hayes watched her. "If they were all your former colleagues, why did you need me?"

She didn't have an answer he would believe. "I needed someone I could trust. Someone whose hands weren't already dirty."

"We should work fast," Hayes said. "Someone had already come after you once. We don't know how much time we have."

She nodded, remembering the sudden cold in the pit of her stomach when she received the USB drive. No note. Just a message on the return address label: REMEMBER. She knew she would remember every moment, every detail of this. She always did.

"I'll call my contact," Gabriela said, reaching for her phone. "See if he can meet us tonight."

"Tonight?" Hayes raised an eyebrow.

"We don't have the luxury of time," Gabriela said, already dialing. The phone rang twice before a familiar voice answered.

"David, it's Gabriela. I need your help." She paused, listening to the response. "I have something... complicated. Financial records, shell companies, names you wouldn't believe. I need someone who can make sense of it, and I need them now."

She listened again, her expression hardening. "I know it's late, David, but this can't wait. Lives are on the line." She glanced at Hayes, a silent message passing between them. This was bigger than either of them had imagined.

"Good," Gabriela said into the phone. "An hour. Last Place Cafe. And David... come alone."

She ended the call and looked at Hayes. "He's in. But we need to be ready for anything. This could get ugly."

Gabriela glanced at the names on the laptop. No, she wasn't ready. She was never ready. She didn't let that stop her.

"We can't let this sit," she said, walking to the door. "The longer it took, the more exposed we were. Let's start making calls."

"Let's hope someone picked up," Hayes said.

Gabriela doubted that anyone would. Not without a fight.

They both stopped talking. Gabriela looked at Hayes, then at the blank cell phone. They waited on the patio of a small café. The last hour stretched time. The tables are filled with people. None of them carried the air of compromise she had expected. The smell of fresh bread mingled with the growing certainty of an ambush. Hayes urged patience. She told him patience was for men with nothing to lose.

"What do you want to do?" Hayes whispered over the lunchtime crowd.

Gabriela watched the sidewalk. "We're too exposed here."

"So, we leave," he said.

"And if David showed up?" She shifted her gaze. "We wait."

Hayes grinned. "You still get nervous."

"Shut up."

"Let's give David another five minutes."

She spotted David. Grayer hair, stooped posture. Gabriela stood and waved. "Five more minutes, huh?"

"I'd be lying if I said no."

David approached, glancing around. He held a manila envelope.

"I thought you ditched me," Gabriela said.

"Almost did. You can't reach out like that."

"You used to enjoy risk."

"Used to. This isn't the time. I thought we were discreet."

"We don't have time," Gabriela said. "Sit."

They moved to a secluded table. David slid into the chair, scanning the patio. The envelope remained untouched.

"Let's hear it," Gabriela said.

"We can't be seen with this."

"Did you look at it?" she asked.

David nodded.

"You realize what you're doing, Gabriela?"

"I realize. Can you help us?"

"We've been through the files."

"Who's 'we'?" Hayes asked.

"Can we trust you?" Gabriela asked.

"You? Yes. Him? Not so much."

"We can't let this get back to us," David continued.

"It won't. What angles do we have?"

"This won't be like your other cases."

Gabriela stiffened. "We know."

"And you still want to do it?"

"Absolutely."

David shrugged. "This information might help. It's a breakdown of some of the financial transactions, the ones Penbrooke was involved in." He slid the envelope across the table. "There are more pieces. You're risking more than your reputation."

"Thank you," Gabriela said.

Hayes laughed.

"We should go," Gabriela said.

Chapter Twelve

In the tense days following the warehouse meeting, the panoramic view of Dallas stretched out from Gabriela's office, and the city lights had begun to prick the darkening sky. Inside, the silence was broken only by the quiet click of the keyboard as she sorted through the envelope. The thin paper rustled like dry leaves, a stark contrast to the digital glow of the laptop screen. Most of it duplicated the information on the flash drive, but some of it looked new, and she had learned not to trust appearances. Hayes paced, his footsteps muffled by the plush carpet, and an unsettling grin tugged at the corner of his mouth.

A faint, distant drone from the city below made her pause. Then, a sharp, metallic click, likely the office printer, caused Gabriela's gaze to flicker to the door. Her senses were on high alert.

"I thought we might have been compromised," he said.

"We had accounted for that already," she replied.

"No," he insisted, holding up a phone. "This was new. Someone logged in last night to one of our backup accounts."

She hesitated, the feeling of betrayal stronger than the fear she pretended was absent. She recalled the unease in her contact's voice, the way they had glanced over their shoulder, and wondered how much they had revealed. “Great,” she said, surprised by her own indifference. “We keep moving.”

“Seriously, Gabriela. You’re fine with this?” he asked.

“I’m used to this,” she replied.

“Was that what it was like in Congress?”

She stared at him, the softness of his face caught between suspicion and disbelief. “Worse,” she said.

He watched her for a moment. “You’re having fun.”

“No,” she replied, though she couldn’t tell which of them she was trying to convince. “Just seeing this through.”

Hayes put down the phone. He opened the laptop and motioned for her to join him. She looked out the window, the horizon blackened by oncoming clouds, and told herself they wouldn’t storm until she was ready.

Gabriela stared at the screen. The facts were there, impossible to ignore. Now came the question of what to do with them. The documents revealed a pattern that was disturbingly familiar, though she couldn’t immediately pinpoint why. Each new detail was filled in the picture. This wasn’t a coincidence. Someone with power had set it in motion, and they were no longer guessing who.

Her eyes burned, and her head pulsed. She had not slept in two days, yet she couldn't pull herself away. Hayes sat beside her, leafing through printouts, pausing to scribble notes before tossing them back onto the table.

"This is big," Hayes said. "Bigger than anything I've seen."

"Did you expect less?" Gabriela didn't answer right away. She had expected less. She thought it was just power games. But this went deeper, and she still didn't know how far it reached.

"I didn't expect this." Hayes pointed to a new document on the screen. It displayed familiar names alongside new ones, each one crossing a border they had not considered until then.

Gabriela closed her eyes, letting the names scroll by like credits to a movie she had already seen. It was all organized crime, offshore laundering, and international trades that shouldn't have connected but somehow did. It felt like there were more players in this than anyone could handle.

"This is dangerous," Hayes said. "We might want to consider backing off."

She laughed, but the sound carried no humor. "You know better than that."

They sat in silence, absorbing the magnitude of what lay before them. Every new document added to the pile, they could barely keep up with. There was more than they could manage, and the smell of ink and old paper became a sharp, persistent memory. Gabriela scanned the data and wondered how much of it was her fault.

The last time she had let herself get this deep, she had lost a case she thought she should have won. But if she turned back now, she knew it would haunt her. Worse than any failure she could have lived with.

The newness of this grew into a familiarity she couldn't ignore. She was running out of names when a message popped up on her screen. The subject line was one word: RESIGN.

"We should," Hayes began, but she held up a hand to stop him. She clicked to open it.

The body consisted of three sentences, and each one rattled her more than the last. "Back off while you still can. It will be your undoing. This isn't a game you can win."

She caught her breath. The emails from her staff had never had this effect. Neither had the press releases from people who wanted her gone. Her pulse raced, and she hadn't felt this terrified in years. It thrilled her in ways that filled her with shame. She told herself she was fine, even though she knew she wasn't.

"You okay?" Hayes asked.

"Do you see who it's from?" she said, her voice breaking over the words like glass falling on a soft surface.

Hayes leaned in closer. "There was no sender. It just showed up."

"I see that."

He shifted his chair toward her, his eyes narrowing. "Then why weren't you freaking out?"

"I was," she admitted.

"Looks like you were loving it."

She exhaled slowly and controlled her breathing. She couldn't let him see how much this rattled her. It wasn't just the threat. It was the clarity of how deeply she was already entangled. "We keep working," she said, though she knew it was too late to pretend she was fine.

Hayes studied her. "You realize what this means, right?"

Gabriela paused, her fingers still on the keyboard. She didn't meet his eyes. "That someone is concerned enough to make their presence known."

"That someone could get to you." Hayes looked at the pile of documents, then at her. He tapped a document, then looked back at her. "The moment we file anything, they'll know."

She leaned back, utterly drained. The hours of sifting through data and the constant tension had all taken their toll. "I appreciate the reminder."

"You don't have to do this."

Gabriela rubbed her forehead, then refocused on Hayes. "We're past that conversation, Hayes."

"I thought you were about justice. This feels…personal."

Gabriela met his gaze. She gave a small, almost imperceptible nod. "Justice should be personal, Hayes. That's why we fight for it. And I won't walk away from this."

Hayes's expression softened, though he remained unreadable.

That night, she barely slept. By sunrise, her mind was still racing, and she needed distance from the screen and the threats that seemed to multiply with every email. She pulled her clubs out of the corner of the garage and drove to Tenison Park, the course where she had first played in Dallas years ago.

The practice range was nearly empty, dew still clinging to the grass. Gabriela teed a ball, settled into her stance, and swung. The familiar crack of the driver echoed across the fairway. The ball soared high, drawing a perfect line against the pale morning sky before dropping near the 250-yards sign.

A young pro picking up range balls stopped and stared. "That's not beginner stuff," he said with a grin. She smiled faintly but said nothing. She didn't need to explain who she had been—a college golfer who nearly won the NCAA championship, a competitor who once thought golf was her future.

She hit another ball, then another. Each swing loosened the tight coil inside her, but the calm never lasted. By the fifth shot, her mind was already back at the office, sifting through names, betrayals, and threats. She set the club down, reminding herself that patience—on the course and in the courtroom—was what had always given her an edge.

By the time she got back to her office, Hayes was already there, papers scattered across the table. The brief calm from the range had disappeared, replaced by the same relentless urgency.

"Let's not waste any more time," she said, turning back to the screen. She began typing faster. "We have work to do."

The documents were a mess of lies and denials that intersected in all the wrong places. She tried sorting them, but the pieces shifted too quickly. Hayes's handwriting was all over the printouts, his questions and thoughts merged with hers. Gabriela had never collaborated like this, and the discomfort of it gnawed at her confidence.

"This is your way out," he said, reading over her shoulder.

"My way out of what?"

"This," he replied, circling a connection she hadn't noticed.

A headline caught her eye: Police investigating major drug cartel for links to the journalist's murder. "You think it's related?"

"I'd bet on it," Hayes said.

"It's a stretch."

"So, were most of your cases," he reminded her.

Gabriela picked up the printout, her hand trembling slightly. She couldn't tell if it was from exhaustion, adrenaline, or something else. "It's too obvious," she said.

"It doesn't matter," Hayes insisted. "We follow it and see where it leads."

"Wasn't that what got us into this in the first place?"

He paused, a questioning look in his eyes. "Do you really want to know the answer?"

She sat quietly, the ticking in her head was growing louder. Perhaps she didn't want to know the answer. Perhaps she just wanted to pretend that it was all she could handle. "We don't stop," she finally said.

"Are you going to lose your edge over this?"

She closed her eyes. "I'm going to find it."

They sifted through the data until the words became shapes that only hinted at meaning. It took an hour, maybe two, yet each minute stretched farther than the one before it. Gabriela read Hayes's notes, most of them pointing to things she had already considered. The advantage of working with him was that he saw her blind spots. The disadvantage was that he knew when she wasn't telling herself the truth. She handed the paper back to him.

"Don't give up on me," she said.

"Wouldn't think of it," Hayes replied.

His smile was genuine, but it didn't reach his eyes. Gabriela felt a slight panic as he pushed the laptop away and turned to face her. She didn't know what he was going to say, but she braced herself. For Hayes, for the threat of a looming failure, for her own inability to stop herself from playing this out until the bitter end.

"Think they'll come after you again?" Hayes asked.

She knew they would. She hoped they did.

Chapter Thirteen

The lights dimmed, leaving her illuminated only by the headlights of passing cars. Hayes didn't know if it was a signal or a coincidence, but either way, he reached for his phone. He watched her through the camera's lens, wanting proof that she had really been there. The restaurant was deserted. He waited another minute, just to be sure, then slid into the booth. At first, he didn't recognize her.

"Christ, Hayes," she said, a bitter laugh cutting through the silence. "I didn't think you'd show. After everything we saw from that flash drive last night, I wasn't sure you'd still answer my calls."

He put his phone away, trying to read her expression. There was more history in her look than he remembered, and he wasn't sure he wanted to unearth it. "I thought you didn't work nights."

"Some exceptions," she replied. She leaned back, her features caught between shadow and streetlight. "Where's Gabriela?"

He watched the door, the unease pressing down like a tidal wave. "Would it have made a difference?"

She nodded, though he wasn't sure whether she meant yes or no. "I assumed she had told you everything."

"Everything she knew."

Her smile was sharp and a little cruel. “That wasn’t much.”

They sat across from each other, letting the conversation weigh down on the table. Hayes said nothing. He wasn’t going to take the bait. She had always been good at laying traps he hadn’t seen until he stepped right into them. She leaned forward, crossing her arms. The lights dimmed again, and this time, there were no car headlights to illuminate her.

“You should be careful with her,” she said, her voice dropping.

“She knows what she’s doing.”

His contact looked up, locking eyes with him. “Not this time.”

“She thought she could handle it.”

“She always could handle anything. She’s fearless in the courtroom.”

He wanted to argue, but he didn’t. Gabriela had more at stake than he did, and for a moment, he wasn’t sure whether he should feel relieved or disappointed. “You’re right. She’s driven.”

“And formidable,” his contact added. “That’s why she takes chances.”

“Not for her.” Hayes picked at the corner of the table. “She’ll be fine.”

His contact shook her head. "Not if she keeps pushing like this."

Hayes leaned back, trying to keep the confidence in his voice steady. "You don't know her as well as you think you do. You only see her from a distance."

She gave him a sharp look. "I knew her before she left Dallas. Before, she was known for anything besides the way she dressed in sharp suits, fitted skirts, and heels that turned heads in every Dallas hallway.

The lights dimmed, leaving her illuminated only by the headlights of passing cars. Hayes didn't know if it was a signal or a coincidence, but either way, he reached for his phone. He watched her through the camera's lens, wanting proof that she had really been there. The restaurant was deserted. He waited another minute, just to be sure, then slid into the booth. At first, he didn't recognize her.

"Christ, Hayes," she said, a bitter laugh cutting through the silence. "I didn't think you'd show. After all the information we saw from that flash drive last night, I wasn't sure you'd still answer my calls."

He put his phone away, trying to read her expression. There was more history in her look than he remembered, and he wasn't sure he wanted to unearth it. "I thought you didn't work nights."

“Some exceptions,” she replied. She leaned back, her features caught between shadow and the faint glow of the streetlight. “Where’s Gabriela?”

He watched the door, the unease pressing down like a tidal wave. “Would it have made a difference?”

She nodded, though he wasn’t sure whether she meant yes or no. “I assumed she had told you everything.”

“Everything she knew.”

Her smile was sharp and a little cruel. “That wasn’t much.”

They sat across from each other, letting the conversation weigh down on the table. Hayes said nothing. He wasn’t going to take the bait. She had always been good at laying traps he hadn’t seen until he stepped right into them. She leaned forward, crossing her arms. The lights dimmed again, and this time, there were no car headlights to illuminate her.

“You should be careful with her,” she said, her voice dropping.

“She knows what she’s doing.”

His contact looked up, locking eyes with him. “Not this time.”

“She thought she could handle it.”

"She always could handle anything. She's fearless in the courtroom and never lets being the only Latina in the room slow her down."

He wanted to argue, but he didn't. Gabriela had more at stake than he did, and for a moment, he wasn't sure whether he should feel relieved or disappointed. "You're right. She's driven. Tough as steel."

"And formidable," his contact added. "That's why she takes chances."

"Not for her." Hayes picked at the corner of the table. "She'll be fine."

His contact shook her head. "Not if she keeps pushing like this."

Hayes leaned back, trying to keep the confidence in his voice steady. "You don't know her as well as you think you do. You only see her from a distance."

She gave him a sharp look. "I knew her before she left Dallas. Before, she had to fight for everything, and before, she was known for her looks and the short skirts she wore back then. I saw what she had to overcome."

"She's fighting for justice."

The contact's expression softened, but her voice still held a trace of concern. "Justice, or a fight she can't walk away from?"

"They're not mutually exclusive."

She hesitated, then said, "Just…be careful, Hayes. And keep her safe," his contact added, her eyes darkening with something Hayes couldn't define. "We both know what she's capable of, but this is beyond even her."

Hayes felt himself wavering. He had heard stories about Gabriela before. Stories of her determination, and that she had threats against her before, and every time, she had insisted she was fine and that she would keep going.

"What are we up against?"

"Something she can't beat," his contact said.

He let the statement linger, wondering if there was anything he could say to refute it. "Then why were you here?"

She hesitated, then reached into her bag and pulled out a small flash drive. "I don't want to see her crash and burn and take me down with her."

He didn't know whether to be grateful or wary. The contradiction gnawed at him, yet he kept his expression impassive, unwilling to reveal his uncertainty.

"You've always had your own reasons for doing things," she said, her voice softening slightly.

"And you haven't?"

She dropped the drive onto the table, where it slid to a stop just before the edge. "This might help. If she's smart enough to use it."

"She is."

The restaurant was too quiet. The lights dimmed, and when they brightened, she was gone, leaving only the flash drive on the table. He snatched it up, the flash drive holding unknown information. *What had she given him?*. I saw what she had to overcome."

"She's fighting for justice."

The contact's expression softened, but her voice still held a trace of concern. "Justice, or a fight she can't walk away from?"

"They're not mutually exclusive."

She hesitated, then said, "Just…be careful, Hayes. And keep her safe," his contact added, her eyes darkening with something Hayes couldn't define. "We both know what she's capable of, but this is beyond even her."

Hayes felt himself wavering. He had heard stories about Gabriela before. Stories of her determination, and that she had threats against her before, and every time, she had insisted she was fine and that she would keep going.

"What are we up against?"

"Something she can't beat," his contact said.

He let the statement linger, wondering if there was anything he could say to refute it. "Then why were you here?"

She hesitated, then reached into her bag and pulled out a small flash drive. "I don't want to see her crash and burn and take me down with her."

He didn't know whether to be grateful or wary. The contradiction gnawed at him, yet he kept his expression impassive, unwilling to reveal his uncertainty.

"You've always had your own reasons for doing things," she said, her voice softening slightly.

"And you haven't?"

She dropped the drive onto the table, where it slid to a stop just before the edge. "This might help. If she's smart enough to use it."

"She is."

The restaurant was too quiet. The lights dimmed, and when they brightened, she was gone, leaving only the flash drive on the table.

He snatched it up, the flash drive holding unknown information. *What had she given him?*

Chapter Fourteen

The glow of the laptop illuminated Gabriela's office, the flash drive lying next to the keyboard. The information that the contact had given them could be the key to everything. Gabriela had worked most of the night and was asleep on the sofa, her head resting on a pile of documents. She stirred when he entered, and by the time he crossed the room, she was alert and reaching for her phone.

"Everything all right?" she asked.

"Good enough," he replied, careful to keep doubt from creeping in.

Gabriela stretched and then nodded toward the flash drive in his hand. "From your source?"

"You could say that."

She took it and inserted it into the laptop. He watched her closely, yet she didn't flinch or hesitate as the data appeared on the screen. Her pulse must have remained steady. Her mind, clear. He envied her resilience, though part of him wondered how long it would last.

"Looks like new evidence," she said.

"It is," Hayes confirmed.

"And you trust it?"

He sat next to her, eyeing the files with caution. "As much as we can trust anything."

She understood what he meant, but she wouldn't let him see her uncertainty. It was a lesson she had learned long ago that had kept her from being dragged under by the current of those who wanted her to sink. She nodded, as much to herself as to him. "Let's keep working."

He should have felt relieved by her determination, but he imagined the worst. Gabriela sat up straighter, her face a mask of concentration.

"Don't lose yourself in this," he said.

"Someone has to," she replied, her eyes locked on the screen.

It was more of an admission than he had expected. She dove back into the data, her attention narrowing on the screen. Hayes wondered if she was losing her touch, or if she had simply been waiting for a chance to prove she hadn't. Either way, he thought, she'd find out sooner than she wanted.

Hours passed as they sifted through the data. Just as the first rays of dawn touched the horizon, a slip of paper was slid under the office door. The message was in black marker, block letters: BE

SMART. Gabriela set the envelope on the table. The handwriting matched her nightmares. It took all she had not to tear it open to find out who they thought she really was. Hayes watched her like she was a time bomb, as if he were waiting for the fuse to burn out. She didn't give him the satisfaction. Not yet.

"What were you waiting for?" Hayes asked, his voice as steady as hers was not.

Gabriela pressed her palms to her thighs. She muttered a quiet, automatic 'Madre mía' under her breath, the kind of phrase that had slipped out since childhood, even when no one was listening. The paper beneath her fingertips felt real enough. "For it to explode."

"Then I'll open it."

His hand reached for the envelope, but she pulled it away, an instinct she couldn't override. It surprised her more than it surprised him. "You'll do no such thing."

"It might help if we knew what it said."

"It might help if it didn't say anything."

She closed her eyes. The red still pulsed behind her lids, matching her quickening breath. Washington had been different, all polished threats and careful smiles that made clear her Latina roots were noted before her arguments ever were. Back then, the pressure came in carefully worded memos or sideways warnings. The threats were wrapped in diplomacy. No one came right out and said what they meant.

"And you enjoyed it? No chance."

"I enjoyed the chase, Gabriela. Not the catch."

She told herself that he was lying. She wasn't convinced.

"Seriously," Hayes said. "Let's get this over with."

Gabriela inhaled, steady and deep. She held her breath and the envelope at the same time. "On three?"

"On one."

She couldn't tell if he was anxious or if he was just playing with her. She never could. It was part of his charm and his curse. She counted down from three in her mind, but he was right. By the time she reached one, her hands were already tearing at the corners.

"Just as you thought," he said, nodding to the paper she held with white knuckles.

The message was short and clear: Be smart. The letters burned into her eyes, each one taking her back to the last time she had let herself get in over her head. She could still taste the shame of her loss. The metallic tang of what-ifs haunted her every step until she convinced herself it was behind her.

"Well?" Hayes asked.

"Well, what?" Her voice wavered.

"Were you going to listen to them?"

She let the paper drop to the table. "Who said I hadn't been?"

Hayes sighed. He watched her with a concern that might have been feigned, though she wasn't sure why he would bother.

Hayes hadn't known her long. They'd only met when this case began. But he'd known her long enough to recognize when she was coming apart.

"I could handle it," she said, more to herself than to him.

"You sure about that?"

"About as sure as I'd ever been."

"Not a glowing endorsement."

Gabriela closed her eyes again, letting the darkness and the dull throb consume her. "We kept going," she said, her voice stronger than it had been in days. "We had to."

"Even if it ended the same way it did before?"

The question cut through her, but she knew he wasn't trying to hurt her. He had never tried to hurt her, which was more than she could say for most of the people who were supposed to be on her side.

"It wouldn't," she said, and she tried to believe it.

He reached for her hand, but she pulled it away before he made contact.

"Because this time was different," she added, though she had no idea if that was true.

She heard him inhale sharply. He didn't need her to say it. He already understood.

"Do you have a plan?" Hayes asked.

She nodded, even though her plan was as threadbare as the envelope. Even though every time she thought she knew where this was leading, something else shook her.

"You are more afraid of failing than anything else," he said.

"Is that right?"

"You know it is."

She stood, the force of her motion sending the table quivering beneath their documents. Her tailored skirt and heels gave her the boardroom poise she'd mastered long ago, though inside she knew the effort took more energy than she had left.

"I am afraid of losing," she said.

"Same thing, Gabriela."

Her mind raced, trying to keep up with all the possibilities, all the ways this could have turned out worse than the last time. Her failure had been an embarrassment in Washington, but at least she had known what to expect. At least she had known who to blame.

"What if you are wrong?" she asked.

"What if I am right?"

She stared at the envelope, the bold letters blurring in and out of focus. It was the same kind of threat she was used to, only now she didn't have a team to protect her. She had no one but Hayes and his own brand of dubious loyalty.

"Then I will have gone too far," she said, letting the admission take root.

"And if you are wrong?"

"Then it is just far enough."

He smiled, though there was an edge to it that she hadn't seen before. It was a combination of pity and admiration, but it made her stomach twist more than the warning on the table. "Were you convinced?"

She hesitated. Her mind, filled with uncertainty and fear of what came next. She told herself that that was how it should be, that anything worth doing required some level of terror. "I was."

"Then let's get back to it."

Gabriela breathed in, filling her lungs with a courage she hadn't known was still there. "They are just words," she said.

"You are sure about that?"

She nodded, but her heart betrayed her with its uneven tempo.

"Then we kept working."

They moved through the data one file at a time. Each one underscored the risk she was taking. Hayes didn't interrupt, but she caught him watching her more than the screen.

"Don't say I didn't warn you," he said.

She glared at him, grateful and irritated by the smirk that had begun to form. "Just don't say anything," she replied.

He didn't. And for a time, she let herself believe that he was wrong.

Chapter Fifteen

June had finally arrived, bringing the start of the Morrison trial. Gabriela stood outside the Dallas County Courthouse, staring up at the stone. She'd done this countless times before, nerves steadying just before a trial.

But this time felt different. Maybe because she wasn't sure she was defending an innocent man. She whispered a quiet oración under her breath, a habit her mother had passed down before every difficult day. A prayer for strength.

The culmination of countless sleepless nights and meticulous planning was about to unfold, and she knew that every word, every gesture, would be scrutinized.

Inside, the trial of Phillip Morrison was about to begin. The courtroom was already stirring with anticipation. Gabriela had spent weeks preparing for this day and this trial, and she knew the stakes were high. There was a billionaire's empire, a murdered journalist, and her own reputation on the line. Court TV cameras lined the entrance, broadcasting the spectacle nationwide.

Judge Harold Thompson presided, his tall, imposing figure filling the bench, his silver hair neatly combed. An elderly jurist known for his strict adherence to courtroom decorum, he surveyed the room with a stern, weathered face.

Years ago, when Gabriela was a young attorney, he had gruffly said to her: "Ms. Sanchez, are you aware this is not a courtroom in the Rio Grande Valley? Here, we expect a certain level of professional decorum in dress."

Now a seasoned lawyer, Gabriela understood the unspoken rules of the room. She wore a tailored blazer, a pencil skirt, and modest heels, a blend of professional respect and her culture had taught her never to hide.

As he adjusted his glasses, a habitual gesture indicating contemplation, Judge Thompson's gaze lingered on Gabriela, a flicker of something unreadable in his eyes. The threat she'd received the night before was a constant, unwelcome companion. The trial had begun, and the stakes were real.

The jury selection had been a tense, drawn-out process that consumed the entire morning. Gabriela approached jury selection not just as a lawyer seeking impartiality but as a former congressional representative attuned to the nuances of public sentiment. She listened not only to their answers but also to the language they used, the issues they were passionate about, and the subtle biases that colored their responses. Her time on Capitol Hill had provided a crash course in understanding the fault lines of public opinion, the hot-button issues that could sway judgment. She recognized the coded language of certain political affiliations, the underlying skepticism towards authority in others. This political savvy allowed her to identify potential jurors who might be predisposed to certain narratives, for or against Morrison, insights that went beyond the standard voir dire questions.

As the final twelve jurors were seated, Gabriela's unease grew. There were a few faces that worried her: a stern-looking businessman with a tight jaw, a woman who seemed overly deferential to the judge, and a man whose eyes flickered nervously around the room. She worried that they might be too quick to judge, too easily swayed by the prosecution's narrative, or too intimidated by Morrison's wealth. She knew that even one or two jurors with preconceived notions could derail her defense.

Judge Thompson called for a lunch break. As Gabriela exited the courtroom, she found Hayes waiting in the witness room.

"You look worried," he said.

"I'm not thrilled with that jury," she said, her voice low. "I see a few faces that make me nervous."

"You'll work with it," Hayes replied, his tone reassuring. "You always do."

Gabriela, Morrison, and Hayes went to a small deli across the street for lunch. Per their plan, they didn't discuss the case. Even over sandwiches, Morrison stayed casual, but Gabriela's mind churned. Trying cases back home with her father, they had strategized over lunch, and that was what she was doing.

After lunch, they walked back to the courthouse. Inside, Judge Thompson was already seated on the bench. The jurors filed back into the jury box, their faces a mix of curiosity and apprehension.

Judge Thompson addressed the jury. "Ladies and gentlemen, before we proceed, I want to remind you that the opening statements you are about to hear are not evidence. They are simply an outline of what each side intends to prove. Please keep an open mind and do not form any conclusions until you have heard all the evidence."

Judge Thompson then turned to the prosecution. "Ms. Mitchell, you may proceed with your opening statement."

District Attorney Laura Mitchell, known for her incisive arguments, stood and began her opening statement. The gallery fell silent except for the low hum of whispered conversations and the steady rustle of papers. Among the onlookers, Chuck Green sat near the gallery, his gaze fixed on every unfolding detail.

"Ladies and gentlemen of the jury," Laura Mitchell declared, her voice firm yet measured, "today we confront a case of cold-blooded murder, where the evidence will show that the defendant, Phillip Morrison, brutally ended the life of investigative journalist Ethan Reyes."

"Mr. Reyes was on the verge of exposing Mr. Morrison's illicit dealings, including his connections to a Mexican cartel and extensive money laundering operations. The evidence we will present will show that Mr. Morrison had a clear motive to silence Mr. Reyes: to protect his vast criminal empire."

Mitchell gestured toward a nearby monitor, where a series of documents and digital files were being displayed. "On the night of the murder, Mr. Reyes arranged to meet a confidential informant behind the Blue Marlin Pub in downtown Dallas. The rain fell steadily as he waited, unaware that this meeting would lead to his untimely death. The informant handed Mr. Reyes a briefcase containing what the prosecution believes to be damning evidence.

"As Mr. Reyes departed, a video camera records him being confronted by an assailant. Despite what appears to be his attempts to defuse the situation, the assailant shot Reyes three times, resulting in his tragic death, and left a briefcase full of evidence that Phillip Morrison was in cahoots with one of the most notorious Mexican cartels.

"The evidence we will present includes," Mitchell paused, her voice taking on a sharper edge.

"Motive: Mr. Reyes was poised to publish an article exposing Mr. Morrison's criminal activities, providing a clear motive for silencing him."

"Murder Weapon: A silver-plated .357 Magnum revolver, registered to Mr. Morrison and bearing his fingerprints, was found at the crime scene."

"Video Footage: Surveillance cameras captured grainy footage of a figure matching Mr. Morrison's height and build, wearing a hat, near the alley where Mr. Reyes was killed."

"Blood Evidence: Traces of Mr. Reyes's blood were discovered in the trunk of Mr. Morrison's car, indicating a connection to the crime."

"Cell Phone Data: Analysis of cell tower records places Mr. Morrison's phone in the vicinity of the Blue Marlin Pub at the time of the murder."

"This compelling evidence will demonstrate beyond a reasonable doubt that Phillip Morrison orchestrated and executed the murder of Ethan Reyes to prevent the exposure of his criminal enterprises. We trust you will carefully consider the facts and deliver a verdict of guilty."

Gabriela, at the defense table, tracked the evidence presented. The growing details emphasized the risks involved, both in and out of the courtroom, and the necessity of their defense. The morning light had shifted. Now only the jurors and spectators watched the unfolding testimony.

The courtroom grew still, a sense of pressure building. Mitchell moved with purpose, her words a well-aimed barrage. She highlighted the motive, the means, and the opportunity. She presented each element of the prosecution's case in clear, concise, and persuasive language, an opening statement that Gabriela had to counter.

"The evidence will show," Mitchell declared, "that Phillip Morrison is guilty of murder, a man who silences threats with deadly force." Her voice echoed, then faded. She returned to her seat. For a moment, the courtroom was still. Gabriela looked over at the jurors and saw several nodding as if buying the story Mitchell had told them. Overcoming Mitchell's version of the case would be a challenge.

"She's laying it on thick," Gabriela murmured to Morrison, her voice low. Morrison gave a slight nod. She whispered, "We have our own story to tell."

Gabriela rose, her presence commanding the courtroom's attention. She began, her voice resonating with sincerity and conviction,

"Ladies and gentlemen of the jury, the prosecution has presented a story. A story, no matter how skillfully told, is not the truth. We are here to seek the truth, and the truth, as you will discover, is far more complex than the prosecution would have you believe. They claim Phillip Morrison is a ruthless criminal, a man who would kill to protect his wealth. But I ask you, look at the man sitting here. He is a husband, a father, and a business leader. He is a man who has built his life on hard work and dedication. Is this the face of a cold-blooded killer? Or is this the face of a man who has been wrongly accused?"

"The prosecution claims Ethan Reyes was killed to protect Phillip Morrison's empire. But Ethan Reyes was a man who lived in a dangerous world, a world of shadows and hidden agendas. He had enemies far beyond Mr. Morrison's business interests."

Gabriela sensed the tension rise as her story began to gain traction. "What if," she proceeded, her voice sharpening to make sure the jury heard her, "the real criminal remains at large? What if Phillip Morrison is merely a scapegoat in an even bigger conspiracy?" She scrutinized the integrity of the evidence, questioned the motives of key witnesses, and cast suspicion and doubt over every aspect of the prosecution's case. Gabriela noticed the jury's interest rising as she dismantled Mitchell's narrative. "We will prove that Reyes's enemies, driven by motives the prosecution ignores, framed Phillip Morrison, using him as a convenient target."

"They tell you of a man who silences his enemies with deadly force." Gabriela paused, her gaze shifting to Ms. Mitchell, then back to the jury. "But I ask you, look at Phillip Morrison. Does he strike you as a man who would commit such a brutal act? Or is he a man who has been caught in a web of deceit, a scapegoat for a crime he did not commit? There will be evidence presented on how these individuals framed Phillip Morrison, using him as a convenient target."

"They speak of digital evidence, of flash drives and timestamps, of data that they claim is irrefutable. But digital evidence, like any other, can be manipulated. We will demonstrate the inconsistencies, the gaps, and the alterations that the prosecution has conveniently overlooked. The facts as they unfold reveal how the digital evidence was tampered with, how the timestamps were altered, how the metadata was changed, all designed to paint a false picture of guilt."

"The prosecution has built its case on assumptions and interpretations, on evidence that is circumstantial and easily manipulated. They have ignored the evidence that points to other suspects, evidence that was conveniently overlooked by the police. They have presented a narrative of certainty, but we will present a reality of doubt. A reality of other suspects. A reality of tampered evidence. A reality of a witness who will tell the truth."

"We ask you to keep an open mind, to examine every piece of evidence with a critical eye. To consider the possibility that the truth is not what the prosecution claims it to be. And when you do, we are confident that you will not deny that the state has proven Phillip Morrison committed this crime beyond a reasonable doubt."

"Furthermore, where is the physical evidence? Where is the DNA? Where are the fingerprints? Where is anything that connects Mr. Morrison to the murder weapon? There is nothing. They have presented a case built on speculation and conjecture, not on facts."

"They want you to believe that Phillip Morrison is a man who silences people with deadly force. But that is not evidence. That is an opinion, a character assassination, nothing more."

"Objection!" Mitchell exclaimed, rising from her seat. "Slander has no place in these proceedings."

"Sustained," the judge ruled. "Ms. Sanchez, please refrain from personal attacks."

"My apologies, Your Honor," Gabriela said, her expression composed. "I meant to say that the prosecution's opinion is not evidence."

Gabriela continued, "In this case, the truth is far more complicated than the prosecution claims. You'll hear the real story, a story of manipulation, of other suspects, of a man framed for a crime he did not commit."

The atmosphere had thickened with anticipation. People leaned in, silent, and waiting to see where Gabriela would take them. She had ended with a final push:

"The prosecution wants you to see only one version of events. We'll present another." She knew her opening statement had accomplished exactly what she intended. She had directly challenged the story Mitchell had told.

She returned to her seat, the courtroom buzzing with the implications of her opening statement. Very little of what she told the jury had been in the media. Gabriela thought she'd given the jury a lot to think about, but she knew the jury's perception was a fluid thing, and she'd have to shape it.

Judge Thompson looked at the clock. "Ladies and gentlemen of the jury, it's getting late. We will reconvene tomorrow morning at 9:00 AM. Please do not discuss the case amongst yourselves or with anyone else. The court is adjourned."

The jurors began to file out, their faces a mixture of contemplation and fatigue. Gabriela gathered her notes, the strain of the day settling upon her. As she walked towards the aisle, her gaze swept across the gallery, a habit ingrained from years in the courtroom. And then she looked up and saw the red light of the Court TV camera fixed on her, a stark reminder of the intense scrutiny surrounding this trial.

Chapter Sixteen

At 9:00 a.m. sharp, Judge Thompson rapped the gavel, the wooden crack turning all heads toward the front of the courtroom. Without pleasantries, he adjusted his spectacles, welcomed the jury back, and peered out at Laura Mitchell. "Ms. Mitchell, you may call your first witness." Reporters sat cross-legged on the hard benches, pens twitching. The Court TV cameras were focused on the proceedings.

"Your Honor, the state calls Officer Benjamin Markham to the stand."

A police officer in his dark, perfectly pressed, blue uniform entered the courtroom from the rear. The TV cameras followed him as he made his way to the front, stood at attention, faced the bailiff, and lifted his hand. His testimony would be the first evidence submitted for this day's consideration. He swore to tell the truth, the whole truth, and nothing but the truth. Laura Mitchell nodded her approval. The jurors watched closely, as if his words would seal the case and let them all go home. From the defense table, Gabriela Sanchez made a note: If they think the day will be that easy, they are wrong.

Mitchell wasted no time getting to the matter at hand. “State your name for the record, please.”

“Officer Benjamin Markham,” he replied, sitting up straight and adjusting his duty belt. His face was chiseled, almost like it had been drawn onto a recruiting poster.

“And your position?”

“Patrol officer with Dallas PD. I’ve been on the force for six years.”

“Officer Markham, can you outline any specific training you’ve received?”

“Yes, ma’am. I’ve completed training in crime scene preservation, evidence handling, first responder procedures, and advanced patrol tactics.”

“And how has this training prepared you for your role as a first responder?”

“It’s given me the tools to properly assess and secure a scene, ensuring evidence is preserved and that I can accurately document my observations.”

“Can you describe your role and duties as a Dallas PD patrol officer?”

“My duties include responding to dispatched calls, conducting patrols, securing crime scenes, and assisting in investigations as needed.”

“I want to take you back to March 22nd of last year. Did you receive a call from the dispatcher that night?”

“Yes, ma’am.”

“What was the nature of the call?”

“Report of a possible shooting, a body found in the alley behind the Blue Marlin Club.”

“What information were you provided in the call?”

“Just the location and that there was a possible deceased individual.”

“You were the first responder to the scene behind the Blue Marlin Club, correct?”

“Yes, ma’am.”

“Upon arrival in the alley behind the Blue Marlin Club, what observations did you make?”

#

"It was raining, dark, and cold. There were no cars in the alley. I observed a briefcase in a clear plastic bag sitting by a body. There was blood on the bag."

Mitchell showed a crime scene photo. Gasps filled the courtroom. She waited before speaking again.

"And what was the condition of the victim?"

"He appeared deceased. He had been shot multiple times. His left hand was clenched, and there was a small, torn piece of fabric near it."

"Did you observe any other individuals present?"

"No. Though I thought I heard a car door slam in the distance, I couldn't be sure."

An older juror with wire-rimmed glasses made a note. The pen scratched softly against the pad.

"Did you open the briefcase?"

"No, I left it as I found it for others on our investigative team."

"Did you immediately secure the scene?" Laura asked, steering the testimony.

"Yes. I called for backup and made sure no one tampered with the evidence. Marked everything with photos and a timeline."

"And was there anything else you found noteworthy?"

"No ma'am."

"No further questions, Your Honor."

Markham's testimony was too textbook and rehearsed. Gabriela watched him from the defense table. He sat upright, delivering each answer like he'd practiced it a dozen times. *He's trying to paint a clean picture, but every crime scene, every investigation, has its flaws. My job is to expose them.* She knew Markham wouldn't be a cooperative witness. He'd been trained to protect the prosecution's narrative, to minimize any potential weaknesses. *But he's also human. He's made observations, followed procedures, and those are the levers I need to pull.*

The victim's position and the sound of a car door are the details that matter. If the assailant killed Reyes to get the briefcase, why would he leave it at the scene? And the fact that he didn't open the briefcase? That was a double-edged sword. *It means he can't testify to its contents, but it also raises questions about the chain of custody, about what might have happened before CSU arrived.*

They're the cracks in the foundation. She needed to challenge his certainty, to plant the seed that things weren't as clear-cut as he made them seem. *The lighting, the mist, and the ten-minute delay were all factors that could have skewed his observations.*

He'll try to deflect, to hide behind protocol. But I'll push. I'll make him admit that things aren't always black and white, that there's room for doubt, for other possibilities.

"You may cross-examine the officer now, Ms. Sanchez," Judge Thompson said. Gabriela pushed back her chair, smoothing the skirt of her suit before stepping toward the podium. *It was time to dismantle his carefully constructed narrative, piece by piece.*

Gabriela leaned forward, her gaze fixed on Officer Markham. "Officer Markham," she began, her voice steady, "You testified that you arrived at 10:47 p.m. Was that the time you were dispatched?"

"Yes, ma'am," he answered curtly.

"And how far was the location of the call from your location when you received the call?"

"Approximately 10 minutes," he said, his eyes straight ahead.

"So, you arrived approximately 10 minutes after the call was dispatched?"

"That is correct."

"Let's talk about your initial observations." Gabriela glanced at the jury, then back at the witness. "You mentioned it was dark. Were the streetlights fully operational?"

"Some of them."

She sensed his reluctance. “So, some were not working?”

“That is correct,” he said, his voice flat.

“And you said it was cold. Was there precipitation?”

“There was a light mist.”

“Would you agree that a dark alley, with partial street lighting, and a light mist could affect one’s visibility?” Gabriela made another quick glance at the jury to make sure they were getting her point.

“I made my observations,” he said, avoiding a direct answer.

“Officer, please answer the question. Could those conditions affect visibility?”

“It could have,” he responded, avoiding her eyes.

“Tell us about the briefcase again,” Gabriela shifted, knowing this was the crux. “You testified you found it by the body?”

“Yes.”

“Did you personally secure it?”

“It was documented and bagged by CSU,” he replied.

“So, you didn’t handle it directly?”

“Not personally, no,” he said, his voice tight.

"Therefore, you cannot testify to the condition of the briefcase when it was found, only to the condition you observed it in?"

"Correct."

"How can you be certain the chain of custody wasn't compromised before the CSU arrived?"

He hesitated, just for a beat. "We followed standard procedures."

"But you did not personally observe the briefcase being secured until the CSU arrived, correct?"

"Correct," he said, his jaw tightening.

"You didn't see anyone else at the scene?"

"Not when I arrived."

"So, it's possible someone was there before you?"

"There was no indication—"

Gabriela cut in. "Just answer the question, Officer."

"Yes, it's possible."

"And it is also possible that someone could have left evidence at the scene before you arrived?"

"Objection, Your Honor, speculation."

Judge Thompson said, “Sustained.”

Judge Thompson’s ruling echoed in the courtroom, cutting off the officer’s potential answer. Gabriela had planted a seed with the jury. She nodded, a subtle acknowledgement of the ruling, and sat down. “No further questions.”

“Officer Markham, you are excused,” Judge Thompson said, looking at Laura Thompson. “You may call your next witness, Ms. Thompson.”

“Your Honor,” Thompson announced, “the prosecution calls Ms. Victoria Ramos, crime scene analyst, to the stand.”

Victoria Ramos, a woman with a no-nonsense demeanor and a neatly tied bun, entered the courtroom. Her eyes, sharp and calculating, scanned the room as she swore the oath and took her seat.

“Ms. Ramos,” Mitchell began, her voice crisp and professional, “please state your name and occupation for the record.”

“Victoria Ramos. I’m a forensic analyst with the Dallas Police Department’s Crime Scene Investigation unit.”

“And how long have you held this position?”

“For twelve years.”

"Could you briefly describe your educational background and professional training?"

"I hold a Master's degree in Forensic Science from the University of North Texas. I've completed extensive training in crime scene analysis, evidence collection, fingerprint analysis, and blood spatter interpretation."

Twelve years, Gabriela thought, observing Ms. Ramos. *Experienced, confident. She'll be a tough one. Ramos's credentials were solid, and her demeanor suggested she won't be easily flustered. Mitchell was playing it safe, established her as an expert, and started to build her narrative with strong evidence. She was avoiding taking risks.* Gabriela noted the way Ramos's eyes flicked to the jury, a subtle attempt to project authority. *But every expert has their blind spots.*

"Ms. Ramos, were you involved in the investigation of the crime scene at the Blue Marlin Club on March 22nd of last year?"

"Yes, I was."

"Can you describe your role in that investigation?"

"I was the lead forensic analyst responsible for the collection and analysis of physical evidence at the scene."

"Let's begin with your arrival at the scene. What were your initial observations?"

"The scene was in an alleyway behind the Blue Marlin Club. It was dark, and there was a light mist falling. The area was secured by patrol officers. I immediately began documenting the scene with photographs and detailed notes."

Dark, misty, Gabriela noted mentally. *Just like Markham said. Consistent, but still potentially flawed. She needed to find the inconsistencies, the points where Ramos's testimony could be challenged. The jury was also taking in every word, and they seemed to be leaning forward.*

"And what evidence did you collect at the scene?"

"We collected several items, including the victim's body, and samples of blood from the surrounding area."

"Specifically, Ms. Ramos, were you involved in the collection of a firearm?"

"No, there was no firearm recovered at the scene."

No gun, Gabriela thought. *That was interesting.*

"And what about the briefcase? What did you do with the briefcase?"

“I documented the briefcase, photographed it, and then I opened it, and documented the contents. The contents were then removed and photographed. All items were then placed into evidence.”

“And what did you find inside the briefcase?”

“There were several documents, some photographs, and a digital storage device.”

“Describe what you found in the documents, photographs, and the digital storage device.”

Gabriela wanted to object, but if she did, then Thompson would have Ramos go over each piece of damning evidence one after another.

“We found photographs of Mr. Morrison with known cartel members, and communications between them about money and drugs.”

#

There it is, Gabriela thought. The crux of their case. The fingerprint match. But fingerprint analysis isn’t infallible. There’s room for error, for interpretation. She knew where she needed to focus her cross-examination.

“Your Honor, I have no further questions,” Mitchell said.

"Ms. Sanchez, you may cross-examine now."

Gabriela stood, her gaze sharp. "Ms. Ramos, can you describe the general procedure for collecting evidence like the revolver?"

"We document its location, photograph it, and secure it in a tamper-proof container," Ramos replied, her voice unwavering.

"Were you present for that process?" Gabriela asked, her tone laced with skepticism.

"No, I received it at the lab."

"So, it's possible something occurred before it reached you?" Gabriela pressed, her voice cutting through the silence. "Tampering, perhaps?"

Ramos's composure wavered slightly. "There is a chain of custody," she stated, her voice a fraction less certain.

"Regarding potential contamination," Gabriela continued, her eyes fixed on Ramos, "is that a possibility?"

"We minimize it," Ramos replied, her gaze unwavering.

"Minimize, not eliminate?" Gabriela confirmed, a hint of steel in her voice.

Ramos hesitated. "It is never completely eliminated."

"And the fingerprint analysis," Gabriela said, pointing to a faint smudge on the chart, "this partial print here, could that affect the results?"

Ramos conceded, "It could, theoretically."

Aha, Gabriela thought, a flicker of triumph. *A crack in their armor*.

"What is the error rate for fingerprint matching?" Gabriela asked, her voice sharp.

"Less than one percent," Ramos replied, her composure beginning to fray. She shifted in her seat, a subtle sign of unease.

"And not zero?" Gabriela pressed.

"Not zero," Ramos admitted, her voice tight.

"The analysis depends on the quality of the print, correct?" Gabriela continued.

"Yes."

"So, if the prints were smudged or incomplete, wouldn't that increase the error rate?"

Ramos replied, "It could, theoretically."

"And the blood in Mr. Morrison's car?" Gabriela asked, her tone even. "Was it fresh blood?"

"It could have been there for some time, perhaps days," Ramos answered.

"Did you find any of Reyes' blood on any clothes owned by Mr. Morrison?"

"No."

"With Mr. Reyes' body having been found at the scene, there was no evidence that the body had been brought from somewhere else and placed there?"

"No, other than the blood found in Mr. Morrison's trunk."

"You didn't find Mr. Reyes' blood anywhere other than the crime scene and Mr. Morrison's trunk, isn't that true?"

"So, you cannot establish a timeframe linking Mr. Morrison to this crime?" Gabriela pressed.

"No," Ramos admitted, her voice barely audible.

Gabriela noticed a juror, a middle-aged woman with a skeptical expression, nodding slightly. *They were listening*, she thought.

"Did you or anyone you know of investigate to determine if the evidence found in the briefcase was legitimate?"

"I'm not sure what you mean by the word legitimate."

"How about authentic? Did you determine whether the documents and photos were authentic?"

"No, we didn't investigate the documents and photos to verify their authenticity."

"So, you somehow concluded that Mr. Morrison murdered Ethan Reyes, leaving blood in his trunk and nowhere else, without determining the authenticity of what you found in a briefcase at the crime scene, and concluding that Mr. Morrison would have left a briefcase with damning evidence about his business in Mexico behind for you to find. Is that true?"

Ramos' jaw tightened almost imperceptibly. A flicker of annoyance touched her brow as she subtly shifted in her seat, her eyes flicking down to the table before meeting Gabriela's unwavering gaze. She inhaled slowly, a barely perceptible preparation for defense.

"Ms. Sanchez," she stated, his voice measured, "standard protocols were followed. The trunk blood matched the victim. The briefcase was at the scene. Eyewitness testimony corroborated his presence. While the briefcase's full authentication continues, its discovery with the other evidence formed our initial assessment." Her tone was firm. "Speculation on a suspect's motives isn't our purview. We gather facts. Any apparent contradictions are for the court's consideration."

"I have no further questions." Gabriela returned to her seat with a subtle sense of victory in her demeanor.

Mitchell rose, her expression determined. "Ms. Ramos, about that partial print Ms. Sanchez mentioned. Was that print included in the final match?"

"No, it was excluded due to its incompleteness," Ramos replied, her confidence restored.

"So, the match was based on the complete, clear prints, correct?" Mitchell asked, her voice sharp and pointed.

"Yes, absolutely," Ramos confirmed, her tone regaining its earlier assurance.

"And the blood in the trunk. Was it fresh?" Mitchell asked.

"It was not possible to determine how fresh it was," Ramos stated.

"And you maintain objectivity in your work?" Mitchell asked.

"Always," Ramos replied.

"Objection, Your Honor. Leading the witness." Gabriela stated.

"Sustained." Judge Thompson ruled.

Mitchell paused, a flicker of annoyance crossing her face, then composed herself. "Ms. Ramos," she began again, her voice clear and firm, "In your professional opinion, based on your years of experience and the rigorous standards you adhere to, was your analysis in this case conducted with complete objectivity?"

"Yes, absolutely," Ramos replied, her voice ringing with confidence.

As the jurors leaned forward in anticipation, a man with wire-rimmed glasses kept his pen poised, as if he were marking the boundary lines in an unyielding battle for truth. Mitchell's questions had been precise and meticulously honed for maximum impact.

"Thank you. No further questions," Mitchell declared, a satisfied smile playing on her lips.

"Ms. Sanchez, do you have any further questions for this witness?"

"Yes, Your Honor."

Judge Thompson glanced at the clock, a hint of impatience in his eyes. *Damn,* Gabriela thought, *He's making it clear he wants this over.*

"Ms. Ramos," Gabriela began, her voice sharp and focused, "You testified about the chain of custody. You received the evidence after it was documented. Isn't it possible that a mistake occurred during that initial stage?"

Ramos's gaze flickered towards Mitchell before she replied, "I have confidence in our process."

"Confidence," Gabriela echoed, her voice laced with skepticism, "but not certainty. You admit there are risks?"

Ramos hesitated, a subtle admission. "There are always risks."

"And the time frame for the fingerprints and blood," Gabriela continued, her voice steady, "You said it was imprecise. How imprecise?"

"Too imprecise to link Mr. Morrison definitively to the crime at the time it was committed."

Gabriela paused, letting the admission hang in the air. *That's it*, she thought, *the seed of doubt.* She had chipped away at the foundation of Ramos's certainty, highlighting the potential for error and the lack of a clear timeline. The jurors' expressions shifted, a subtle acknowledgment of the uncertainty she had introduced.

"No further questions," Gabriela concluded, a quiet satisfaction in her tone.

"All right then, let's take a break for lunch." Judge Thompson said, looking up at the clock. "We'll return at 1:30, and Ms. Mitchell can call her next witness. Remember, ladies and gentlemen, do not discuss the case with each other over lunch."

Gabriela emerged into the cool afternoon light, Phillip Morrison a step behind her. The moment they cleared the heavy oaken doors of the Dallas County Courthouse, a wall of reporters surged forward, microphones thrust, questions shouted.

"Ms. Sanchez, any comment on the fingerprint evidence?"

"Mr. Morrison, did you kill Ethan Reyes?"

Gabriela held up a hand, a silent attempt to create space, but the reporters pressed closer. Morrison's jaw tightened.

"No comment at this time," Gabriela said, her voice barely audible.

A reporter's voice cut through the noise. "Ms. Sanchez! Did you know about the new evidence?"

Gabriela stopped, her eyes narrowing. *New evidence?* She hadn't been informed of anything.

"What new evidence?" she asked, her voice low.

The reporter smirked. "You'll find out in court."

The crowd shifted, pushing Gabriela forward. *New evidence*. She ran the possibilities through her mind, trying to anticipate what Mitchell could have found. *Damn it*. She needed to get back to her office, to her team. This could change everything.

Chapter Seventeen

This Gabriela's phone buzzed with an incoming text. "Meet me back at the office. ASAP. New motion filed." It was from Hayes. She told Morrison to go to lunch, and she walked feverishly towards Field Street, her mind racing. New evidence. The reporter's words echoed in her head.

Hayes was waiting in her office, his face grim, a document clutched in his hand. "Mitchell just filed this. New witness."

Gabriela snatched the motion, scanning it quickly. "Damn it. This is a disaster." She looked up at Hayes. "Get the team together. We need to dissect this witness's statement, find the holes. Now."

"What is it?" Hayes asked, his brow furrowed.

"A bartender from the Blue Marlin," Gabriela said, her voice tight. "He's claiming he saw Reyes leave the bar with someone. And he's identified Morrison."

"Morrison? But why didn't the police interview him before?" Hayes asked.

"Mitchell's claiming he just came forward this morning. Says he was afraid to talk earlier, or that he didn't realize what he saw was important until now. Or some other BS." Gabriela said. "She just filed the motion and handed me this."

"So, he's just now coming forward?" Hayes asked. "That's convenient."

"Too convenient," Gabriela said. "We need to tear this testimony apart. There has to be something we can use. Something to discredit him."

The room was charged with a tense, unmistakable energy. Despite the judge recessing court before lunch, no one had departed; everyone stayed in the gallery, near the body of testimony that lay warm and bloody at their feet. Mitchell arrived early and took her seat at the prosecutor's table. The exhibits were arranged in an orderly row—yellowed documents affixed to charts like items catalogued in a meticulous investigation. She briefly looked up and offered a quick, guarded smile, reminiscent of a silent exchange between adversaries anticipating backup.

Gabriela returned the smile with a measured nod, an unspoken promise not to yield an inch. Soon, the gallery filled with press and curious onlookers, each eager for a new headline, sensation, or a clear explanation for the murder. They shifted their attention back and forth between the defense and prosecution tables, waiting to see who would take the next decisive action. Though the case was soon to be Mitchell's foray, Gabriela had crafted a plan of her own.

Judge Thompson entered the courtroom and commanded silence with practiced authority. "Court is now in session. Call your next witness."

Mitchell wasted no time. "Prosecution calls Officer Vargas."

All eyes turned to the stand. The young Latino officer carried himself with an assured calm as he took the oath and seated himself confidently.

Mitchell approached with her clipboard. "State your name and position for the record."

"Officer Daniel Vargas, Dallas PD."

"Officer Vargas, how long have you been on the force?"

"Four years," he answered, his voice steady.

"Then you were the second officer to arrive at the scene?" Mitchell inquired, her tone suggestive yet careful.

"Yes. I arrived less than a minute after Officer Markham."

"Can you describe what you observed at the scene?"

"I saw a vehicle leaving the area. It matched the description of Mr. Morrison's car."

The courtroom tensed as every eye focused on Mitchell and Officer Vargas, as if witnessing a subtle battle for control.

"And the driver?" Mitchell pressed, her voice deliberate as she connected the elements of the case. "Were you able to identify the driver of that vehicle?"

"Yes, I was."

"And who was the driver of that vehicle?"

Vargas paused, his eyes scanning the courtroom. Then, he pointed directly at Phillip Morrison. "That man there."

Mitchell paused, allowing the jurors to absorb the testimony. A soft rustle passed through the room as papers shifted and anticipation grew. "What did you do next, Officer?"

"I relayed the information and secured the scene with Officer Markham."

"Thank you. No further questions," Mitchell stated.

Gabriela rose and stepped toward the witness stand with calculated precision. "Officer Vargas, let's revisit your observations that night. You stated it was dark. Was the lighting sufficient for a positive identification?"

"The streetlights were on," Vargas replied.

"But were they all functioning? Or were some of them out, as Officer Markham testified?" Gabriela asked.

"Some were out," Vargas admitted, his voice slightly lower.

"You also mentioned about mist. Did that compromise your visibility?"

"No, it did not," he answered, though a slight uncertainty betrayed him.

"You testified that the vehicle matched Mr. Morrison's car. Aside from the make and model, was there anything distinctive about it? A dent? A sticker? Anything?"

"No additional features," he admitted.

"And are you absolutely sure it was Mr. Morrison you saw? Were you able to see his face clearly?"

"Enough to identify him."

"Enough, but not clearly?" Gabriela pressed, her voice sharp. "Was it just a quick glance?"

"It was a brief observation," Vargas conceded, his gaze shifting slightly.

"You mentioned dispatch had identified him prior to your arrival. Could that have influenced your observation?"

"No," he replied, though a hint of doubt crept in.

"Would that information have affected your expectations? Would you have been more likely to see what you were told to see?"

"Objection, Your Honor. Speculation," Mitchell objected. "Sustained," Judge Thompson ruled.

"How many vehicles did you see at the scene?" Gabriela asked, pressing on.

"Just one."

"And how many individuals?"

"Only the driver."

"Not two, not three, just one?"

"Just one," he confirmed.

Shifting her tone to probe further, Gabriela asked, "So, if earlier information was incorrect, you wouldn't have had any way to know it, would you?"

Vargas hesitated just a moment. "Not without more evidence."

Gabriela noticed a juror, a middle-aged woman with a skeptical expression, leaning forward. They were listening, she thought.

"Thank you, Officer. No further questions," Gabriela concluded, noting the room's cautious return to focus.

Mitchell then rose, determined to solidify her case. "Officer Vargas, how far were you from the vehicle when you saw it?"

"A couple hundred feet. And the vehicle was moving quickly."

"Was anyone else leaving the scene when you arrived?"

"No, only the driver."

"And you're certain of your observations?"

"Absolutely," Vargas replied, though his voice lacked its earlier conviction.

Mitchell faced the jury, her confidence unwavering. "No further questions."

Officer Vargas stepped down, his testimony lingering in the courtroom as everyone contemplated its implications.

Judge Thompson cleared his throat, his gaze sweeping across the courtroom. "Members of the jury," he began, his voice authoritative, "it is now late in the day. We will adjourn until 9:00 a.m. Monday morning. During this time, I must once again remind you: do not discuss this case with anyone, including each other. Do not conduct any independent research, and do not allow yourselves to be influenced by any media coverage."

He paused, his eyes settling on Gabriela. "Ms. Sanchez, Ms. Mitchell, please approach."

Gabriela rose, a flicker of unease in her stomach. What was this about? Mitchell looked equally puzzled as they approached the bench.

"I've just received a communication," Judge Thompson said, his voice low, "regarding a potential issue with one of the upcoming witnesses. I'll need to discuss this with you both in chambers before we proceed tomorrow."

Gabriela's mind raced. *What issue? Which witness?*

"We'll discuss this first thing Monday morning, before the jury is brought in," Judge Thompson continued, his expression unreadable. "Court is adjourned."

The gavel fell with a sharp crack, the sound echoing through the suddenly quiet courtroom. Gabriela's thoughts turned to this question. *What could possibly be so urgent that the judge wanted to talk to us before court starts?*

Chapter Eighteen

It was Monday morning when Gabriela and Morrison arrived at court. Judge Thompson's words from Friday afternoon, about a potential issue requiring a meeting in chambers, still lingered in the quiet of the courtroom. Before they could settle at the counsel table, the bailiff approached. "Judge Thompson will see you now."

The clock on the wall of the chambers ticked slowly. Gabriela felt the tension build with each passing second. It was 9:00 a.m. sharp. Judge Thompson, his face drawn, sat behind his desk. Mitchell was already seated across from him, her posture rigid.

"Ms. Sanchez. Ms. Mitchell," Judge Thompson began, his voice low, "late Friday afternoon, I received a communication from the husband of one of our jurors."

Gabriela looked up sharply. A juror's husband receives a threat, and she's excused? That wasn't a coincidence. It was deliberate. Chosen for maximum impact and minimal trace.

She didn't need to hear more to know what it meant. Someone wanted that juror off the panel. And they didn't mind letting the judge think it was random or unrelated.

Her thoughts narrowed. She'd received threats, too. Hand-delivered. Targeted. Now this?

The message was clear. Control the jury. Shape the outcome. Eliminate the risk.

If the same people were behind both threats, they weren't trying to help the prosecution. They were trying to bury the truth. And if Morrison really had nothing to hide, then someone had gone to a lot of trouble to make him look guilty.

Morrison sat quietly beside her, his expression unreadable. But the timing was too precise to ignore. The threats against her. Now this juror's removal

Someone's manipulating this trial. And it's not just Mitchell.

Mitchell leaned forward. "What kind of communication, Your Honor?"

The judge slid a manila envelope across the desk. "The husband says this was delivered to their home. Since the juror is sequestered, she doesn't know about the note. He wasn't sure what to do."

Judge Thompson opened the envelope and removed several photocopies of handwritten pages. The message was short and direct:

"Persuade your wife to vote guilty. We know where your children go to school. We're watching them."

"Death threats?" Gabriela asked quietly.

The judge nodded. "The husband believes so. We've taken steps to ensure his family's safety."

Mitchell's mouth tightened. "This is outrageous."

"We agree on that," the judge said. "But we can't allow it to derail the trial. I've decided to excuse Juror No. 6, Karen Delgado, and seat an alternate. She'll be told there's been a family emergency. She won't be informed about the note."

Gabriela gave a slow nod. "Understood."

Mitchell's brow furrowed. "Do you believe she would have voted for acquittal?"

"We'll never know," the judge said. "And that's how it needs to stay."

Gabriela met the judge's eyes. "I've received threats, too. Emails. A letter last week. They said I should walk away from this case or regret it."

Mitchell looked over, surprised. The judge didn't.

"Have you reported those to the marshals?" he asked.

“I did,” Gabriela said. “They’re looking into it.”

Judge Thompson gave a single nod. “Let’s keep this trial on course. Ms. Mitchell, you may call your next witness when we reconvene.”

Back in the courtroom, the jury filed into the box. Judge Thompson waited for them to settle, then addressed them evenly.

“Before we continue, you’ll notice one juror is no longer present. Due to a private matter unrelated to this case, Juror No. 6 has been excused. An alternate has been seated in her place.”

He gave a slight pause. “You are to draw no conclusions from this and continue your service without speculation.”

Gabriela scanned their faces. If anyone suspected more, they didn’t show it.

Judge Thompson turned toward the prosecution. “Ms. Mitchell, you may call your next witness.”

Mitchell stood, her composure regained. “The state calls Dr. Zofia Nowak, medical examiner.”

Dr. Nowak, a woman with a calm and professional demeanor, took the stand. Her testimony would focus on the victim’s injuries and the cause of death. But in the back of Gabriela’s mind, the image of the threatening notes lingered, a dark shadow hanging over the proceedings.

"Please state your name and occupation for the record," Mitchell started. With deliberate care, the coroner eased into the witness chair and cleared her throat as if drawing time itself into her pause. "Dr. Zofia Nowak, medical examiner, Dallas County."

Gabriela watched intently as Dr. Nowak fumbled slightly with the microphone. Mitchell waited for Dr. Nowak. "Dr. Nowak, can you detail what you discovered regarding Mr. Reyes's injuries?"

The jury collectively leaned forward, their morbid fascination evident as Dr. Nowak began her account. "We conducted a full autopsy on the victim, Ethan Reyes. He sustained multiple gunshot wounds," she recounted in a measured cadence that lent a clinical finality to each word. "The primary cause of death was massive hemorrhaging from the bullets that struck his chest and temple."

Gabriela absorbed every syllable with a deceptive calm that belied the rapid, strategic calculations swirling in her mind. Her fingers flew across the keyboard to connect to her iPad, notes populating the glowing screen in rapid strokes; each detail was logged, catalogued, and weighed for how it might undercut the prosecution's case.

She noted subtle shifts in the jurors' expressions, an eyebrow raised here, a slight grimace there, each reacting to those words. Beneath every clinical detail, however, lingered the memory of a critical inconsistency. The trajectory described did not fully match the ballistic evidence implicating Morrison. It was a small discrepancy, but it could eventually erode the prosecution's airtight narrative.

Dr. Nowak continued, oblivious to the growing tension. "One bullet was fired at close range, entering the right shoulder and exiting the back." Adjusting her glasses, she briefly met Gabriela's unyielding gaze. "The total number of wounds was three, consistent with a .357 Magnum revolver." Gabriela's gaze quickly moved from one juror to the next, noticing some of them visibly wincing at something Dr. Nowak said.

"Dr. Nowak, in your expert opinion, what was the manner of death?" Mitchell asked, Gabriela noted the smug certainty in Mitchell's stance, a posture of one who believed she held all of the power. She registered every nuance, already plotting how to strike back at the narrative being woven against her client. Dr. Nowak cleared her throat once more, a deliberate pause that commanded every eye in the room.

"Homicide," she declared, the stark finality of the word landing with stark finality. In an instant, the atmosphere cracked with whispered reactions and Mitchell's barely contained triumph. Though Gabriela had anticipated this moment, hearing the charge spoken aloud sent an unwanted shiver down her spine. She scanned the report once again in her mind's eye, seeking that elusive misstep, that discrepancy which might expose an overlooked detail hinting that Morrison's involvement was nothing but a convenient set-up.

"Thank you, Dr. Nowak," Mitchell said briskly, "I have nothing further."

Judge Thompson looked over the rim of his glasses. "Ms. Sanchez, you may cross-examine the doctor."

Gabriela locked eyes with the coroner for a fleeting second as she stepped down, already orchestrating her strategy for cross-examination. Despite the compelling nature of the coroner's testimony, the slight misalignment in the bullet trajectories, and Mitchell's troubling certainty, she stayed focused.

Gabriela rose, her movements deliberate, her gaze steady on Dr. Nowak. "Dr. Nowak," she began, her voice calm but firm, "you stated that the victim sustained three gunshot wounds. Is that correct?"

"Yes, that's correct," Dr. Nowak replied, her tone professional.

"And you concluded that the manner of death was homicide. Based on your expert opinion?" Gabriela asked.

"Yes, absolutely." Dr. Nowak said.

"And you testified that one bullet entered the right shoulder and exited the back. Could you describe the trajectory of that bullet?"

Dr. Nowak hesitated slightly. "It was a relatively straight trajectory, angled slightly downward."

"Slightly downward," Gabriela repeated, her voice thoughtful. "And you are absolutely certain of this trajectory?"

"Based on my examination, yes."

"Is it possible, however remote, that the trajectory could have been slightly different?"

Dr. Nowak paused, her gaze shifting slightly. "In theory, yes. There is always a degree of interpretation."

"So there is a degree of interpretation?" Gabriela said.

"Yes." Dr. Nowak said.

"And the other wounds. Were their trajectories perfectly aligned with the .357 Magnum revolver found in the dumpster near the scene?"

"They were consistent with the weapon," Dr. Nowak replied, her voice carefully neutral.

"Consistent, but not perfectly aligned?" Gabriela asked, her voice low. "Could they have been inflicted from a different angle, a different position, perhaps even by a different weapon?"

Dr. Nowak's composure wavered slightly. "They were within the expected range for the weapon found in the dumpster."

"Expected range," Gabriela echoed, her voice laced with skepticism. "So, not definitive. Not conclusive. Just...expected. Meaning, there are other possibilities?"

Dr. Nowak hesitated, a flicker of uncertainty in her eyes. "There are always possibilities."

"Dr. Nowak, from your analysis of the wounds, are you able to determine if the shooter held the gun in his right hand or left hand?"

"I wasn't asked to make that analysis."

"I'm asking you to make the analysis now."

"Based on the angle and entry points, the wounds are consistent with a right-handed shooter. But without additional evidence, we can't say that definitively."

Gabriela paused, giving the jury a moment to absorb the admission. "Thank you, Dr. Nowak. No further questions."

Judge Thompson looked at the clock. "Let's take our morning break. We'll reconvene at 10:45."

As the courtroom buzzed with activity, Gabriela went down the hall into the conference room and pulled Hayes aside. "Hayes, anything on that bartender yet?" she asked, her voice urgent. "We need to find something to discredit him."

Hayes leaned toward her, eyes fixed on his laptop. "Name's Jimmy Malone. Got a few petty theft and assault charges. Nothing major, but it shows a pattern."

"Petty crimes. That's not much to discredit him. Pattern of what?" Gabriela pressed, her brow furrowed, a hint of disappointment in her tone.

"Pattern of being unreliable," Hayes replied, scrolling through the documents. "And he was fired from his last two bartending jobs. Claims it was unfair, but both places cited 'dishonest behavior.'"

Gabriela's voice became low and more intentional. "Dishonest behavior? That's not great, but at least it's something we can use. Any witnesses to these incidents?"

"Working on that," Hayes said. "But the most interesting thing I found is this: he has a significant gambling problem. He owes money to some...questionable people."

Gabriela leaned closer, her mind racing. "Questionable people? Could they have pressured him to testify?"

"It's a possibility," Hayes said. "I'm digging into that angle now. But there's still the question of why he waited until now to come forward. That's the real key, Gabriela. Why now?"

Gabriela paused, considering the implications. "Exactly. Why now? That's what we need to figure out. If we can show he had a motive to lie, or was pressured, we can tear his testimony apart."

She dropped into the chair at the table, motioning for Hayes to clear space. Legal pads and highlighters scattered as she began jotting a list: visibility, lighting, distance, bias. If the officer were young, she'd challenge his certainty. If he were seasoned, she'd test his memory against the conditions that night.

Hayes glanced at her notes. "Don't forget the chain of custody."

"I won't," Gabriela muttered, underlining the word in thick strokes. Her father's voice echoed in her head: *No witness is perfect, mija. They all bleed if you press in the right place.* She steadied herself.

"I'm on it," Hayes said. "I'll keep digging."

Gabriela nodded. "Good. We don't have long." She closed the pad, tucking it into her briefcase.

By the time she returned to the courthouse, the jury was filing back into the box, and the gallery had hushed to a low murmur.

Judge Thompson adjusted his glasses, signaling the session's return to order.

Without hesitation, Mitchell rose and addressed the court in a measured tone. "The prosecution calls Andrew Harper to the stand."

Andrew Harper walked to the witness box, pausing briefly as the bailiff prepared the oath. When the formal words were recited, Harper lifted his right hand and answered solemnly, "I do."

Mitchell started. "Mr. Harper, please state your name and occupation for the record."

"Andrew Harper. I am a forensic ballistics analyst."

"Mr. Harper, could you please outline your qualifications and experience in this field?"

"I have over twenty years of experience in forensic ballistics. I hold a Master's degree in Forensic Science from the University of California, Davis, and I've testified as an expert witness in numerous cases."

"And are you certified in forensic ballistics?"

"Yes, I am certified by the Association of Firearm and Tool Mark Examiners."

"Your Honor," Mitchell said, turning to Judge Thompson. "The prosecution moves to qualify Mr. Harper as an expert in forensic ballistics."

Judge Thompson nodded. "Any objections, Ms. Sanchez?"

Gabriela rose. "No objection, Your Honor."

Judge Thompson turned back to the witness. "Mr. Harper, you are qualified as an expert in forensic ballistics."

Mitchell stepped forward. "Mr. Harper, in your professional opinion, is there any doubt that these bullets came from the defendant's weapon?"

Harper adjusted his glasses. "In this particular case, I was assigned immediately after the weapon was recovered from the scene. My role was to compare the bullets to the alleged murder weapon…"

Harper carefully held the revolver in his hands, his tone imbued with quiet authority. "None whatsoever," he stated clearly. "Upon testing, I determined that these bullets were fired from the .357 Magnum revolver before me. Every firearm leaves distinctive markings on its ammunition due to the unique pattern of its barrel and grooves. In this instance, the patterns match perfectly, providing unequivocal evidence linking the bullets to the weapon."

Mitchell then motioned toward the evidence table. "Let's demonstrate this for the jury." Harper moved deliberately to the table, treating the revolver and spent cartridges with meticulous care. Utilizing a laser pointer, he guided the court's attention to the microscopic markings that, in his expert view, affirmed the connection between the weapon and the materials recovered at the scene.

The jurors observed intently, their expressions reflecting varying degrees of engagement and concern as they absorbed the significance of his analysis.

Gabriela, who had been watching every gesture, narrowed her focus as she mulled over the chain of custody. Rising steadily, she interjected with unwavering clarity. "Objection," she declared, her voice measured and deliberate. "There is a significant possibility that the chain of custody for both the weapon and the bullets might contain discrepancies. The witness cannot account for any potential errors or contamination in handling this evidence."

All eyes turned to Judge Thompson as he weighed the objection. After a brief pause, he responded evenly, "Overruled."

Mitchell offered a faint, challenging smile toward Gabriela, who maintained steady eye contact, unwilling to yield even for a moment.

Unperturbed by the objection, Harper proceeded. “The evidence stands on its own merit,” he said firmly before returning the firearm to the bailiff. His methodical explanation and the clarity in his demonstration underscored the gravity of the findings.

“No further questions, Your Honor,” Mitchell said.

Judge Thompson turned to Gabriela. “Ms. Sanchez, you may cross-examine.”

Gabriela stood slowly, eyes on Harper. “Mr. Harper,” she said, “you testified that the patterns on the bullets ‘match perfectly’ with the .357 Magnum revolver. Is that correct?” “Yes, that’s correct,” Harper replied, his tone professional.

“And you stated that this ‘unequivocal evidence’ links the bullets to the weapon. Is that correct?” Gabriela asked.

“Yes, absolutely,” Harper said.

“And you are absolutely certain of this match?”

“Yes,” Harper said.

"Are you aware of the exact chain of custody of this weapon from the moment it was recovered from the scene until it reached your lab?"

Harper hesitated slightly. "I received it with proper documentation."

"Proper documentation," Gabriela repeated, her voice thoughtful. "But you weren't present for the initial recovery, were you?"

"No," Harper said.

"And you don't know the exact conditions under which it was stored or transported, do you?"

"I assume standard procedure was followed," Harper replied.

"Assume," Gabriela echoed, her voice laced with skepticism. "So, you can't testify with absolute certainty that there was no possibility of contamination or tampering?"

Harper paused, his gaze shifting slightly. "We have protocols to minimize those risks."

"Minimize," Gabriela said. "But not eliminate. Is that correct?"

"There are always potential risks," Harper said.

"And the bullets themselves," Gabriela continued, her voice steady. "Were they handled with the same level of care?"

"Yes, of course," Harper said.

"But again, you weren't present for their recovery, were you?"

"No," Harper said.

"So, you can't testify with absolute certainty that they weren't contaminated or tampered with, can you?"

Harper hesitated, a flicker of uncertainty in his eyes. "We follow strict procedures."

"Procedures," Gabriela echoed, her voice low. "But not guarantees. Thank you, Mr. Harper. No further questions."

Harper stepped down, his testimony hanging in the air. The jury's faces were a mix of contemplation and unease. Had the evidence been handled perfectly? Was there a chance, however slight, that something had gone wrong?

Judge Thompson glanced at the clock. "It's nearly lunchtime. We'll reconvene at 1:30. Ms. Mitchell, please have your next witness ready."

As the courtroom began to empty, Gabriela turned to Hayes, her expression grim. "We need to find something solid on that bartender. Something that explains why he's coming forward now."

"I'm working on it," Hayes replied, his eyes still fixed on his laptop. "But I just got something else. From the video analyst's file."

Gabriela's focus sharpened. Sounding suspicious, she asked, "What is it?"

Hayes hesitated, his gaze shifting to the departing jurors. "It's...complicated. It looks like the surveillance footage might have been altered."

Gabriela's breath hitched. "Altered? How?"

"I'm not sure yet," Hayes said, his voice low. "But there are inconsistencies. Time stamps that don't match, missing frames...it's like someone tried to edit it."

Gabriela's mind raced. Edited footage? That could change everything. If the surveillance footage was manipulated, it would cast serious doubt on the prosecution's timeline and Morrison's alleged presence at the scene.

"This could be huge," she said, her voice barely a whisper. "We need to verify this. And we need to do it before the video analyst takes the stand."

Hayes nodded, his expression grim. "I'll start digging."

As they left the courtroom, Gabriela's mind was a whirlwind of questions. Who would alter the footage? And why? Was it part of a larger setup? She knew one thing: the afternoon session was about to get very interesting.

Court reconvened at 1:30 PM. Judge Thompson turned to Mitchell. “Ms. Mitchell, please call your next witness.”

“The prosecution calls Mr. Robert Timmons,” Mitchell announced.

Robert Timmons took the stand and was sworn in.

“Please state your name and occupation for the record,” Mitchell began.

“Robert Timmons. I’m a forensic video analyst employed by the Dallas Police Department,” Timmons replied.

“Mr. Timmons, how long have you been working in that capacity?” Mitchell asked.

“Approximately twelve years.”

“Briefly describe your training and expertise in video analysis.”

“I hold a master’s degree in digital forensics and certifications in advanced video enhancement techniques. I’ve analyzed and testified regarding video evidence in numerous criminal cases.”

“How did you become involved in the Morrison investigation?” Mitchell continued.

"I was assigned by the detective bureau to analyze surveillance footage obtained near the Blue Marlin Pub on the night of the murder."

"What was the condition of the footage when you received it?"

"The original footage was grainy, low-resolution, and poorly lit, making it difficult to discern specific details clearly."

"Explain to the jury what steps you took to enhance the footage."

"Using specialized software, I applied digital enhancement techniques including brightness adjustment, contrast sharpening, noise reduction, and frame-by-frame analysis to improve image clarity and detail visibility."

"After these enhancements, what were you able to determine about the figure in the video?"

Timmons indicated the screen. "The enhanced footage shows an individual approaching the alley near the Blue Marlin Pub at approximately 9:05 p.m. The figure's attire, build, and height closely match those of Mr. Morrison on the night in question."

"Did your enhancements alter or add anything to the original video content?"

"No. Enhancements clarify existing details. They do not create new elements or alter content."

"In your professional opinion, does the enhanced footage accurately represent the scene as recorded by the original camera?"

"Yes, it does."

"Thank you, Mr. Timmons. No further questions."

"Ms. Sanchez, you may cross-examine now."

Gabriela rose. "Mr. Timmons, the original footage was quite unclear, wasn't it?"

"Yes, that's correct," Timmons confirmed.

"You testified you used various digital enhancements to improve the clarity?"

"That's correct."

"But enhancements, by their nature, can also amplify artifacts or introduce subtle distortions, can't they?"

"If improperly applied, that could happen, yes."

"Can you guarantee your enhancements introduced absolutely no distortion?"

Timmons hesitated. "No enhancement process is entirely without some minimal risk of artifacting, but I carefully monitored—"

Gabriela interrupted gently. "Thank you. Now, this individual in the video wears a dark suit and a hat, correct?"

"Yes."

"Did you identify the person's face?"

"The face remained obscured."

"So, you cannot say for certain the individual in this footage is actually Mr. Morrison, can you?"

"Based purely on the footage, I cannot confirm the facial identity conclusively."

"Meaning it could reasonably be someone else, dressed similarly, couldn't it?"

"Theoretically, yes."

"Did the prosecution specifically request these enhancements to help identify the figure as Mr. Morrison?"

"They requested clarity to determine identification."

"Clarity to match Mr. Morrison, or clarity in general?"

"Clarity in general."

Gabriela then turned to the Judge. "Your honor, I would like to request that the original footage be admitted into evidence, along with the enhanced version."

"Objection, Your Honor," Mitchell said. "The original footage is too grainy to be of any use."

"Overruled." Judge Thompson said. "The original footage will be entered into evidence."

Gabriela nodded, a flicker of satisfaction in her eyes. Let them see the truth, she thought. She turned back to the witness. "No further questions, Your Honor."

Judge Thompson addressed Mitchell. "Ms. Mitchell, redirect?"

Mitchell, her expression tight, shook her head. "No redirect, Your Honor."

Timmons stepped down, his testimony lingering in the air. The jury's faces were unreadable. They had seen the enhanced footage, but now they would also see the original, flawed version. What would they make of it?

Judge Thompson turned to Mitchell. "Ms. Mitchell, call your next witness."

Mitchell hesitated, her gaze shifting to her notes. A flicker of unease crossed her face. "Your Honor," she began, her voice slightly strained, "the prosecution...requests a brief recess."

Judge Thompson raised an eyebrow. "On what grounds, Ms. Mitchell?"

"To...review some evidence," Mitchell stammered, her eyes darting towards the gallery.

Gabriela's senses sharpened. Something was wrong. Why the sudden recess? What evidence did Mitchell need to review? And why was she so flustered?

Judge Thompson's expression hardened. "Very well. We will take the afternoon break now. Ten minutes. No more."

The gavel fell, its sharp crack echoing through the courtroom. As the jury filed out, Gabriela saw Chuck Green, and he walked out with her. "Something's not right," she whispered. "Why the sudden recess?"

Green shrugged, his eyes scanning the courtroom. "I don't know. But I don't like it."

Chapter Nineteen

The sharp crack of the gavel still echoed in Gabriela's ears as she followed Morrison out into the hallway. The sudden recess had thrown her off balance. Morrison kept shifting his weight, his fingers drumming a restless rhythm on his phone. He avoided her gaze, his jaw tight. She saw Chuck Green, and she walked with him outside the courtroom.

"We need to figure out what's going on," she said, her voice low. "Ten minutes," she added, glancing at her watch. "Ten minutes to find out what Mitchell's hiding."

Before Green could respond, Gabriela's phone buzzed with a text. It was from an unknown number: *They are watching you. Be careful.*

Gabriela's eyes widened. She showed the text to Green.

Greens' eyes scanned the text. "What the hell?"

Ten minutes had passed, and Judge Thompson was ready to resume. They headed back into the courtroom. Gabriela's jaw was tight, her steps measured. Green took his seat in the back, while she and Morrison settled at the defense table. Mitchell was already at the prosecutor's table, her composure regained, but her eyes held a sharp, predatory gleam.

Judge Thompson addressed the court. "Please be seated. Ms. Mitchell, you may proceed."

Mitchell rose, her voice now steady. "Your Honor, during the recess, the prosecution reviewed some evidence. It appears there was a clerical error in the chain of custody documentation for the video evidence."

Gabriela's eyes narrowed. *A clerical error?*

Mitchell continued, "The error has been corrected, and it does not affect the integrity of the evidence itself. The enhanced video accurately represents the original footage."

Clerical error, my ass, Gabriela thought. Mitchell hadn't been caught off guard—she'd been scrambling. And scrambling meant weakness.

Judge Thompson nodded. "Very well. Let's move forward. Ms. Mitchell, call your next witness."

Mitchell rose, her movements precise. "The prosecution calls Mr. Arthur Vance."

Arthur Vance, a man with the meticulous air of a data analyst, took the stand and was sworn in.

"State your name and occupation for the record," Mitchell began.

"Arthur Vance. I am a forensic cell phone data analyst."

"Mr. Vance, please describe your qualifications and experience in this field."

"I have a master's degree in telecommunications engineering and over fifteen years of experience analyzing cell phone data for law enforcement. I've testified as an expert witness in numerous cases involving cell phone location and tracking."

"Your Honor," Mitchell said, turning to Judge Thompson, "the prosecution moves to qualify Mr. Vance as an expert in forensic cell phone data analysis."

Gabriela rose, her expression neutral. "No objection, Your Honor."

Judge Thompson nodded. "Mr. Vance is qualified. Please proceed, Ms. Mitchell."

"Mr. Vance," Mitchell continued, "how did you become involved in the Morrison investigation?"

"I was assigned to analyze the cell phone data associated with Mr. Morrison's phone on the night of the murder."

"And what did your analysis reveal?"

"Based on the cell tower data, the phone was in the vicinity of the Blue Marlin Pub at the time of the murder."

A ripple of gasps and murmurs spread through the gallery. Gabriela watched, her eyes narrowed, her mind already dissecting Vance's words.

"Can you be more specific?" Mitchell asked, her voice sharp.

"The data indicates the phone was within a one-mile radius of the pub, and the time stamp matches the window of the shooting. Furthermore, the phone's movement indicates that it was approaching the area around the time of the murder."

Jurors exchanged glances, their expressions a mix of curiosity and concern. Her fingers flicked rapidly across her keyboard, bullet points stacking up in neat columns. One-mile radius. Time stamp. Movement.

"And in your expert opinion, Mr. Vance," Mitchell asked, her voice laced with confidence, "is this data reliable?"

"The data is extremely reliable. Cell tower triangulation provides a high degree of accuracy."

Mitchell allowed herself a faint smile. "Thank you, Mr. Vance. No further questions."

Judge Thompson turned to Gabriela. “Ms. Sanchez, you may cross-examine.”

Gabriela rose, her gaze steady on Vance. “Mr. Vance, you stated that the data is ‘extremely reliable.’ However, cell tower ranges can overlap, can’t they?”

“Yes, they can.”

“And these ranges can give false impressions of location, correct?”

“There’s a margin of error.”

“A margin of error,” Gabriela repeated, her voice thoughtful. “How large of a margin?”

“It varies depending on the tower density and signal strength.”

“So, a one-mile radius could actually be two miles, or even more, in some cases?”

Vance hesitated. “Theoretically, yes.”

“And the time stamps,” Gabriela continued, “are they precise to the second?”

“No. They’re based on tower pings, which can vary slightly.”

“Slightly,” Gabriela echoed. “Meaning minutes, not seconds?”

“Potentially.”

"And the phone's 'movement' you described," Gabriela pressed, "was that based on a series of tower pings?"

"Yes."

"Meaning it's an approximation, not a precise tracking of the phone's location?"

Vance's composure wavered slightly. "It's an accurate approximation."

"Accurate, but not exact," Gabriela said, her voice low. "Thank you, Mr. Vance. No further questions."

A quiet shift settled over the courtroom. Gabriela's questions had undermined the expert's seemingly solid testimony.

Judge Thompson turned to Mitchell. "Ms. Mitchell, redirect?"

Mitchell shook her head, her expression tight. "No redirect, Your Honor."

"Very well," Judge Thompson said. "Mr. Vance, you may step down. Ms. Mitchell, call your next witness."

Mitchell rose, a practiced confidence in her movements. "The prosecution calls Ms. Dana Carter."

Dana Carter took the stand, her eyes scanning the courtroom with a focused intensity, as if dissecting every detail. She was sworn in.

Mitchell began, "State your name and occupation for the record."

Dana Carter responded, "Dana Carter. I'm a digital forensic analyst specializing in data recovery and authentication."

"Ms. Carter, can you describe your role in the Reyes murder investigation?"

"I was tasked with analyzing the digital files found in a laptop recovered from Mr. Reyes's home."

Mitchell paused for a moment, "And what did your analysis reveal?"

"We found files containing sensitive information about Mr. Morrison's business dealings. The data includes evidence of payments originating from accounts associated with Mr. Morrison's businesses."

"Ms. Carter, did your analysis reveal the recipients of these significant transactions originating from Mr. Morrison's accounts?"

"Yes." Carter turned to the jury. "A substantial portion of the payments was directed to an entity called 'Inversiones del Sol' in Mexico."

Mitchell then asked, "And did you find any information on Mr. Reyes's laptop that might shed light on Mr. Reyes's understanding or interpretation of these payments to 'Inversiones del Sol'?"

"Yes, we recovered some of Mr. Reyes's personal notes and draft articles where he appeared to be investigating Mr. Morrison's business dealings in Mexico. In these files, Mr. Reyes made certain connections and drew his own conclusions about the nature of 'Inversiones del Sol.'"

Mitchell prompted, "Could you elaborate on those connections and conclusions?"

"Yes," Carter said. "Mr. Reyes's notes contained his suspicions that 'Inversiones del Sol' might be a front for illicit activities, potentially involving cartel connections, given the region of operation and the lack of publicly available information about the entity."

Gabriela rose to her feet. "Objection, Your Honor. The witness is characterizing Mr. Reyes' notes."

Before Judge Mitchell ruled, Mitchell continued. "I'm putting printouts from Ethan Reyes' computer on the screen. Is this what you are referring to as suspicions and conclusions?"

Mitchell took Carter through each page.

"Yes, this is a complete digital record we recovered. The files were unaltered and authenticated by timestamps and metadata."

Mitchell then asked, "Ms. Carter, during your analysis of Mr. Reyes's laptop, did you recover any communications that might be relevant to his investigation or his state of mind prior to his death?"

Dana Carter answered, "Yes, we found a text message received by Mr. Reyes approximately one week before his death from an unknown number."

Mitchell put the message on the screen and asked, "Can you read that text message to the court?"

Dana Carter read, "'I know about the payments to Inversiones del Sol. I have proof of the real reason. Meet me if you want the truth.'"

Mitchell inquired, "Did Mr. Reyes respond to this text message?"

Dana Carter replied, "We could find no record of a direct reply on the phone associated with the laptop."

Mitchell concluded, "Thank you," signaling the end of her direct examination.

Judge Thompson turned to Gabriela. "Ms. Sanchez, your cross-examination."

"Ms. Carter," Gabriela began, her voice calm and measured, "you testified to finding evidence of payments related to Mr. Morrison on Mr. Reyes's laptop. Can you elaborate on the specifics of these payments?"

Carter met her gaze steadily. "The data includes records of wire transfers and electronic payments originating from accounts associated with Mr. Morrison's businesses."

"And to whom were these payments directed?" Gabriela asked, her tone pointed.

Carter consulted her notes. "The majority of the payments we could trace were directed to an individual or entity identified as 'Inversiones del Sol' in Mexico."

"'Inversiones del Sol,'" Gabriela repeated, allowing the name to resonate in the courtroom. "Did your analysis uncover the identity of the specific individual or individuals behind 'Inversiones del Sol?'"

"No, the publicly available records and the information on Mr. Reyes's laptop did not provide a direct link to a specific person or persons."

"So, the prosecution is presenting evidence of Mr. Morrison's company making payments to a business entity in Mexico, the specific ownership of which remains undisclosed based on your analysis of Mr. Reyes's laptop?" Gabriela clarified.

"That is an accurate representation of the information we were able to extract from the laptop."

"You also mentioned that Mr. Reyes was a journalist, correct?" Gabriela continued, shifting the focus to the deceased's profession.

"Yes, our information indicates Mr. Reyes was employed as a journalist."

"A journalist who, we might assume, investigated various individuals and entities as part of his work?" Gabriela suggested.

Mitchell objected. "Objection, speculation."

Judge Thompson nodded. "Sustained, Ms. Sanchez. Rephrase."

"Ms. Carter," Gabriela continued, undeterred, "in your analysis of Mr. Reyes's laptop, did you find any of his journalistic work? Any research notes, drafts of articles, or communications related to his investigations?"

"Yes, we recovered numerous documents and files related to Mr. Reyes's journalistic activities."

"And among these journalistic files, did you find any indication that Mr. Reyes was actively investigating Mr. Morrison's business dealings, particularly his operations in Mexico?" Gabriela asked, leading the witness.

Carter hesitated. "There were notes and some draft articles that touched upon Mr. Morrison's company's presence in Mexico and some of the challenges of operating in that region."

"Challenges such as?" Gabriela prompted.

"The notes referred to issues like fuel theft and the need for enhanced security measures."

"Did these notes or draft articles make any specific allegations of wrongdoing on the part of Mr. Morrison or his company?" Gabriela pressed.

Carter looked at the notes that were on the screen for the jury and courtroom spectators. "Some of these notes contained Mr. Reyes's own interpretations and theories, including speculation about potential connections between legitimate businesses and illicit activities in Mexico."

"Speculation," Gabriela repeated, emphasizing the word. "Isn't it true that none of these notes or draft articles that Ms. Mitchell has shown the jury provide any concrete evidence of Mr. Morrison or his company knowingly engaging with cartels or illegal activities?"

"No, Mr. Reyes only expressed his suspicions."

Gabriela glanced from Carter to Judge Thompson. "I have nothing further, Your Honor."

Judge Thompson's voice broke the tension. "Court is adjourned for the day," he said, and the courtroom began to clear.

Gabriela slipped her files into her bag as the courtroom emptied. When she glanced at her phone, a message waited from her father: *Call me when you're done. I want to hear how it's going.*

She stepped into a quiet alcove and dialed. Roberto answered immediately.

"¿Cómo vas, mija?" His voice was calm, but she heard the undercurrent of worry.

"Tired," she admitted. "And Mitchell's throwing everything she has. Today it was cell data, digital files, payments in Mexico…"

Roberto was silent for a moment. "And Morrison?"

"He keeps his head down. But Papá, someone's pulling strings. A juror's family was threatened. I've had threats, too."

His exhale was heavy. "Eso no es un juicio limpio. You know what that means. But listen to me, Gabriela. Don't let fear dictate your pace. Keep the jury with you. Show them you believe your own arguments."

Her throat tightened. "I'm trying. It feels like every time I close a gap, Mitchell opens another."

"That's her job. Yours is to hold steady. Confía en tu preparación. Step by step. The truth will hold."

"I know, Papá. Gracias."

The line clicked silent. Gabriela slipped the phone back into her bag—only to see another notification appear. Hayes's text: *Bartender has a criminal record. Call me now.*

When the call ended, another notification appeared on her screen. Hayes's text. *The bartender has a criminal record. Call me now.* Gabriela stared at the message, her pulse quickening. She'd find a way to use it to her advantage.

Chapter Twenty

Gabriela checked her watch, then called Hayes. She tapped her foot as the phone kept ringing. Come on, Hayes. The silence on the other end made everything worse. Too much was at stake for Morrison and for her. Reyes's final words stayed with her, sharper now than before.

On the sixth ring, Hayes answered. "Gabriela?"

"Hayes, the bartender," she said, her voice tight. "What have you got?"

A pause. "He's got a record. Fraud, extortion. Possible ties to their investigator."

"Ties?" Gabriela asked, her gaze narrowed. "What kind?"

Hayes sighed, a long, drawn-out exhale. "Fraud, extortion. Arrests. Messy."

"Fraud," Gabriela repeated, her grip tightening on the phone. *Mitchell's playing a dangerous game*. "Are you certain it's him?"

"Confirmed."

Gabriela glanced at the files on her desk. An unreliable witness. This could break their case. "I need everything on him by morning. Before court."

"Plan?"

"Destroy him on the stand," Gabriela said, her gaze fixed on the rising sun. "They won't recover."

"Understood. I'll call with updates."

"Hayes," Gabriela said. "Don't miss anything. Mitchell doesn't make mistakes."

"Got it."

Gabriela ended the call. *Something's wrong.* She gathered her notes. *Every word counts.*

She stood, her gaze hard. *Tomorrow, this breaks.* She walked to the elevator.

Gabriela met Hayes in a quiet corner of the courthouse café the next morning. "Anything new?" she asked, her voice low. Hayes slid a file across the table. "Everything you asked for. And then some." She scanned the documents, a grim satisfaction settling in her stomach. *Cortez won't know what hit him.*

Gabriela strode through the crush of reporters, her briefcase a sharp counterpoint to their shouted questions. *Ignore them*. Her gaze remained locked on the courtroom doors.

"Gabriela! How do you plan to handle today's witness?" a reporter yelled.

"Is Morrison's empire about to fall?" another voice demanded.

Morrison's name. *A challenge.* She pushed through the crowd, their questions a blur. *Don't give them anything.*

Inside, the courtroom buzzed with expectation. Gabriela took her seat, her eyes meeting Mitchell's. *She's ready.*

"Your Honor, the prosecution calls John Cortez," Mitchell announced.

Cortez took the stand, his eyes shifting, his smile too smooth. He's hiding something.

"State your name," Mitchell instructed.

"John Cortez."

Gabriela watched the jury, their eyes fixed on Cortez. *He's well-rehearsed.*

"Where were you on April tenth?"

"Blue Marlin Pub."

.

"Did you see anyone in the courtroom there?"

Cortez looked out at Gabriela and Morrison.

"I saw the man sitting at the table over there," pointing at Morrison.

"Was anyone with him?"

"There was another man across from him."

"Anything unusual?"

Cortez shifted. "The man over there," he gestured towards Morrison, "was angry."

"What did he say?"

Here it comes.

"He threatened the other man."

"How?"

"Stay out of my business. I'll ruin you."

"Anything else?"

"He left after a call."

Mitchell was playing it tight. Gabriela's mind raced. *He was trying to cut off the alibi.* She watched the jury.

"Did you tell anyone?"

"A few friends," Cortez said, a smirk flickering.

"No further questions," Mitchell said.

A ripple of sound moved through the courtroom. Gabriela rose.

"Mr. Cortez," Gabriela began, her voice cutting through the murmurs, "is this your first time testifying?"

Cortez's eyes flickered. "Yeah."

"Ever been in court before?"

"Objection," Mitchell snapped. "Relevance."

"Credibility, Your Honor," Gabriela said, her voice calm.

Judge Thompson nodded. "Overruled. Answer."

Cortez hesitated. "Yeah."

"How many times?"

He shifted. "A few."

"Five? Ten?"

"Around that."

"Criminal charges?"

The room stilled.

"Yes."

"Fraud?"

"Yes."

"Extortion?"

"Yes."

A faint rustle moved through the gallery, the jurors shifting in their seats. Cortez's shoulders hunched as if bracing for the next blow. Gabriela kept her expression neutral, giving them all a moment to absorb the admissions before pressing again. "You've lied for money."

"That was then."

"You've done it."

"Yes."

"Experience," Gabriela said, staring at the witness. "How much is your testimony worth?"

"I saw what I saw."

"Paid to see it?"

"Objection!" Mitchell said.

"Sustained."

"Expect anything?" Gabriela asked.

Cortez hesitated. "No."

"Pressured?"

"No."

"Contact with the prosecution?"

"Investigator, once."

"Anyone else?"

"No."

"Lying about that, too?"

"No!"

"The phone call. What kind?"

Cortez blinked. "What?"

"The phone."

"I don't remember."

"But you remember a conversation across the room?"

"I—"

"Misheard?" Gabriela cut in.

"I heard him."

"Booth. How far?"

"Tables away."

"Loud?"

Cortez nodded.

"So, unsure of the words. Unsure of the speaker?"

"It was the man at the table."

"Sure?"

"Yes."

"Or told to say it was?"

"Objection!" Mitchell said.

"Sustained."

"Why should we believe you, Mr. Cortez?"

"I'm telling the truth." His voice wavered.

"No further questions."

Gabriela sat, focusing her attention on the jury. *They're doubting him.*

Judge Thompson cleared his throat. “Court will take a brief recess.”

Fifteen minutes later, Gabriela and Morrison were back in their seats. After the jury was seated, Judge Thompson said, “Ms. Mitchell, you may call your next witness.”

Mitchell replied, “The prosecution calls, Marissa Ortega.”

Gabriela knew Marissa could not have been more reluctant to be a government witness. She had called when she received the subpoena and asked if she had to testify. Gabriela told her she had to comply with the subpoena.

As she approached the witness stand, Marissa looked over at Gabriela.

Mitchell frowned and then started her questioning with practiced calm. “Please state your name for the record.”

“Marissa Ortega.”

“Ms. Ortega, where are you currently employed?”

“Morrison Oil,” Ortega replied clearly. “I serve as Mr. Morrison’s executive assistant.”

“How long have you held that position?”

“Five years.”

"And during that time, did you work closely with Mr. Morrison?"

"Yes," Ortega answered cautiously. "We worked closely."

Mitchell continued carefully. "Over those five years, did you become familiar with Mr. Morrison's business dealings?"

"I did," Ortega said quietly. "But over time, things changed. Once Morrison Oil started drilling in Mexico, there were new people and private meetings. I noticed a difference."

Marissa had told Gabriela how things had changed, but it still bothered her hearing Marissa express it in court.

"And when did you notice these changes?" Mitchell asked.

"Around the time Mr. Morrison became aware of Ethan Reyes's investigation."

"Investigation?" Mitchell asked, her voice sharp. "What kind of investigation?"

"Mr. Reyes was a journalist," Ortega clarified. "He was looking into Morrison Oil's operations in Mexico. Mr. Morrison was very concerned."

"Concerned how?" Mitchell pressed.

"He was more stressed, more agitated. He was having private meetings, making calls at odd hours."

That's not how Marissa had expressed it to Gabriela in their meetings. After telling Gabriela she didn't want to testify, Marissa must have met with Mitchell, and she or someone pressured Marissa.

"Ms. Ortega, during the two weeks prior to Mr. Reyes's death, did you observe any specific interactions between Mr. Morrison and Mr. Reyes?"

"Yes. Mr. Reyes called the office four times," Ortega replied.

"And what was the nature of those calls?"

"He told me he was working on an article about Morrison's Mexican connections."

"Do you know if Mr. Morrison ever met with Mr. Reyes?"

"Yes, once. Three days before Mr. Reyes was found dead."

"And can you tell the jury how Mr. Morrison seemed after that meeting?"

Gabriela rose. "Objection, Your Honor. This witness is in no position to tell the jury how Mr. Morrison seemed."

"Your Honor, she can tell the jury what she saw."

“I’m going to allow the witness to answer the question, but be careful, Ms. Mitchell.”

“Mr. Morrison was very upset and angry. When I asked about the meeting, he said, “It’s being handled,’ and changed the subject.”

Mitchell narrowed her questioning further. “Did Mr. Reyes contact Mr. Morrison again before his death?”

Ortega paused briefly. “Yes, the afternoon before Mr. Reyes died, Mr. Morrison received a call from Mr. Reyes. Mr. Morrison was out, so I asked Mr. Reyes if I could tell Mr. Morrison what he was calling about. I wrote down that Mr. Reyes was calling about some problems he had uncovered regarding Morrison Enterprises' drilling operations in Mexico, and he thought Mr. Morrison would want to address them before he published his findings."

Did you tell Mr. Morrison, and how did he react?”

“I showed him the note I had written. He was even more angry than before and said, ‘I have to take care of this now.’ He left abruptly, visibly upset. When he returned, at nearly 4 PM, he said he had taken care of something urgent.”

Gabriela rose again. “Your Honor, I ask that the witness’s testimony be stricken from the record and that you instruct the jury to disregard it. Ms. Mitchell asked if the witness could recall any instance when Mr. Morrison was upset with Mr. Reyes. The witness testified Mr. Morrison was upset after a call, but there is no evidence that the call was from Mr. Reyes."

"Ms. Sanchez, I think you've made your point. The jury can take that point into consideration."

Mitchell asked pointedly, "Ms. Ortega, during your time as Mr. Morrison's assistant, did you ever become aware of him possessing a firearm?"

Ortega hesitated, her eyes darting to Morrison, then back to Mitchell. "Yes."

"And what type of firearm was this?"

"A handgun," she said quietly. "A .357 caliber."

A collective gasp rippled through the courtroom.

Mitchell paused, allowing the significance of the statement to settle. "And when did you last see this firearm?"

Ortega's voice trembled slightly. "That afternoon when he left to… 'take care of something urgent.'"

Gabriela stopped breathing for a moment. *No.*

Mitchell stepped back, a subtle, satisfied smile playing on her lips. "No further questions, Your Honor."

Despite Ortega's denial earlier, Gabriela saw the damage clearly. Mitchell had placed Morrison, leaving in a hurry, returning shortly after, and possessed the same caliber weapon used in the murder, all in the afternoon before Reyes died. Gabriela glanced toward the jury, their expressions now a mix of shock and suspicion. *This is it. This is where it all falls apart.*

Morrison's voice, a low hiss, cut through the sudden silence. "She's lying."

Gabriela's head snapped towards him, her eyes searching his. *She'd trusted Marissa. She'd believed Morrison. But this was a direct contradiction.*

Gabriela rose slowly, gathering herself and quickly reviewing each contradiction she needed to highlight. This was her opportunity to regain control. *A .357 caliber? How would she know?* She felt the momentum slipping away, yet her resolve grew stronger in response. *She had trusted Marissa. She had lied.* As she approached the witness stand, Gabriela knew she had reached the trial's most dangerous moment. Now, she had to prove Marissa was lying.

"Ms. Ortega," Gabriela began firmly, her voice steady but sharp, "you worked for Phillip Morrison for how long?"

Ortega shifted in her seat. "Five years."

"And you were loyal to him?"

Ortega nodded, slowly, her eyes briefly lowering.

"And you still are?"

"Yes," Ortega said, but a subtle uncertainty slipped through.

Gabriela pressed. "Did you ask him about this case?"

"No," Ortega said, then hesitated. "Not directly."

"Why not?"

"I was told not to talk to him about the case."

"Who told you not to talk to Mr. Morrison?"

"Ms. Mitchell and a policeman."

Gabriela paused, letting the implication hang in the air. "You were cooperative with the defense, Ms. Ortega. You spoke with me. You were helpful. Then, abruptly, you stopped. Why was that?"

Ortega's voice trembled. "Ms. Mitchell said... she said I could get into trouble if I helped you."

"Trouble how?" Gabriela asked, her voice sharp. "What kind of trouble?"

Ortega looked down, her voice barely a whisper. "She didn't say. But she made it sound serious."

"Serious enough to make you change your story?" Gabriela pressed.

"No!" Ortega said, her voice rising slightly, then falling again. "I'm telling the truth."

"The truth as Ms. Mitchell told you to tell it?" Gabriela asked, her voice laced with skepticism.

"Objection!" Mitchell said, her voice sharp. "Badgering the witness!"

"Withdrawn," Gabriela said, her voice still sharp. "Ms. Ortega, you previously told me that you helped Mr. Morrison prepare the stolen gun report, correct?"

Ortega's eyes flickered towards Mitchell, then back to Gabriela. "Yes."

"And you are aware that the police report states that Mr. Morrison's .357 caliber handgun was stolen three weeks before the murder?"

Ortega hesitated. "Yes."

"And you are aware that this report mysteriously disappeared from the police system, and was only found buried in county records?"

"No." She replied.

"Ms. Ortega, you are Mr. Morrison's executive assistant, and you have been to his home, correct?"

"Yes," Marissa answered.

"You are aware he kept the gun in a safe at his home, correct?"

"Yes."

"And you are aware he rarely accessed the gun, correct?"

"Yes."

"So, Ms. Ortega, you claim you saw Mr. Morrison with the same gun he reported stolen weeks before. Are you mistaken?"

Ortega's voice trembled. "I don't know."

"Did anyone tell you what to say about the gun?" Gabriela asked, turning toward Mitchell and the detective at her side.

Ortega did not respond.

Gabriela continued, her voice sharp. "How do you know it was a .357 caliber handgun?"

Ortega hesitated. "The police told me."

"The police told you?" Gabriela asked, her voice incredulous. "Or did Ms. Mitchell tell you?"

"Objection!" Mitchell said. "Badgering the witness."

"Withdrawn," Gabriela said. "Are you familiar with handguns, Ms. Ortega?"

"No."

"Then why are you so sure of the caliber?"

Ortega shifted in her seat. "I... I don't know."

"You mentioned Mr. Morrison's closed-door meetings. Do you know what they were about?"

"No."

"But you admit something changed in him?"

"Yes."

"Isn't it true you're guessing about other things?"

"No," Marissa insisted, but her voice wavered.

"You don't know if Mr. Reyes was planning to write something negative about Morrison Enterprises drilling in Mexico. Isn't that true?"

"I assumed…"

"You assumed? Ms. Ortega, Ethan Reyes never said in his conversation with you that he was planning to write a negative story about Mr. Morrison, did he?"

"He was an investigative reporter. I don't recall him writing positive articles about people he was investigating. Plus, any time I mentioned him, Mr. Morrison was angry."

"After Mr. Morrison met with Mr. Reyes, he told you everything was okay, didn't he?"

"Yes," Ortega replied, nodding.

"Isn't it true your testimony omits important details?"

Marissa hesitated.

Mitchell stood quickly. "Objection, Your Honor. Speculation. Badgering the witness. No foundation."

Judge Thompson considered, then looked at Gabriela. "Ms. Sanchez, do you have any foundation for this line of questioning?"

"Your Honor," Gabriela said, "the witness has already testified that Ms. Mitchell and the police told her not to talk to the defense. I am merely exploring the implications of that testimony."

Judge Thompson nodded slowly. "Objection overruled. The witness will answer."

Marissa remained silent, her eyes fixed on the floor. Finally, she looked up, her voice trembling. "Yes. They have threatened me."

A collective gasp sounded through the courtroom. Gabriela tracked the jurors instead of the noise. One pressed his lips together. Another scribbled a hurried note. She had given jurors a reason to doubt Mitchell's case and find Morrison not guilty.

Gabriela paused, letting the implications sink in. "I have no further questions."

Gabriela stepped back, turning to look at the jury. *Doubt.*

Mitchell's jaw tightened, her eyes flashing with suppressed alarm. She quickly turned to Judge Thompson. "Your Honor," she said urgently, "I request a brief recess."

Judge Thompson nodded, his expression serious. "The court will recess for fifteen minutes."

During the break, Gabriela closely observed Mitchell huddling with her team around, speaking quickly, her movements sharp and tense. Gabriela could tell that Mitchell was rattled.

When the court reconvened, Mitchell moved decisively to the witness stand, her composure carefully restored, though her eyes were noticeably colder. "Your Honor, at this time, I request the court declare Ms. Ortega an adverse witness. Her testimony is clearly hostile to the prosecution's case."

Judge Thompson considered the request, scrutinizing Marissa closely. "Ms. Mitchell, the motion is granted. You may proceed with Ms. Ortega as an adverse witness."

Mitchell turned sharply back to Marissa, her eyes intense. "Ms. Ortega, let me ask you directly: No member of the police department threatened you in any way, isn't that true?"

Marissa hesitated, then replied. "Yes, no member threatened me."

"Did I or any member of the police department coerce you into giving any specific testimony?"

"No."

"Isn't it true that the only instruction I gave you was to tell the truth?"

"Yes, that's what you told me, but…."

"You've answered the question. So, to be clear, Ms. Ortega, you are now testifying that you were not threatened, and that you were only instructed to tell the truth?"

Marissa's voice was barely audible. "Yes."

"And you understand that you are under oath, and that making false statements is a crime?"

"Yes."

Mitchell paused as if thinking. She looked at the jury and said, "No further questions, your honor."

Ms. Sanchez, do you have any more questions? Judge Thompson asked.

Gabriela looked over at the jury, noticing some had crossed their arms. Others were slowly shaking their heads. She quickly assessed how Mitchell had regained some lost ground, but only with a few jurors. *The damage is done. But now they will wonder why she changed her story. And what else they're missing?*

Gabriela turned and looked over at Judge Thompson. "No further questions, Your Honor."

As she sat down, Gabriela's gaze lingered on the jury. *Something isn't right. There's a piece of this puzzle they haven't seen. And I need to find it before it's too late.*

Chapter Twenty-One

Judge Thompson, with a curt nod and a firm grip on the gavel, called the courtroom to order. The sharp crack echoed, silencing the lingering buzz. Gabriela, seated at the defense table, maintained a steady focus. Her gaze swept over the jury.

Judge Thompson's voice boomed across the silent room. "Ladies and gentlemen of the jury, this concludes the state's case. You are dismissed for the day. Please remember not to discuss the case among yourselves or with anyone else until you return at nine o'clock tomorrow morning."

Chairs creaked as the jurors rose. One young man rolled his neck, his jaw set in a hard line. Another scratched notes furiously, unwilling to lose a thought. A middle-aged woman adjusted her scarf, her gaze distant, as if already weighing testimony against Morrison.

The doors swung shut, and Gabriela stood. "Your Honor," she began, voice poised and confident, "I move for a directed verdict of not guilty. The state has failed to meet its burden. The evidence is entirely circumstantial, and the testimony lacks credibility." She'd never had a judge grant a motion for a directed verdict, and she didn't expect this to be the first time.

Morrison watched her from his seat at the defense table. He knew what the stakes were, but Gabriela's unwavering presence gave him confidence. He clung to her words, hoping Judge Thompson would agree with her carefully constructed argument.

Judge Thompson listened, his expression unreadable. He let a moment of silence linger after Gabriela finished. "The court finds that there is sufficient evidence for the jury to consider. Motion denied. The defense must proceed with its case."

Morrison leaned toward Gabriela, voice barely above a whisper. "What does this mean for us?" His eyes searched hers, trying to pierce through his uncertainty.

"We're still in a strong position," Gabriela assured him. Her words were firm, but that was a lie. Her father had once told her that in many criminal trials, the defense's case often peaked when the prosecution rested. At that point, the jury was most ready to doubt. As she looked at Morrison, knowing he would take the stand, she was pretty sure her father was right.

After Morrison left with his wife, Gabriela found Hayes. "We have work to do."

As they exited, Gabriela caught Mitchell's eye briefly, noting the quiet confidence in her opponent's expression.

Returning to her office, Gabriela dropped her bag onto her desk and immediately opened her files. Thoughts raced through her mind as she sorted through papers and documents.

She turned sharply to Hayes. “I’m worried about Marissa’s testimony. She put the gun, which Mitchell claims is the murder weapon, right into Morrison’s hands the day before Reyes was killed. We need to create a different story for the jury, one where that detail doesn’t condemn Morrison.”

“You think they manipulated evidence or testimony?” Hayes asked.

“Almost certain,” Gabriela replied, determination edging her voice. “We have these flash drives. They hold the pieces of our story, the one that Mitchell is ignoring.”

Gabriela plugged the flash drive into her laptop, quickly navigating through folders. Her focus intensified as she identified critical financial records.

“Penbrooke’s transactions clearly link him to everything we’ve suspected,” Gabriela said urgently, highlighting specific entries. “This is the start of our story, Hayes. Penbrooke’s story.”

Hayes leaned closer. “Reyes was killed on the seventeenth, and these transactions with sums disappearing from Penbrooke’s account occur right around that date. They look like payoffs. This is the motive in our story."

Hayes pointed at another section of data. "Reyes spoke to these officers, but several never followed up. The police ignored critical leads. This is the police's story, and it's full of holes."

"This is exactly the proof we need to tell our story," Gabriela affirmed confidently. "We need to show the jury the story the police missed. The story where Morrison is not the killer. "

"Mitchell will come after us hard," Hayes cautioned. "She has her own story."

"Let her," Gabriela replied firmly. "We will tell a more compelling story." Hayes left her, and Gabriela turned off the light in her office, took the elevator to the ground floor, and took the parking garage elevator to the second floor.

As she stepped into the parking garage, the lightbulb above flickered, casting wild shadows across the concrete floor. Gabriela unlocked her car and gripped her car door. A voice, low and slightly raspy, sliced through the darkness, stopping her in her tracks.

"Keep pushing, and you'll end up like Rodriguez. Walk away, Sanchez. You'll burn too."

Her breath caught before she turned. The garage was empty. Just before the voice, she had heard the faintest sound, like fabric brushing against concrete. The threat stayed with her. Someone knew the cartel had ordered the killing of a Dallas lawyer. Maybe that same someone was watching her now. Had they ordered her death, too?

Gabriela gripped her handbag tighter and walked toward her car, alert to every sound. Her heels hit the concrete, each step loud in the silence. Her heart pounded. Every instinct told her to run, but she forced herself to stay calm. Panic wouldn't help.

The encounter rattled her. She thought of Rodriguez. Steady. Unshaken. Until the day his car exploded. He had known he was in danger. He hadn't gotten out. Had she made the same mistake?

She sat in the driver's seat, letting the fear come and go. What was left wasn't calm. It was resolved. She wouldn't back off. She wouldn't give them that. She would keep going. And she would win.

The drive home passed in a blur. Every headlight looked like a threat. At each turn, she checked her mirror. No one followed. But it wasn't just fear that kept her eyes moving. It was anger.

Anger that the threat was both so personal and so invasive. Anger that they thought they could scare her off. She gripped the wheel with white knuckles, and the enormity of the case and the risks loomed larger than ever.

By the time Gabriela reached home, she was still scared. She pulled into the driveway and sat in the car for a moment, eyes scanning the shadows. She didn't see anyone.

She stepped inside, her thoughts still racing about the thousand different threads connecting Penbrooke to the cartel and to the threats against her. She thought about her father and the dozens of times he'd been threatened. He'd never backed down, and neither would she.

The next morning, the courtroom buzzed with anticipation. Gabriela, her face a mask of composure, entered with Hayes. She scanned the gallery, searching for any sign of Penbrooke or anyone connected to him. Judge Thompson entered, and the room fell silent.

"Ms. Sanchez, you may call your first witness," Thompson stated, his voice booming.

Gabriela rose. "We call Samuel Hayes to the stand."

Samuel Hayes approached the stand, his face serious. Gabriela began her direct examination, her questions precise, each one a scalpel slicing through the prosecution's narrative.

“Mr. Hayes, you testified that you analyzed the financial records from the flash drive. What did you find?”

“I found a series of transactions linked to shell companies controlled by Stephen Penbrooke. These transactions occurred around the time of Ethan Reyes’s murder.”

Gabriela stood at the lectern, glancing at Judge Thompson. “Your Honor, with the court’s permission, we would like to display the surveillance footage on the courtroom monitor.”

Judge Thompson nodded. “Permission granted.”

The court’s technology personnel activated the large screen facing the jury. The lights dimmed slightly, and the footage appeared on the screen.

Gabriela turned to Hayes. “Mr. Hayes, what can you tell us about this surveillance footage?”

Hayes replied confidently, “This footage was on a second flash drive that I personally obtained during my investigation. I analyzed the footage myself and then turned it over to the court and the prosecution team two days ago.”

Mitchell rose, her voice sharp. “Objection, Your Honor. The witness has not established any qualifications to analyze this footage. The defense cannot simply assert authenticity without an expert witness."

Judge Thompson turned to Gabriela. "Ms. Sanchez, the prosecution's objection is well-founded. You must establish Mr. Hayes' qualifications before we can consider his analysis."

Gabriela nodded. "Understood, Your Honor." She turned back to Hayes. "Mr. Hayes, could you please explain your professional experience with video analysis?"

Hayes responded clearly, "I have over fifteen years of experience as a private investigator. I have conducted digital forensic analysis on hundreds of cases, including analyzing surveillance footage, authenticating video evidence, and presenting my findings in court. I have received certification in digital forensics from the National Institute of Justice."

Gabriela glanced at Judge Thompson, who nodded. "You may proceed, Ms. Sanchez."

Gabriela continued. "Mr. Hayes, after personally analyzing this footage, what did you find?"

Hayes pointed to the screen. "The footage shows a man, not Phillip Morrison, entering the alley where Ethan Reyes was killed. The timing aligns with the estimated time of death."

Gabriela leaned in, her tone thoughtful. "Can you describe any distinctive features of the man shown in the footage?"

Hayes nodded. "The man is wearing a dark hoodie pulled low over his face. As he moves under the alley light, there's a brief glint from his left wrist. It looks like a reflection from a watch or bracelet with a bright, almost metallic band. It's only visible for a split second when he turns his hand."

Gabriela glanced at the screen. "Were you able to identify the object?"

"No, the footage quality isn't high enough to make out specific details. It just appeared to catch the light momentarily. I didn't consider it significant in identifying the man."

"Is there anything else you made note of from the video?"

"Yes. The man draws the gun out of his pocket with his right hand."

Gabriela nodded, satisfied. "And to your knowledge, was this footage ever investigated by the police?"

"No. It appears they focused solely on Mr. Morrison."

Gabriela moved on to the financial records, her tone steady and deliberate. "Mr. Hayes, can you explain the connection between these transactions and Mr. Penbrooke?"

Before Hayes could answer, Mitchell stood swiftly. "Objection, Your Honor. Lack of foundation. The witness hasn't established personal knowledge of these financial documents."

Judge Thompson looked toward Gabriela. "Ms. Sanchez, please establish a proper foundation first."

Gabriela nodded calmly, refocusing her questioning. "Mr. Hayes, did you personally examine these financial records?"

"Yes, I did," Hayes replied firmly.

"What is your professional experience or expertise regarding financial investigations?" Gabriela continued.

"It's the same as I testified earlier about the video. I also have over fifteen years of experience as a financial investigator, specializing in tracing complex financial transactions and uncovering fraud," Hayes explained.

Gabriela glanced at Judge Thompson, who nodded approvingly. "Proceed."

Returning to the key point, Gabriela asked again, "Now, Mr. Hayes, based on your analysis, can you explain the connection between these financial transactions and Mr. Penbrooke?"

Hayes walked the jury through the maze of shell companies, tracing each suspicious transfer. Gabriela watched the jurors closely;

a few leaned forward, pens scratching, catching the significance of dates that lined up too neatly with Reyes's death.

"Mr. Hayes," Gabriela continued, shifting the focus, "earlier you mentioned that the police investigation appeared to focus exclusively on Mr. Morrison. In your investigation, did you uncover evidence suggesting the police considered other suspects?"

Mitchell rose again sharply. "Objection, Your Honor. Calls for speculation."

"Sustained," Judge Thompson said calmly. "Ms. Sanchez, rephrase your question."

Gabriela adjusted her approach smoothly. "Mr. Hayes, during your investigation, did you find documented evidence that indicated police followed up on other potential suspects?"

"No, I did not," Hayes answered clearly. "Several key leads and witnesses were never pursued further."

"Regarding the list of police contacts you mentioned earlier, specifically those names crossed off on the second flash drive, what did you find?" Gabriela asked carefully.

Hayes explained directly, "Those officers had interviewed Reyes in the weeks prior to his death. My review showed notations indicating these officers had relevant information, but the records confirm they were never questioned further or pursued by investigators."

Gabriela paused briefly before continuing. "In your professional opinion, what did your findings reveal about the nature of this police investigation?"

Hayes responded without hesitation. "The records show that the investigation narrowly targeted Mr. Morrison without adequately following up on other critical evidence or potential suspects."

Gabriela stepped back, addressing the jury clearly. "Thank you, Mr. Hayes. No further questions, Your Honor."

Mitchell rose, her expression carefully composed. "Mr. Hayes," she began, her voice sharp and pointed, "you claim to have personally analyzed the surveillance footage. Can you tell the court what specific methods you used to verify its authenticity?"

Hayes replied confidently, "I used industry-standard digital forensic techniques, including metadata analysis and frame-by-frame examination, to confirm that the footage had not been altered or tampered with."

Mitchell frowned. "And you are not a certified forensic video analyst, correct?"

Hayes remained composed. “That’s correct. I am a licensed private investigator with certification in digital forensics.”

Mitchell moved closer, her tone skeptical. “But you’re not claiming to be an expert specifically in video authentication?”

“No, I am not. I have, however, authenticated video evidence in numerous cases, including those where my analysis has been accepted by the court,” Hayes clarified.

Mitchell nodded slowly. “Mr. Hayes, you also testified that the financial transactions occurred ‘around’ the time of the murder. Can you provide the exact dates of these transactions?”

Hayes consulted his notes. “The largest transfer of funds occurred three days before Mr. Reyes’s death, and another significant transfer took place two days after.”

Mitchell raised an eyebrow. “And isn’t it possible that these transactions were entirely unrelated to the murder?”

Hayes didn’t hesitate. “It is possible, but highly improbable, given the timing, the amounts involved, and the specific accounts linked to Mr. Penbrooke.”

Mitchell gave a tight smile. “So, you’re asking the jury to believe your analysis based on your own experience rather than the expertise of a certified video analyst?”

"I'm asking the jury to consider the evidence as presented, including the corroborating details," Hayes responded.

Mitchell leaned in. "You have a history of conducting independent investigations, sometimes pushing the limits of standard procedures. Isn't it true that you might have a personal bias in implicating Mr. Penbrooke?"

"Objection, Your Honor!" Gabriela interjected. "Counsel is improperly questioning the witness's integrity without a basis."

"Sustained," Judge Thompson said. "Ms. Mitchell, keep your questions relevant."

Mitchell gave a curt nod. "No further questions, Your Honor."

Judge Thompson addressed the jury. "Ladies and gentlemen, we'll break for lunch. Please remember my previous instructions. We will reconvene at 1:00 p.m. Ms. Sanchez, call your next witness at that time."

As the jurors filed out, Gabriela noted the sideways glances and the half-whispered exchanges the bailiffs tried to hush. The story was shifting. It was not won, not yet, but it was shifting.

Chapter Twenty-Two

The courtroom emptied as Judge Thompson called for the lunch recess. Gabriela, Hayes, and Morrison retreated to a small, private room. Gabriela's gaze was sharp as she addressed Hayes.

"That objection from Mitchell about your qualifications almost derailed us," Gabriela said. "Good thing we established your credentials after that."

Hayes gave a slight nod. "I should have anticipated that. I didn't think she'd challenge it so aggressively."

Morrison, leaning back in his chair, offered a placating smile. "We all have our secrets, don't we? What matters is that we get through this." The way he said it, with a slight emphasis on "secrets," made Gabriela's instincts as a trial lawyer uncomfortable. She studied him, searching for a tell, but his expression remained open, supportive.

"We need to shift the jury's focus," Gabriela said, turning back to Hayes. "We're calling Marcus Patel and then Detective Navarro. Their testimony will undermine the police investigation and give us room to introduce Elizabeth, you, and Penbrooke at the end."

They discussed Patel's and Detective Navarro's testimony, outlining the key points Gabriela wanted to emphasize: the inconsistencies in the investigation, the ignored leads, the missing gun report, and the early suspicion of Penbrooke.

"We have to build a narrative," Gabriela stressed, "a story where the police dropped the ball. A story where Morrison is not the killer."

The lunch break ended, and they returned to the courtroom. Judge Thompson took his place on the bench, and the jury returned to their seats, some glancing at each other with a mix of curiosity and unease, still digesting the morning's testimony. Gabriela straightened her notes, her mind already forming the path to expose the investigation's flaws. Mitchell had landed a few punches in the morning, but this was her chance to turn the tide.

Gabriela, her face composed, rose. "Your Honor, the defense calls Marcus Patel to the stand." A low murmur rippled through the room, the audience sensing a shift as Patel approached the stand.

The courtroom quieted as Marcus Patel, the digital forensics expert, took the stand. Gabriela approached him, her questions precise and deliberate. She established his expertise and then guided him to his analysis of Ethan Reyes's laptop. Marcus explained his examination of the metadata associated with the article incriminating Morrison, clearly stating that the file's modification date was after Reyes's death. He detailed how metadata acts as a digital history, a point he emphasized for the jury's understanding.

With visual aids displayed on courtroom monitors, Patel walked the jury step by step through the differences between the initial drafts of Reyes's article and the final version recovered by the police. He highlighted the specific, detailed allegations of Morrison's cartel involvement that were added after Reyes was no longer alive to make those changes.

A hush fell over the courtroom, thickened as Marcus described his efforts to trace the IP address that accessed the laptop. He explained the complexities of VPNs and how he meticulously followed the digital breadcrumbs, ultimately locating the originating point to a high-end residential building downtown, though the specific unit remained elusive. Gabriela ensured Marcus concluded by stating that this post-mortem manipulation strongly indicated a deliberate attempt to frame her client.

With Patel's final words hanging in the air, Gabriela stepped back, a sense of having landed a significant blow evident in her posture. The focus now shifted as Laura Mitchell rose to cross-examine.

Laura Mitchell rose to cross-examine, her voice sharp with professional skepticism. She immediately questioned Marcus's impartiality, emphasizing his employment by the defense. Mitchell then delved into the intricacies of tracing IP addresses through VPNs, suggesting his findings were more speculative than definitive and that the ultimate user remained unidentified.

She proposed the possibility that Reyes himself intended to include the damning allegations, arguing that the writing process is not always linear and that digital timestamps don't capture every intention. Mitchell painted digital forensics as open to interpretation, implying Patel's conclusions were only one reading of the data.

Despite Mitchell's pointed questions, Marcus maintained his composure, carefully explaining the logical inferences drawn from the consistent digital evidence of post-mortem alteration.

Having concluded Marcus Patel's impactful testimony, Gabriela simply stated, "The defense calls Detective Linda Navarro to the stand, Your Honor."

Gabriela heard a buzz of hushed conversation as Patel stepped down. She turned towards the jury and saw them exchanging glances. She hoped their focused expressions suggested they were considering the implications of the manipulated digital evidence.

Detective Linda Navarro, a woman with a history within the Dallas Police Department, made her way to the witness stand, her presence promising a potentially explosive turn in the proceedings.

She was a woman in her late forties, with a no-nonsense demeanor and a steady gaze.

As Navarro took the stand, Gabriela established her credentials and experience before turning to the Reyes investigation. She asked Navarro about her involvement in the early stages, and Navarro confirmed she was part of it.

Gabriela then inquired if Navarro had observed any inconsistencies during her involvement. Navarro stated that she had, pointing to a premature focus on Mr. Morrison and the failure to follow up on several potential leads. When pressed for specific examples, Navarro detailed the lack of follow-up on witness statements, the dismissal of alternate suspects, and the missing gun report, emphasizing that she had expressed her concern about the missing report at the time, considering it highly irregular.

Gabriela then shifted her questioning to Stephen Penbrooke, asking if Navarro had any concerns about him. Navarro replied affirmatively, stating that she had brought him up as a person of interest early in the investigation, but her concerns were dismissed. Gabriela further elicited testimony about the pressure Navarro felt from her superiors to close the case quickly and the reasons that ultimately led to her resignation from the police force.

Laura Mitchell rose for cross-examination, her voice carrying a note of skepticism. She immediately questioned Navarro's resignation, implying it occurred under less than amicable circumstances. Navarro countered that she resigned due to her disagreement with how the Reyes investigation was handled. Mitchell sharpened her tone, suggesting Navarro's testimony was based on personal grievances rather than objective facts, but Navarro firmly maintained her testimony was based on professional observations.

Mitchell then argued that these "professional observations" were influenced by Navarro's frustration with the department, leading to Gabriela's objection on the grounds of being "Argumentative," which Judge Thompson sustained.

Shifting tactics, Mitchell inquired if any of Navarro's fellow detectives had supported her concerns. Navarro hesitated before admitting they had not, but she insisted this did not invalidate her concerns. Mitchell pounced on this, suggesting Navarro's interpretation was based on personal bias rather than evidence. Navarro straightened, stating that she had followed the evidence, but higher-ups had pressured them to close the case.

Mitchell offered a tight, dismissive smile and asked if Navarro had any direct evidence linking Mr. Penbrooke to the murder. Navarro conceded she did not, but reiterated her concerns about the evidence that was ignored. Mitchell raised an eyebrow, characterizing Navarro's testimony as "concerns, not facts" and questioning if the jury should accept them over the "thorough investigation" of her colleagues, leading to Gabriela's objection of "Mischaracterizes the witness's testimony," which Judge Thompson sustained.

Concluding her cross-examination, Mitchell asked no further questions. Judge Thompson then announced the afternoon break.

Gabriela and Morrison walked back to the witness room, where they found Hayes sitting, listening to something on his iPad.

Morrison sat and leaned back. "Are you sure calling Penbrooke's accountant and Penbrooke as the last witnesses after me is the best strategy?"

"Yes," Gabriela said. "We need to present a clear alternative for the jury to consider. The order of our remaining witnesses is designed to do just that."

Hayes added, "It's about showing them the full picture, Phillip, not just the one the prosecution wants them to see."

"Your alibi has to be airtight. And we'll reinforce it before then."

The courtroom reconvened after the afternoon recess. Judge Thompson called the court back to order. "Counsel, are you ready to proceed?"

"Yes, Your Honor," Gabriela replied, rising with a composed demeanor. "The defense calls Dr. Mei Chen to the stand."

Dr. Chen, a forensic pathologist with a reputation for meticulous analysis, approached the witness stand. Gabriela established Dr. Chen's extensive qualifications and experience before turning to the autopsy of Ethan Reyes.

Gabriela directed Dr. Chen to the autopsy report and the findings related to potential physical altercations. Dr. Chen, speaking with a precise and measured tone, confirmed the presence of small cuts and bruises on Reyes's hands, injuries consistent with a struggle. Gabriela then asked Dr. Chen about the expected trace evidence in such a scenario. Dr. Chen explained that a physical struggle typically results in the transfer of biological material like skin cells, fibers, or hair between the victim and the attacker. She stated that the Medical Examiner's report indicated a thorough search for such evidence under Reyes's fingernails and on his clothing, and crucially, no material matching Phillip Morrison was found.

Gabriela then addressed the prosecution's likely argument about gloves and protective clothing. Dr. Chen acknowledged this possibility but pointed out the additional layer of complexity it added to the timeline of events Morrison would have had to execute between the murder and his appearance at the charity gala.

Gabriela nodded slowly, a thoughtful expression on her face as she absorbed Dr. Chen's points. *The missing trace evidence, the timeline... It's all adding up to a picture that doesn't quite fit Morrison as a lone, careless killer.* "Thank you, Dr. Chen. No further questions at this time, Your Honor."

Judge Thompson turned to the prosecution. "Ms. Mitchell, you may cross-examine the witness."

Laura Mitchell rose for her cross-examination, her focus sharp. She began by questioning Dr. Chen about the limitations of trace evidence analysis. Mitchell suggested that the absence of Morrison's DNA or fibers did not definitively exclude him as the attacker, as transfer rates can vary, and evidence can be easily lost or degraded.

Mitchell then pressed Dr. Chen on the possibility of Morrison having used gloves and protective clothing, effectively minimizing the significance of the missing trace evidence. She argued that a meticulous killer would take such precautions. Mitchell also questioned the certainty of linking the hand injuries solely to a struggle with the attacker, suggesting they could have been caused by other means prior to the murder.

Dr. Chen, while acknowledging the variables involved in trace evidence transfer and the possibility of protective measures, maintained that the complete absence of any matching material, given the presence of struggle indicators, was a notable inconsistency that warranted consideration. She emphasized that while not definitive proof of innocence, it certainly did not unequivocally link Morrison to the physical act of the murder.

As Dr. Chen concluded her testimony, the jury absorbed the implications of the missing trace evidence, another crack appearing in the prosecution's seemingly solid case.

Judge Thompson looked over at Gabriela. "You may call your next witness."

Gabriela's gaze swept the courtroom before she announced, "Your Honor, the defense calls Elizabeth Morrison."

Elizabeth Morrison took the oath and ascended the stand with the assured poise of a woman who'd rehearsed every word.

"State your name for the record, please."

"Elizabeth Morrison," she said, her voice steady and clear, but with a slight, almost imperceptible emphasis on each word.

Gabriela pointed over at Phillip Morrison. "And your relation to Mr. Morrison?"

"I'm his wife."

"How long have the two of you been married?"

"Forty years."

"Mrs. Morrison, I want to ask you some questions about your husband. Does he eat right-handed or left-handed?"

"Left-handed."

"Does he write with his right hand or left hand?"

"Left hand."

Having made her point, Gabriela started questioning about the night Reyes was murdered. "Mrs. Morrison, can you tell us where Phillip was on the night of October 26th, 2023?"

A brief pause, then Elizabeth answered, "He was with me at a charity gala."

Gabriela leaned forward, eyes focused on the jury. "And what time did you both arrive at this gala?"

"Approximately nine-thirty," Elizabeth replied, maintaining her composure, but her eyes flickered momentarily toward the gallery.

Gabriela's lips curled into a knowing smile as she pressed further. "And where did Phillip tell you he was departing from to go to this gala?"

"His office."

"And you departed from your home?"

"Yes."

"So, you two did not travel together?"

"No."

Gabriela continued, "And what was the last time you spoke with him before meeting him at the gala?"

"He called me from his office at around 8:10 pm."

Gabriela then asked. "And what was the first time you saw him at the gala?"

"Approximately 9:30 pm."

Gabriela then continued. "And after your arrival at the gala, you stayed together?"

"Yes. Phillip mingled a bit while I stayed by his side the entire time." The details flowed smoothly, almost too smoothly, Gabriela thought.

A ripple of murmurs passed through the courtroom, and Gabriela raised her hand for silence before continuing with deliberate cadence. "Mrs. Morrison, you've testified that Phillip called you from his office at 8:10 p.m. Is that correct?"

"Yes."

"And you've also testified that you met him at the gala at 9:30 p.m. Is that correct?"

"Yes."

"And you arrived at the gala from your home?"

"Yes."

"So, you did not travel with your husband?"

"No."

"And you've testified that he was with you the entire time at the gala?"

"Yes."

"Where was Morrison between 8:10 pm and 9:30 pm? She has no idea."

Elizabeth shifted slightly but maintained her placid expression. "Yes."

"Is this type of evening common for you both?" Gabriela asked, her voice cool and incisive.

"Very common," Elizabeth replied with a polite smile that barely masked a slight tension in her jaw.

Gabriela then inquired, "Did anyone else verify your presence at this gala that night?"

"The event staff and numerous attendees can confirm we were together," Elizabeth responded, her tone soft yet resolute.

After a measured pause meant to let every word sink in, Gabriela eyed the jury before turning back to Elizabeth. “Did Phillip ever slip away, perhaps unnoticed in the midst of the gala?”

“No,” Elizabeth stated firmly. “We stayed together the entire event.”

“Any unusual occurrences that evening?” Gabriela continued.

“None whatsoever,” Elizabeth replied, her voice a blend of gentleness and quiet hurt. “It was a typical evening until the news about Ethan came the next morning.”

Gabriela shifted her focus, her precision unwavering. “According to your account, he was with you the whole night. You arrived at approximately 9:30 pm. Can you reiterate, Mrs. Morrison, what time your husband called you from his office?”

“At approximately 8:10 pm,” Elizabeth replied, her composure unwavering.

“And you did not see him again until you met at the gala around 9:30 pm?” Gabriela clarified.

“That is correct,” Elizabeth confirmed. Gabriela felt the urge to exhale in relief, but held it back, keeping her expression composed as she scanned the courtroom. “Thank you, Mrs. Morrison. No further questions at this time, Your Honor.”

Judge Thompson glanced at the clock on the wall. "Ladies and Gentlemen," he announced, his voice firm but tired, "it's 5:20 PM. We will reconvene on Monday morning when Ms. Mitchell can cross-examine Mrs. Morrison. Mrs. Morrison, you are still under oath." He then addressed the jury. Remember my instructions: do not discuss this case amongst yourselves or with anyone outside of this courtroom. We stand adjourned until 9:00 AM Monday."

As she made her way out of the courtroom, she spotted Chuck Green near the back, leaning against the wall, his expression unreadable. He'd been a silent observer all day, a familiar anchor in the turbulent waters of the trial. She nodded to him, a silent acknowledgment, and they met near the exit.

The drive back to Parker & McEvoy was quiet. The Dallas skyline, usually vibrant, seemed muted in the late afternoon light.

She walked from her car in the parking garage to the elevator and then to her office, where Chuck Green was waiting. He was watching a video on his iPad.

"What are they saying?" Gabriela asked.

"Court TV commentators are already picking Elizabeth's testimony apart," Green replied, frustration evident in his voice. "They claim she didn't help your defense."

She wasn't surprised. Elizabeth had seemed too perfect, her story overly rehearsed. Gabriela wished she hadn't put Elizabeth on the stand. And Mitchell hadn't even begun her cross yet.

Chapter Twenty-Three

On Saturday morning, after her morning run, Gabriela was in her office preparing to go back to court on Monday. She had done as much as she could to prepare Elizabeth for Mitchell's cross.

She brewed more coffee and spread the files across her desk, cross-referencing Morrison's claimed timeline against the evidence. The gaps glared back at her, every inconsistency ready to blow the case wide open. Morrison had assured her repeatedly that he was innocent of Reyes's murder, but Gabriela's instincts told her he was hiding something. Marissa's testimony that she'd seen Morrison with a handgun the day before Reyes was killed made her more uneasy.

Hours passed, and exhaustion crept in. She promised herself rest, but she was still troubled by something as she packed the files away.

Returning to her computer, Gabriela took a breath and steadied herself. Morrison's confidence bordered on delusion. He believed he could bend the truth to his will, but Gabriela feared the jury would see straight through him. She had seen defendants like Morrison before, powerful men who thought they could outsmart justice. They were always wrong.

She closed her eyes briefly, trying to shake the doubt that kept resurfacing. They had one chance to get this right. Morrison had to be ready. Because if he wasn't, his arrogance would sink them both. His confidence had been a shield against reality, and Gabriela feared it would shatter spectacularly once he took the witness stand.

Gabriela spent the rest of Saturday morning at her desk, reviewing evidence and reorganizing her case files. When Morrison arrived that afternoon, he displayed his usual confidence, leaning back casually as if the trial posed no real threat.

"Mitchell doesn't have a case," Morrison said dismissively. "Her timeline is a joke."

Gabriela held her gaze steady. "It's not a joke to the jury. Elizabeth's testimony raised doubts, and Mitchell hasn't even asked her the first question."

Morrison didn't look up. He waved his hand as if Mitchell cross-examining Elizabeth would be no problem. "Elizabeth was nervous, but you handled it well. She'll be ready for Mitchell on Monday. Besides, you plan to make it clear that Penbrooke could've easily committed this murder. All the jury needs to acquit me is a reasonable doubt. I will tell my side of the story, and there's no way the jury will find me guilty."

Gabriela shifted in her chair. The last time a client insisted on testifying against her advice, it ended in disaster. She could still picture Sparks Duval on the stand, overconfident and polished, convinced the jury would believe him. Instead, their faces turned colder with every answer. The guilty verdict didn't surprise her. What still bothered her was how easily he had ignored her warnings. Only the D.C. prosecutor's reckless tweets saved him from prison. The damage was done. A smart businessman knows when to stay quiet. Duval didn't.

Morrison thought he could do better. She had seen jurors turn in an instant, their sympathy evaporating with one careless phrase. Morrison believed he could charm them, but charm was a fragile shield in court.

"Mr. Morrison," Gabriela began, "I understand that you think you can persuade the jury. However, you must understand the immense risks involved. Your friend, Sparks Duval, had said the same thing. He was convinced he could persuade the jury. "

"Yeah, yeah, but that was Sparks. I can handle this."

"That's what Sparks and his high-powered PR firm said."

Gabriela sighed. Turning back to Morrison, her expression serious, Gabriela continued, "However... the prosecution has built a narrative. To counter that effectively, the jury needs to hear your voice, your explanation. It's a risk we have to take. But we need to be absolutely, unequivocally prepared, more prepared than we've ever been before." She had not forgotten the memory of Duval's self-destruction. She wouldn't let Morrison take the stand unprepared.

Gabriela studied him, fighting back frustration. "We can't rely solely on shifting blame to Penbrooke. The jury expects your story to hold up."

"It does," Morrison insisted. "My alibi is solid."

Gabriela shook her head slowly. "Not solid enough. Marissa's testimony about seeing you with the handgun complicates everything."

Morrison looked away. "It wasn't the same handgun." Gabriela wasn't convinced.

"The jury might still wonder why you were seen with one," Gabriela said, leaning forward. "Mitchell will seize on every inconsistency. Your arrogance puts you at risk."

Morrison studied her for a moment, then gave a slight nod. "You've done good work, Gabriela. I trust your judgment. But Mitchell won't rattle me."

She didn't respond. His praise meant nothing if he wouldn't listen. After he left, Gabriela returned to her files, cross-checking dates and timelines. Morrison had praised her plan to implicate Penbrooke, but shifting blame wasn't enough. Mitchell would see through it. Gabriela suspected Morrison's calm was a cover for something he hadn't told her.

By Sunday afternoon, Gabriela felt anxiety returning. She reviewed the threatening messages again, worried about their implications. Gabriela called her parents, urging them to stay vigilant.

"We're safe," her father reassured her. "Don't worry so much."

But she couldn't help worrying. Someone's connections reached further than she first realized. The missing handgun, Marissa's testimony, and Morrison's evasive answers troubled her. As evening fell, Gabriela stacked her files neatly, determined to rest but unable to escape the uncomfortable feeling someone was watching her.

Driving home, Gabriela checked her mirrors more than usual. A dark SUV made the same turns she did, and headlights flared behind her at every stoplight. Morrison's arrogance kept him from seeing the danger. She couldn't afford that. Something was off, and if she didn't get to the bottom of it soon, it could cost them both.

Just as Gabriela was pulling into her driveway, her cell phone buzzed. She looked at the dashboard screen and saw that it was Morrison. She pressed accept and waited for him to talk. His usual confident tone was gone, replaced by a raw edge of panic. “Gabriela,” he said, his voice strained, “Elizabeth… she’s terrified. Something happened. She doesn’t think she can face Mitchell on Monday. I… I think someone got to her.”

#

Chapter Twenty-Four

Monday morning, a familiar tension gripped the courtroom as Gabriela and Phillip Morrison entered. Morrison's face was etched with a mixture of anxiety and resignation, the strain of his wife's fear evident in his drawn features. Gabriela offered him a small, reassuring nod as they took their places at the defense table, but beneath her calm exterior, her mind raced with the implications of Morrison's panicked call about Elizabeth, a call that had kept her up most of the night.

Moments later, Judge Thompson entered, his usual somber expression slightly more pronounced.

The jury followed, watching Elizabeth Morrison closely. She sat upright, calm on the surface, but Gabriela saw the tension in her hands.

"Mrs. Morrison," Judge Thompson addressed her, his voice steady. "You may resume the witness stand. Please remember, you are still under oath." He then turned his attention to the prosecution. "Ms. Mitchell, you may now cross-examine the witness."

Before Elizabeth could fully settle herself, Laura Mitchell stepped forward, her eyes sharp and fixed on Elizabeth Morrison.

"Mrs. Morrison," she began, her voice cutting through the quiet of the courtroom, "you testified yesterday that your husband was at the gala with you the entire evening. But wouldn't a routine like that, a common occurrence as you described, sometimes include the possibility of late meetings or brief departures that you might not necessarily be privy to?"

Elizabeth hesitated a moment and then looked at Mitchell's piercing gaze. "Not that night."

"And how can you be so absolutely certain?" Mitchell said, giving no room to dodge the question.

"Because he was with me the entire time," Elizabeth said, her tone defiant but strained.

Mitchell smiled briefly and then moved on. "Is it not possible," she pressed, "that while you were engaged at the gala, your husband might have briefly dashed off, perhaps unnoticed?"

A flicker of uncertainty crossed Elizabeth's face. "No," she replied, though her tone wavered ever so slightly.

"Were your eyes glued to him every single second of a crowded gala? Isn't it plausible he could have moved through the crowd unnoticed by you for a crucial few minutes?"

"We moved through the crowd together."

Gabriela analyzed Mitchell's strategy. She had anticipated Mitchell attacking the pre-gala timeline, but this relentless focus on their time at the gala felt like a subtle trap. Was Mitchell trying to lure Elizabeth into a contradiction, no matter how small, that could then be used to discredit her entire testimony?

Mitchell stepped closer, her presence compressing the space between certainty and doubt. "Isn't it a fact, Mrs. Morrison, that your husband has, on occasion, worked late without mentioning it?"

"That did not happen that night," Elizabeth countered, defensiveness tinging her gentle voice.

"But it has happened before?" Mitchell asked provocatively as she circled the witness like a predator.

"Yes," Elizabeth whispered, regret and sorrow woven through her words.

Mitchell's gaze locked on hers as she continued, "Could he have slipped out from the gala while you were momentarily distracted in another room?"

"No," Elizabeth repeated, this time with firmer resolve, though a note of vulnerability seeped through.

"Did you ever leave the vicinity at all to make a call or check on something?" Mitchell prodded, her inquiry slicing through the mounting tension.

Elizabeth hesitated, searching her memory before saying, "I don't recall doing so."

"So, it's possible?" Mitchell seized the pause with clinical exactness.

"I suppose," Elizabeth conceded softly, "but he didn't leave the gala."

"Or perhaps you stepped out briefly, was it not to read a message?" Mitchell pressed her and kept staring at her.

"I read the updates in the same room," Elizabeth replied, her voice barely above a whisper.

"Yet, is it not possible, at a different moment within the event, you were in another room?" Mitchell suggested slyly.

"Sometimes," Elizabeth acknowledged, her tone a blend of resignation and distress.

"And on the night in question?" Mitchell demanded.

"In the same room," Elizabeth said, striving for firmness despite the tremor of uncertainty in her voice.

Mitchell then pivoted. “You and your husband did not travel together to the gala. Is that correct?”

“Yes. I left from home, and he left from the office.”

“Why was that?”

“It was more convenient.”

“More convenient than riding together?”

“Yes.”

“More convenient for whom? Was it perhaps more convenient for your husband to have a window of unaccounted time before meeting you? Is it common for you to travel separately to events?”

Gabriela leaped to her feet and objected. Judge Thompson sustained her objection.

Mitchell paced slowly, her steps deliberate and imposing. “Did you ever leave him alone at any point during the gala?”

“No,” Elizabeth responded firmly. “We were together the entire time.”

With every question, Mitchell chipped away at the fragile alibi.

“And you mentioned earlier,” she said, pacing a step closer to the witness box, “that your husband eats with his left hand.”

Elizabeth nodded, guarded. “Yes.”

"He also writes with his left hand?"

"Yes."

Mitchell arched an eyebrow, the gesture subtle but deliberate. "Interesting," she said, almost musing aloud. "And are those the only activities you've observed him doing with his left hand?"

Elizabeth hesitated. "No. I've seen him play tennis, pickleball, and other sports. He's left-handed."

Mitchell's gaze narrowed. "Have you ever seen him shoot a gun?"

"No."

"Ever watched him at a shooting range? Practicing? Hunting?"

Elizabeth's brows pulled together slightly. "No. I don't hunt and I'm not really a... gun person."

A pause. Then, Mitchell tilted her head slightly, her voice soft but carrying. "So, you wouldn't know which hand he uses to fire a weapon."

Elizabeth shifted in the chair. "No. I wouldn't."

Mitchell didn't smile this time. She didn't need to. The doubt had been placed.

Turning to the jury with a piercing gaze, Mitchell concluded, "No further questions, Your Honor."

Judge Thompson looked towards the defense table. "Ms. Sanchez, do you have any redirect examination?"

Gabriela rose, her expression thoughtful. She approached the witness stand, her demeanor calm but focused, a contrast to Mitchell's sharp intensity. "Mrs. Morrison," Gabriela began, her voice gentle but firm, "Ms. Mitchell asked you several questions about the possibility of your husband having brief departures or late meetings being a routine occurrence. While you acknowledged that, on occasion, your schedules might differ, I want to be perfectly clear about the night of October 26th. Was there anything about that specific evening that made it stand out from a typical gala night for you and Phillip?"

Elizabeth's gaze met Gabriela's, a flicker of relief in her eyes. "Yes. It was a particularly important event for the charity. Phillip was a major sponsor, and we both felt it was crucial for us to be present and engaged throughout the evening to show our support."

"And did Phillip indicate to you at any point that he needed to step away for a call or a meeting?" Gabriela continued.

"No, not at all," Elizabeth replied with more certainty. "He was very attentive to the guests and the organizers. We were circulating and speaking with people together for the entire time."

Gabriela paused, allowing the jury to absorb this. "Ms. Mitchell also questioned you about brief moments of potential distraction on your part. Mrs. Morrison, considering the importance of this event and your commitment to being there together, would you have noticed if your husband had left your side, even for a short period?"

Elizabeth hesitated for a moment, considering her answer carefully. "Yes," she said finally, her voice regaining some of its earlier firmness. "Given the nature of the event and our intention to be there together, I believe I would have noticed if he had left, even briefly."

Gabriela nodded, satisfied. "Thank you, Mrs. Morrison. No further questions, Your Honor."

Judge Thompson looked at his watch. "We will take a fifteen-minute break."

When she was leaving, Chuck Green called her aside. "How is Morrison holding up? Is he ready to testify?"

Gabriela sighed before answering. "I've worked with him for hours, but he's... difficult. He thinks he's smarter than both Mitchell and me. It's been a constant battle to keep him focused. I just hope he doesn't blow it on the stand."

"Morrison thinks he's smarter than Mitchell," Gabriela continued, "but he's not prepared for what's coming. Mitchell's sharper than he realizes."

Gabriela walked down the hall to the witness room. Morrison returned from the bathroom and sat across from her.

She looked intently at him. He appeared confident, composed, and ready, though Gabriela wasn't convinced. She leaned toward him and spoke quietly.

"Stick to the alibi exactly as we rehearsed," she said. "Mitchell will test every detail."

Morrison nodded, his eyes steady. "She can try."

Gabriela chose not to argue. Morrison's confidence was part of the problem.

After 15 minutes, the bailiff came to the door. "They're ready," he said.

After sitting at the counsel table, Gabriela briefly reviewed her notes as Judge Thompson looked directly at her. "Ms. Sanchez, call your next witness."

Gabriela stood without hesitation. “Defense calls Phillip Morrison.”

Morrison rose and walked confidently to the witness stand. The bailiff administered the oath, and Morrison affirmed clearly. Gabriela watched as he sat down, adjusted the microphone, and faced the jury.

She moved from behind the defense table to the podium, prepared to guide him carefully through the testimony. The weekend of preparation had been long and tense, but the time for doubts had passed. Morrison was on the stand, and Gabriela knew everything depended on his answers now. She paused briefly, ensuring the jurors were attentive before beginning.

“Please introduce yourself to the jury.”

“My name is Phillip Morrison.”

“Mr. Morrison, briefly describe your business.”

“I’m in the oil and gas industry. My company specializes in exploration, drilling, and production.”

Morrison shifted in his chair and, as instructed, turned toward the jury. “We primarily operate here in Texas, but we also have significant drilling operations in Mexico.”

"Your company has been highly profitable. Why take the risk of drilling in Mexico if you were already successful here?"

Morrison leaned forward in the witness chair. "I built my business on taking smart, calculated risks. Drilling in Mexico meant more jobs, lower gas prices, and economic benefits on both sides of the border. I never imagined the cartel would make it personal."

"When did you first begin operations in Mexico?"

"About four years ago."

"Have your operations in Mexico been successful?"

"Yes, very successful. We discovered several large deposits of oil and quickly became profitable."

"Did that success create any problems?"

"Yes. Mexican cartels became aware of our success and tried to muscle in. They wanted a piece of our profits."

"What did the cartel do specifically?"

"Initially, they tried intimidation: threats, sabotage, demands for protection money. Later, threats escalated, targeting me personally and trying to steal oil from our sites."

"How did you respond?"

"I hired private security to protect our operations and reported each incident to Mexican authorities and U.S. federal agencies."

"Did you personally cooperate with American and Mexican law enforcement investigations about these cartel threats?"

Morrison turned once again toward the jury. "Yes. I provided everything the authorities requested, including detailed reports, surveillance footage, and financial records. I had nothing to hide."

Gabriela paused briefly, letting the jury consider Morrison's words before moving forward.

"Mr. Morrison, did you know Ethan Reyes?"

"I knew who he was. He was a journalist."

"Were you aware that Mr. Reyes was planning to publish an article about you and your company's relationship with the Mexican cartel?"

"Yes, I was aware. Reyes made no secret of it. He had openly accused me of corruption and claimed I was paying off cartel leaders."

"Did you ever speak with Reyes about his article?"

"Yes, once. He reached out for a comment. I agreed to meet him to set the record straight."

"What happened during that meeting?" Gabriela looked briefly at her notes. That was her signal to Morrison to look over at the jury when answering, and he did.

"We met briefly at my office. I explained to Reyes that I was the victim, not the partner, of cartel activity. I shared documentation proving we'd reported every incident to authorities." He paused to let his testimony sink in. "I hoped he'd correct his story."

"How did Reyes respond?"

Mitchell rose from her seat. "Objection, Your Honor. The witness is offering hearsay."

Judge Thompson quickly responded. "Overruled, you may continue, Mr. Morrison."

"He was skeptical. He said his sources were credible. He promised to consider my evidence but made no assurances."

"Were you afraid of Reyes' article damaging your reputation or your company?"

Morrison responded calmly. "I was concerned but not afraid. Negative stories happen. I've faced criticism before. My business is built on facts and proven results, not rumors."

"Did you threaten or intimidate him during that meeting?"

"Absolutely not. It was a professional conversation. I tried to reason with him, nothing more."

"After your meeting, did Reyes publish his article?"

"No. He never got the chance. He was killed before he could."

Gabriela paused again, then carefully turned to the events surrounding Reyes's death.

"Mr. Morrison, let's talk about the night Ethan Reyes was murdered. There's been testimony that you met your wife at a charity gala alone that evening. Why did your wife not ride with you?"

"We planned to ride together, but I had some last-minute business in my office. I called Elizabeth and told her to meet me there."

"Why did you arrive so late that evening?"

"The business meeting at my office ran longer than expected. The gala was important, so I decided to go even though I would be arriving late."

"Describe the route you took to the gala."

Morrison paused briefly. "I drove along Oak Lawn Avenue, then took Cedar Springs toward Turtle Creek. It wasn't my usual route, but traffic was lighter. I remember glancing at the dashboard clock. It read exactly 9:22 when I passed the Crescent Hotel. I was concerned I might have missed the keynote speech at the gala."

Gabriela stepped closer to the jury, framing her next questions deliberately.

"Earlier in this trial, Marissa Ortega testified she saw you with a handgun the day before Mr. Reyes was murdered. Did you hear that testimony?"

"Yes, I did."

"Was Marissa mistaken?"

"She was mistaken about the handgun. I own several firearms, and the gun Marissa saw me holding that day wasn't the stolen .357 caliber handgun tied to this case."

"Then, what gun was it?"

"It was an antique revolver, a Colt from the early 1900s. It's part of my collection. I planned to display it at a gun collectors' event that weekend."

"Why did you have it out?"

"I'd removed it from my office safe to clean and inspect it. Condition is important to collectors, and I wanted it ready for the show."

"Describe for the jury the differences between the two handguns."

"The antique Colt revolver is unmistakable. It's large, engraved, silver-plated, with a polished wooden handle. The stolen .38 is compact, modern, black metal. It's a completely different weapon. You couldn't confuse the two."

Gabriela allowed a brief pause, emphasizing the difference between the guns.

"Did you report another handgun, a .357 caliber pistol, stolen shortly before Reyes was killed?"

"Yes, I reported that gun stolen three weeks before Reyes's murder."

"When did you notice it missing?"

"I discovered it missing the morning I made the police report."

"Did you suspect who took it?"

"No. At the time, I assumed it had to be an employee, a visitor, or someone else with access."

Gabriela looked Morrison directly in the eye.

"Mr. Morrison, did you have anything to do with Ethan Reyes's murder?"

"No, absolutely not."

"Were you anywhere near the alley at the time of his death?"

"No. I was at the gala, surrounded by dozens of people."

"Did you have any motive to kill Ethan Reyes?"

"No. Killing Reyes wouldn't silence suspicion. Instead, because he was planning to publish a negative story about me, it would only focus on me. His death harmed me, not helped."

Gabriela paused one last time, scanning the jury, then returned to Morrison.

"How did you learn Reyes had been killed?"

"My assistant, Ms. Ortega, told me the next morning. My first thought was shock, followed by disbelief. Then I realized people might assume I was responsible, and I immediately contacted the police myself."

"So, you've cooperated fully with authorities investigating this case?"

"Yes, fully, from the beginning."

Gabriela stepped away from the podium, moving closer to the jury box, her voice taking on a slightly more serious tone.

"Mr. Morrison, the prosecution has presented evidence indicating that Mr. Reyes's blood was found in the trunk of your car. Can you explain that to the jury?"

Morrison's composure, which had been carefully maintained, tightened slightly. He turned directly towards the jury, his expression earnest.

"Yes, I can. That is deeply troubling to me, and frankly, it's further evidence of what I believe is happening in this case: I am being framed."

Gabriela nodded slowly, allowing his words to sink in. "Please elaborate, Mr. Morrison. How could Mr. Reyes's blood have ended up in your car?"

Morrison leaned forward, his gaze sweeping across the jury. "I have no idea how his blood got there. I never transported Mr. Reyes in my car, dead or alive. I was at my office and then at the gala that entire evening, as many witnesses can attest. The only logical explanation, the only one that makes any sense to me, is that whoever murdered Mr. Reyes and is now trying to pin this crime on me could have planted that blood in my car while I was out. I was at a public event with hundreds of people. My car was parked in a public parking area. Someone with the means and the motive to frame me had ample opportunity to access my vehicle and plant evidence."

Gabriela paused, allowing the jury to consider his explanation. "Mr. Morrison, did you give anyone permission to use your car that evening?"

"No, absolutely not. I drove myself to my earlier meeting and then directly to the gala. My car remained parked there until I drove home later that night."

Gabriela returned to the podium, her voice firm. "So, to be clear, Mr. Morrison, you are stating unequivocally that you did not put Mr. Reyes's blood in your car, and you believe it was placed there by someone else?"

"That is exactly what I am saying, Ms. Sanchez. I am innocent of this crime, and I believe this blood evidence is part of a deliberate attempt to frame me for a murder I did not commit."

"Have you ever concealed or destroyed evidence?"

"Never."

Gabriela turned to Judge Thompson, signaling clearly she had covered her points.

"Nothing further, Your Honor."

Judge Thompson looked up at the clock and then surveyed the tense courtroom. "The court will break for lunch and reconvene at 1:30." The sharp crack of his gavel punctuated the silence as the jury began to file out, their expressions a mixture of contemplation and concern. Gabriela watched Morrison. His usual swagger was gone. He kept his eyes down as he walked toward the witness room.

Chapter Twenty-Five

To avoid reporters outside the courthouse, Hayes had ordered lunch for them, and they chose to eat in the small witness room. Holding a sandwich, Gabriela paced restlessly, anticipating Mitchell's sharp questions. Hayes was quietly reviewing his notes, his brow furrowed. Morrison had excused himself again to use the restroom, leaving the tension in the room.

"What are they saying?" Gabriela asked Hayes, her voice low, glancing towards the closed door Morrison had disappeared behind. "Court TV... what's the spin?"

Hayes looked up, a thoughtful expression on his face. "They're divided. Some commentators think Morrison held up okay during your direct, presented a charming front. But others... they're picking up on the evasiveness during some of the key questions. Mitchell's cross is being anticipated as the real test. They're saying if she can crack his composure, it could be devastating."

Gabriela nodded slowly. "So, the jury is likely feeling the same uncertainty." She stopped pacing as the door creaked open and Morrison re-entered, attempting to regain his earlier air of confidence.

At 1:25, the bailiff came by to get them back in the courtroom. Gabriela's stomach tightened; Morrison was walking back in with the same misplaced swagger.

"Alright, let's get back out there," Morrison said, adjusting his tie with a dismissive flick of his wrist. "That Mitchell woman thinks she can rattle me. She's in for a surprise."

Gabriela met his gaze, her expression firm but calm. "Phillip, listen to me. Mitchell is experienced. She's going to try to provoke you, to make you angry or defensive. Don't give her that satisfaction."

She continued, her voice measured, "Stick to the facts. Answer her questions directly and concisely. Don't volunteer information, and for God's sake, don't try to be clever. Your charm didn't seem to sway her, and it could easily backfire with the jury now."

Gabriela paused, trying to gauge if her words were sinking in. "Remember what we discussed. Focus on the timeline as you remember it. If you don't recall something, it's okay to say you don't recall. But do not contradict yourself, and do not get drawn into arguments with her."

Morrison gave a curt nod, a slight smirk playing on his lips. "Gabriela, relax. I've handled tougher board meetings than this. Let Mitchell throw her best punches. I can take it." He clapped her on the shoulder with a condescending air before heading towards the courtroom door.

Gabriela exchanged a worried glance with Hayes. Morrison's arrogance was a dangerous liability.

As Gabriela followed a still-sulking Morrison back into the tense courtroom, she anticipated the jury would be scrutinizing her as well as Morrison. Mitchell was already at her table, composed and seemingly confident, reviewing her notes. Judge Thompson entered, and the hushed silence fell once more.

As the bailiff announced the return of the jury, a heightened tension spread throughout the courtroom. The jurors settled back into their seats, their eyes now focused intently on Phillip Morrison, waiting to see how he would fare under the prosecution's scrutiny.

Judge Thompson called the court to order. "Mr. Morrison, you are still under oath." He turned to Laura Mitchell at the prosecutor's table. "Ms. Mitchell, you may proceed with your cross-examination."

Mitchell rose from her seat with a composed and purposeful air. She approached the witness stand slowly, her gaze fixed on Morrison. Her initial tone was calm, almost conversational, a predator lulling its prey. Morrison adjusted his tie and squared his shoulders, trying to appear confident.

Mitchell approached the witness stand, her expression calm and confident. She held a folder in one hand, tapping it lightly as she spoke.

"Mr. Morrison," Mitchell began, her tone almost conversational, "you testified earlier that your business dealings are entirely legitimate and unrelated to criminal activity. Is that correct?"

"Yes," Morrison replied, his voice steady.

Mitchell opened the folder, pulling out a glossy photograph. "Your Honor, I'd like to present People's Exhibit 37." She handed the photo to the court clerk, who displayed it on the screen for the jury and the witness to see.

Morrison's face tightened as he recognized the image. It showed him shaking hands with Carlos Delgado at a private airstrip, Morrison's jet visible in the background. Gabriela's pulse skipped. This was exactly the kind of exhibit she had feared Mitchell was saving.

Mitchell didn't give him a moment to collect himself. "Mr. Morrison, do you recognize the man in this photograph?"

Morrison hesitated, clearly unsettled. "Yes, that's me."

Mitchell kept her tone neutral, though her eyes were fixed on him. "And the man you're shaking hands with?"

His jaw tightened. "That's Carlos Delgado."

Mitchell took a step closer, her voice a little sharper. "Would you tell the court who Carlos Delgado is?"

Morrison swallowed. "I... I believe he's connected to some criminal organizations."

Mitchell arched an eyebrow. "You believe? Are you aware that Carlos Delgado is a known associate of one of the most violent cartels operating along the Texas-Mexico border?"

Morrison glanced nervously at Gabriela before nodding. "Yes."

Mitchell didn't miss a beat. "When did you first become aware of his cartel connections?"

Morrison hesitated. "After this photo was taken. I wasn't aware at the time."

Mitchell leaned in, her voice crisp. "You didn't know you were meeting with a mid-level executive of a notorious cartel when you arranged a private meeting at an airstrip?"

"No," Morrison insisted. "It was a business meeting. Delgado was introduced to me through an intermediary as a potential partner to address theft issues in my energy operations."

Mitchell narrowed her eyes. “Theft issues?”

Morrison paused before answering. “There were reports that cartels had been stealing from American energy producers, including some of my companies. Delgado claimed he could help mitigate the problem. He was offering a... solution.”

Mitchell tilted her head. “And did this solution involve any form of payment or incentive on your part?”

Morrison hesitated, then cleared his throat. “There was talk of facilitating security measures in exchange for... financial support. It wasn’t bribery. It was securing my investments.”

Mitchell’s voice grew sharper. “Securing your investments by dealing with a cartel operative? Did it not cross your mind that paying a known criminal might constitute bribery?”

Morrison looked visibly rattled. “At the time, I believed it was a business arrangement. I didn’t know his full background.”

Mitchell paused, letting the tension hang in the air. “And where was this photograph taken?”

“At a private airstrip just outside the city,” Morrison said reluctantly.

Mitchell pressed on. "And would you care to explain why a real estate investor would need to meet at a private airstrip rather than an office or a more public location?"

Morrison glanced at the photo again. "That was his choice, not mine. He insisted on a private meeting."

Mitchell didn't let up. "Did it not strike you as unusual that a potential partner in an energy theft mitigation plan would meet you at a private airstrip rather than a business office?"

Morrison stammered slightly. "At the time, I... I didn't think much of it. Sometimes high-profile clients prefer discretion."

Mitchell nodded, appearing to consider his response. "So, to be clear, you met with a known cartel associate about a security problem related to cartel theft, and despite the unusual circumstances, you didn't investigate his background before or after the meeting?"

Morrison shifted uncomfortably. "No, I didn't follow up. I thought the intermediary had vetted him."

Mitchell's voice turned cold. "So, you relied on a third party without doing your own due diligence, even when it involved dealing with a potentially criminal figure?"

"Yes," Morrison admitted, his tone subdued.

"Mr. Morrison, let's turn to another subject. You testified that on the night of October 26th, 2023, you were at your office in a meeting before heading to a charity gala to meet your wife. Is that correct?"

"Yes, that's correct," Morrison replied, attempting a confident smile.

"Who was in the meeting with you?"

Morrison paused his eyes moving upward. "I don't specifically recall."

"What were you meeting about?"

Morrison's mouth opened slightly, "I don't recall that either. I just recall calling Elizabeth and telling her to meet me at the gala."

"You stated you left your office around 8:10 PM to meet Mrs. Morrison at the gala at 9:30 PM. That's a significant amount of time, Mr. Morrison. What exactly were you doing during that hour and twenty minutes?"

Morrison shifted slightly in his seat, his fingers tapping nervously on the armrest. "Just... finishing up some work. Making a few calls before the evening."

Mitchell took a step closer, her voice remaining level but gaining a sharper edge. "Specific work, Mr. Morrison? Specific calls? Can you recall any of these crucial tasks or conversations that occupied over an hour of your time before a major social event?"

Morrison hesitated, his expression hardening as he glanced at Gabriela, searching for reassurance. "General business matters. I don't recall the specifics at this moment."

Mitchell leaned forward slightly, folding her hands together. "General business matters that are so easily forgotten, Mr. Morrison, despite the shadow this murder investigation has cast over your life for months?" She let the question hang in the air.

A faint rustle moved through the gallery, and Gabriela noticed one juror exchange a glance with another, clearly intrigued. She couldn't tell if it was skepticism toward Mitchell or suspicion aimed at Morrison.

"Isn't it true, Mr. Morrison, that when investigators reviewed your phone records from that evening, they found no outgoing calls from your office line or your cell phone between 8:10 PM and 9:30 PM? Not one?"

Morrison blinked, momentarily off-balance. He cleared his throat, his hands tightening around the edges of the witness stand. "I don't recall. Maybe not."

Mitchell tilted her head slightly, her gaze unyielding. “In fact, there was no activity from your phone at all. No texts, no emails sent. Does that sound familiar now?”

Morrison looked down briefly, then straightened up, forcing his voice to remain steady. “As I said, I was catching up on paperwork.”

“Mr. Morrison, less than five minutes ago, you testified you were making a few calls,” Mitchell said evenly. “Now, you are saying it was paperwork. Which was it, Mr. Morrison?”

Morrison shifted again, visibly flustered. “I forgot earlier. It was paperwork.”

Mitchell didn’t miss a beat. “Describe the paperwork that you so conveniently remember.”

Morrison hesitated, licking his lips. “I believe it was accounting records.”

Mitchell paused deliberately, then let her gaze sweep briefly over the jury. “Now, you testified you didn’t travel to the gala with your wife. Why the separate journeys?”

“It was more convenient,” Morrison stated, a touch of defensiveness creeping into his tone. “She was coming from home, I from the office.”

Mitchell's gaze sharpened, her voice gaining an accusatory edge. "Convenient, Mr. Morrison, or a way to have an unaccounted-for period of time before meeting her?"

"Objection!" Gabriela interjected. "Speculation, Your Honor."

"Sustained," Judge Thompson said, but the seed of doubt had been planted. Gabriela saw a few jurors shifting in their seats, clearly considering Mitchell's implication.

Mitchell turned her attention to Marissa Ortega's testimony. "Mr. Morrison, your executive assistant, Marissa Ortega, testified that she saw you with a handgun in your office the day before Mr. Reyes's death. You recall that testimony, correct?"

Morrison's fingers clenched the armrest tighter. "Yes, I do."

"And you have stated to this court that the handgun Ms. Ortega observed was your antique Colt revolver, which you were planning to take to a gun show. Is that your testimony?"

"Yes, that's correct," Morrison affirmed. "It was carefully wrapped, ready to go."

"A gun show, Mr. Morrison. Where was this gun show held?"

Morrison hesitated for a fraction of a second. "It was... over at the Will Rogers Memorial Center."

"The Will Rogers Memorial Center in Fort Worth, Mr. Morrison?"

"Yes, that's right," Morrison confirmed, but his voice was less certain.

Mitchell went back to her table and picked up the document that an assistant had brought her earlier. She approached Morrison, placing it carefully in front of him. "Mr. Morrison, I'm handing you a list of all scheduled public events at the Will Rogers Memorial Center during the weekend following October 26th, provided by their director. Can you find your gun show listed there?"

Gabriela quickly rose. "Objection, Your Honor. Foundation."

Judge Thompson considered briefly. "Overruled. You opened the door, Ms. Sanchez. Mr. Morrison, please answer the question."

Morrison scanned the document, face reddening. A murmur ran through the gallery. "It appears it's not listed."

Mitchell took a step back, her face calm but intense. "In fact, there was no gun show at the Will Rogers Memorial Center that weekend, was there, Mr. Morrison?"

Morrison shifted uncomfortably, beads of sweat appearing on his forehead. "I must've been mistaken about the location."

Mitchell remained still, her eyes fixed on him. "Or mistaken about your story entirely?"

Mitchell moved closer, lowering her voice but making sure each word landed. "Mr. Morrison, isn't it true that you had a powerful motive to silence Ethan Reyes? That his investigation threatened to expose not just financial irregularities, but something far more damaging?"

Morrison's face flushed. "That's outrageous!" he exclaimed, his voice rising.

Mitchell remained still, letting the jury take in Morrison's outburst. She turned toward them, speaking evenly.

"Outrageous, Mr. Morrison? Or exactly what we'd expect from someone who's lost control of their story?"

Gabriela stood. "Objection. Argumentative."

"Sustained," Judge Thompson said.

Mitchell didn't move. She kept her eyes on Morrison. "You claim to have been working late, then heading to a gala. You had a meeting with the victim, threatened him, and possessed a handgun of the same caliber that killed him. Your executive assistant saw that gun the day before the murder, despite your stolen report."

"No. That's not true," Morrison managed to force out, glaring at Mitchell.

"No further questions, Your Honor," Mitchell said, then stepped back, giving the jury a moment to take it in.

As Mitchell returned to her table, the courtroom seemed to exhale, the tension slowly easing. Gabriela remained seated, her eyes fixed on Morrison. His shoulders had slumped slightly, and his face bore the strain of the relentless questioning.

From where she sat, Gabriela could see the confusion in his eyes, the flicker of hurt still etched in his expression. He looked over at her, almost pleading for reassurance, and she gave him a small nod. Despite everything Mitchell had thrown at him, Gabriela still saw the same man who had come to her office weeks before. Then and now, he was adamant about his innocence and determined to clear his name.

Gabriela glanced at the jury, noting their varied reactions. Some seemed wary, but a few looked more curious than convinced. A young woman juror who had seemed most skeptical of the prosecution's case early on still appeared thoughtful, as if not entirely swayed by the cross-examination.

Gabriela knew that Mitchell had left a mark, but she also knew that the truth wasn't as simple as Mitchell had made it seem. She had seen defendants break down, seen the guilty crumble when caught in a lie. But Morrison's anger wasn't the explosive defensiveness of a man caught out. It was the frustration of a man that boiled over when falsely accused. She had watched him as Mitchell pressed him on the missing hour and the gun show, and despite his faltering, his reaction was genuine.

She believed him.

Still, belief alone wouldn't save him. Gabriela straightened her posture, her mind already spinning through how to address the damage during the redirect. She couldn't afford to appear rattled, not now. The jurors needed to see someone confidently still fighting for the truth, no matter how the cross-examination had gone.

She took a deep breath, setting her face with a calm resolve. This was where her experience came into play. A skilled defense lawyer didn't just react to the prosecution's attacks; she anticipated them, turned them to her advantage. Gabriela wasn't finished. She would make sure the jury remembered that Mitchell's cross-examination, no matter how relentless, didn't change one critical fact: there was still no proof that Morrison had killed Ethan Reyes.

She glanced once more at Morrison, giving him a firm, reassuring look. Whatever happened next, she would not let him face it alone.

Gabriela stood calmly, approaching the podium with measured confidence. She knew the jury had just seen him at his weakest, and she had to move carefully but firmly. She paused, took a breath, and glanced toward the jury before speaking.

“Mr. Morrison, Ms. Mitchell questioned your inability to recall specific phone calls or paperwork from several months ago.” She gestured briefly toward the prosecutor’s table. “Can you explain why those details are difficult to remember?”

Morrison shifted slightly in the witness chair and looked toward the jury. “Because at the time, they were routine emails, paperwork, and daily phone calls. They seemed ordinary, not something I’d recall months later, especially with the stress of being wrongfully accused.”

Gabriela nodded slowly, as though absorbing his answer. She glanced briefly at her notes and then looked back at Morrison.

“Earlier, Ms. Mitchell questioned why you recalled seeing the dashboard clock read exactly 9:22 near the Crescent Hotel.” Gabriela took a small step closer to the jury. “Why do you specifically remember that detail?”

Morrison exhaled, visibly relaxing a little. “I was running late and worried about missing the keynote speech at the gala. When you’re anxious about time, you notice details.” He paused, spreading his hands slightly. “It stuck in my mind because at that moment, I knew I’d missed most of the evening.”

Gabriela turned slightly toward the jury, letting Morrison’s explanation linger for a moment. She saw a few jurors nod almost unconsciously; anchoring the timeline in something ordinary, like watching a dashboard clock, was landing. Then she turned back to him.

“Regarding the antique Colt revolver, Ms. Mitchell questioned you about the gun show at the Will Rogers Memorial Center.” Gabriela’s voice was patient, calm. “Is it possible you mistakenly named the wrong venue or weekend?”

Morrison rubbed his chin thoughtfully. “Yes, it’s entirely possible. I regularly attend collector events throughout Texas.” He shook his head briefly. “I might have confused locations or weekends under questioning. But the fact remains, the antique gun Marissa saw was not the stolen .38.”

Gabriela stepped back toward her table, picked up a pen briefly as if checking something off a list, then returned her attention fully to Morrison.

“Ms. Mitchell implied you had a motive to harm Ethan Reyes. Did you believe Reyes’s investigation was truly a threat to you or your company?”

Morrison leaned forward earnestly. "No, I didn't. Reyes had suspicions, yes, but I gave him documents to prove I had nothing to hide. Killing him would only have drawn more suspicion onto me." He spoke with conviction. "I cooperated fully with authorities precisely because I had nothing to fear."

"Mr. Morrison, when Ms. Mitchell questioned you earlier, you seemed unsure about some details. Can you explain why you might have been uncertain about specific times or tasks from that evening?"

"Yes. I've been over those events so many times in my head, trying to make sure I get everything right. Sometimes it feels like the more I think about it, the harder it is to remember clearly. I just wanted to be accurate, but with so much pressure, I second-guessed myself."

Gabriela glanced deliberately at the jurors, gauging their reaction. She could feel the tension easing slightly, but knew she needed one final reassurance from Morrison.

"Finally, Mr. Morrison, Ms. Mitchell's questioning caused you to become visibly upset." Gabriela's tone softened. "Can you explain to the jury why her accusations provoked such a strong reaction?"

Morrison sat quietly for a second, then met the eyes of several jurors in turn. His voice was calm but carried clear emotion. “Because being accused of murder is horrifying. For months, I’ve lived under suspicion. It’s been devastating to me, to my family, and to the people who trust and rely on me.” He took a breath, his voice steadier. “I reacted strongly because I’m innocent, and the accusations hurt.”

As Morrison spoke, Gabriela noticed one of the older jurors nodding slowly, as if acknowledging the seriousness of what he was saying. Another juror, a young man in the front row, leaned forward slightly, his expression softened.

Gabriela nodded gently, her expression conveying quiet confidence. She briefly scanned the jury again and then turned to Judge Thompson.

“Nothing further, Your Honor.”

Judge Thompson cleared his throat, looking at the clock. “Counsel, given the time, we will take the afternoon break. Members of the jury, please remember my instructions. Do not discuss this case with anyone, and do not conduct any independent research. We will reconvene at 3:30.” He gaveled the court into recess.

As the jury filed out, Gabriela watched Morrison, his face pale and his earlier confidence completely shattered. Mitchell turned back to her table, a barely perceptible smile playing on her lips. Gabriela refused to look away. Whatever damage Mitchell thought she'd done, Gabriela knew the fight wasn't over.

Chapter Twenty-Six

The small defense conference room felt quiet and cramped during the afternoon break. Morrison held a glass of water, staring at nothing in particular. Hayes flipped through his notes without a word. Gabriela stayed focused on what came next.

"Hayes," she said quietly, "I'm more convinced than ever that calling Vance and then Penbrooke last is the right move. Mitchell did a damn good job in that cross-examination. We need to shift the focus and create real doubt."

"Arthur Vance?" Hayes asked.

"Penbrooke's former accountant," Hayes said.

"He can raise doubts about Penbrooke," Gabriela said. "We build our narrative."

Hayes nodded. "Arthur can testify to financial motives and Penbrooke's pressure."

"He isn't loyal to Penbrooke?" Morrison asked.

"He left six months before Reyes was killed," Gabriela said. "Around the time these transactions started."

"Interesting, or suspicious?"

"Suspicious. Offshore accounts and shell companies. The timing of Reyes's murder. It directs suspicion to Penbrooke."

"You think this works?"

"Yes. We establish a financial motive and frame Penbrooke."

The conversation in the conference room moved in short bursts, each suggestion was met with a challenge before they moved to the next. Finally, Gabriela nodded, her decision made. "This is our path. We establish Penbrooke's motive, then present Morrison's airtight alibi. And then...we let Mitchell unravel."

Hayes and Morrison exchanged a look, a silent acknowledgment of the risk. But the plan was in place.

Gabriela and Morrison headed back into the courtroom, leaving Hayes behind in the witness room. After Judge Thompson and the jury were seated, the judge looked toward Gabriela.

"Ms. Sanchez, call your next witness."

Before calling Mr. Vance, Gabriela took a deliberate breath. Having anticipated what happened to Morrison, this was the gamble she had to take. She knew once Vance spoke, there was no turning back. If his testimony faltered, Penbrooke's shadow over the case would vanish, and Morrison would stand alone before the jury.

"Yes, Your Honor," Gabriela replied. "The defense calls Arthur Vance to the stand."

The rear courtroom door swung open, and Arthur Vance, a man with a slight stoop and a worried expression, was escorted in by the bailiff. He took the oath, looking nervously from the judge to the jury, then to the attorneys.

"Mr. Vance," Gabriela began, her voice calm and direct, "please state your name and occupation for the court."

"Arthur Vance. I am an accountant," Vance replied.

"And what was your professional relationship with Stephen Penbrooke?"

"I was his accountant for five years, until six months before Ethan Reyes's murder."

"Why did you leave Penbrooke's employment?"

"I became concerned about certain financial transactions."

"Can you describe those transactions?"

"They involved shell companies and offshore accounts. The timing of these transactions was suspicious."

Though focused on Vance, Gabriela felt a subtle shift in the atmosphere at the defense table. She caught a slight movement from the corner of her eye, a barely perceptible tightening in Morrison's posture as Vance described the offshore accounts. Several jurors scribbled notes. That was a good sign. They were listening.

"Can you be more specific about the timing?"

"Large sums of money were moved between accounts in September through December 2023."

"Did you observe any changes in Mr. Penbrooke's behavior during this period?"

"Yes. He was unusually stressed and secretive. He was also making large cash withdrawals."

"And what was your impression of these transactions?"

"They were irregular. They didn't align with Penbrooke's usual business practices."

"During your time as Penbrooke's accountant, did you become aware of Ethan Reyes?"

"Yes."

"How did you become aware of him?"

"I learned he was investigating some of Penbrooke's business transactions."

"And when did you learn this?"

"In the weeks leading up to my departure from Penbrooke's company."

"Did Mr. Penbrooke make any comments about Ethan Reyes?"

"He was very concerned. He said Reyes was 'prying into things he shouldn't be.'"

"Thank you, Mr. Vance. No further questions."

"Ms. Mitchell, you may cross-examine now."

Mitchell rose, her voice sharp and direct. "Mr. Vance," she began, "let's be clear. You're not currently employed by Penbrooke, are you?"

Vance's voice was tight. "No, I am not."

"Not now, and not at the time of Mr. Reyes's murder, correct?"

"That's correct."

"You testified you left due to concerns about financial practices. Yet, you couldn't convince anyone else?"

Vance hesitated. "I expressed my concerns."

"Isn't it true you're simply a disgruntled former employee with an axe to grind?"

"I left because of those transactions."

"And started working for the defendant shortly after, correct?"

"Yes."

Mitchell turned to the jury and then back at Vance.

"Sounds like you had a grudge, Mr. Vance."

"That's not true."

"I bet," Mitchell replied.

Gabriela stood. "Your Honor, Ms. Mitchell can't offer commentary on Mr. Vance's testimony. I ask that her comment be stricken, and the jury informed to ignore it."

"Ms. Mitchell, you know better. Ladies and Gentlemen, please ignore Ms. Mitchell's comment. You may continue, Ms. Mitchell."

"Now, Mr. Vance, you mentioned shell companies and offshore accounts. Are those not common in many business sectors?"

"Not in the way Penbrooke was using them."

"But you weren't there when these transactions were completed, were you?"

"No."

"And your concerns about the timing of these transactions are those based on assumption?"

"Based on the records I kept, yes."

"Records from before you left. You have no direct knowledge of Penbrooke's business after you left, do you?"

"I know what I saw."

Mitchell moved closer to the jury. "But you can't prove these transactions are linked to Mr. Reyes's murder, can you?"

Vance leaned forward. "I know he was investigating Penbrooke."

"Investigating what exactly?" Mitchell pressed. "You don't know the specifics of his investigation, do you?"

"No."

"And your testimony about Penbrooke's behavior, his stress, his cash withdrawals. Isn't that just your interpretation?"

"It was what I observed."

Mitchell gave him a final, dismissive glance. "Again, you don't know. No further questions, Your Honor." She walked away with a confident stride.

Judge Thompson addressed the jury. "Ladies and gentlemen, we'll adjourn for the day. Please remember my previous instructions. We will reconvene at 9:00 a.m. tomorrow."

Gabriela packed her briefcase slowly, her mind still on Vance's testimony. It had helped, but the sense of being watched lingered.

After the courtroom emptied and Morrison left with his wife, Chuck Green caught up with her.

"Chuck, what did you think of Vance's testimony?" she asked.

"He planted the seeds of doubt," Green replied. "But Mitchell did a good job of minimizing the damage. We need something more concrete."

Later, when she returned to her office, the only sound was the steady hum of the air conditioning. Gabriela paused. Something felt off. Her eyes landed on a white envelope placed neatly on her otherwise organized desk. It hadn't been there that morning.

Inside was an old photograph of her father. Young, confident, and standing outside the Cameron County Courthouse. On the back, someone had scrawled a message: *The past always returns.*

A chill ran up her arms. She was still staring at the words when the shrill ring of her office phone made her jump. A distorted voice followed. "You can't protect them all."

Gabriela left the office, her mind on the courtroom battles still ahead and the unsettling message about her father. The sun was setting, casting long shadows over the downtown streets. She pulled her phone from her bag and dialed her father's number.

He picked up after two rings. "Mija, how did it go today?"

Gabriela paused while gripping the steering wheel as she navigated through the evening traffic. "It was tough, Papá. I also questioned Penbrooke's former accountant today. He testified that Penbrooke was involved in some very shady business dealings and that Reyes was investigating those dealings. Mitchell did everything to destroy their credibility, but I think I got the points across." She tried to keep her tone steady, but she knew her father could sense the strain.

There was a pause on the line, just long enough for Gabriela to hear the weariness in his breathing. "You'll handle it," Roberto said, his voice calm and reassuring. "You always do."

Gabriela bit her lip. "Something happened today at my office. There was an envelope on my desk. No return address. Inside was a photo of you with a message on the back: 'The past always returns.'"

Her father was silent. She could almost see his face—jaw clenched, eyes narrowed. "What else, Gabriela?"

"A phone call right after I opened it. Distorted voice. Said I couldn't protect everyone."

Roberto let out a slow breath. “You think it’s related to the case?”

“I’m sure it is,” Gabriela replied. “I think you and Mom may be in danger.”

Roberto hesitated. “It wouldn’t be the first time I’ve received a death threat. You know I’ve defended some bad men, Gabriela. Powerful men. But most of them were here in Texas, not across the border. If this is from the cartel, it’s different. Cartels don’t forget Gabriela. And they don’t forgive.”

A thought struck her, and she gripped the phone tighter. “Papá, have you gotten any messages lately? Anything unusual?”

“No,” he replied. “Nothing out of the ordinary.”

“Be careful, Papá,” Gabriela said, her voice barely above a whisper. “This feels different.”

“You too, mija. I’ll reach out to a few people. Quietly. If someone’s dredging up old history, I need to know who’s talking—and why.”

As she pulled into her driveway, Gabriela’s mind raced; she couldn’t dismiss the cartel threat. Why target her father if they wanted to scare her? It had to be about the case, about Morrison.

They wanted her distracted, worried about her family, not the trial. Not the holes in Mitchell's case she still had left to expose.

Chapter Twenty-Seven

Gabriela sensed the tension in the courtroom as she watched Judge Thompson enter and take his seat. The jury filed in, clearly anticipating what they would hear that morning.

"Ms. Sanchez," Judge Thompson said, his voice resonating through the room, "you may call your next witness."

Gabriela rose. "Your Honor, the defense calls Stephen Penbrooke."

Gabriela heard murmurs as Penbrooke entered, escorted by the bailiff. He walked in like he'd rather be somewhere else. His eyes moved over the room, not stopping on anyone. He raised his hand for the oath, but didn't seem to care much about the formality.

Gabriela didn't waste time. "Mr. Penbrooke, state your name and occupation for the record."

"Stephen Penbrooke," he said, leaning back in the chair. "Businessman."

"Mr. Penbrooke, you knew Ethan Reyes, correct?"

"Yes," Penbrooke said without looking at her. "We had some professional dealings."

"And were you aware that Mr. Reyes was investigating certain financial transactions involving companies you control?"

"He asked some questions," Penbrooke conceded, sounding annoyed.

"Questions that could have exposed irregularities, perhaps even illegal activities?" Gabriela pressed.

"That's a rather dramatic interpretation," Penbrooke scoffed. "He was simply looking into standard business practices."

"Standard business practices that involved shell companies and offshore accounts?" Gabriela asked, her skepticism clear.

"Mr. Penbrooke," Gabriela began, her voice calm but firm, "you've stated that Mr. Reyes's investigation was simply 'looking into standard business practices.' Is that correct?"

"Yes," Penbrooke replied, while rolling his eyes.

"And you've also stated that the financial transactions in question were 'perfectly legal and common practices.' Is that also correct?"

"Of course," Penbrooke said, sounding more defensive.

"Yet, when I asked about the potential impact of these transactions, you described my questions as 'rather dramatic interpretations.' Could you explain why you find those questions dramatic?"

"Because they imply wrongdoing where none exists," Penbrooke replied.

"And when I asked about whether these practices were something you wanted kept hidden, you responded, 'I have nothing to hide.' Is that correct?"

"Yeah, that's what I said."

"Mr. Penbrooke, you are stating that Reyes's investigation was routine, that the transactions were legal, and that you have nothing to hide. However, you are also characterizing my questions as 'dramatic interpretations' and displaying a clear reluctance to engage directly with the details of those transactions. Could you explain this discrepancy?"

Penbrooke hesitated before asserting. "There's no discrepancy. I'm simply stating the facts."

"The facts, or your interpretation of them?" Gabriela asked, her voice low. "Your Honor, Mr. Penbrooke's responses are consistently dismissive and evasive, demonstrating a clear unwillingness to provide direct answers. This pattern of behavior, coupled with his characterization of my questions, indicates a level of hostility that warrants his designation as an adverse witness."

Gabriela turned back to Penbrooke. “Let’s talk about the night Ethan Reyes died. Isn’t it true you were near the South Dallas alley where Mr. Reyes was found that night?”

Penbrooke’s composure cracked slightly. He drummed his fingers on the table. “I might have been in the general area. But I didn’t see Reyes.”

“Why were you in that area, Mr. Penbrooke?”

“Personal business.”

“Personal business in an alley in South Dallas, the same night Reyes was murdered?”

“It had nothing to do with him.”

“Yet you didn’t think to mention this to the police? When they were investigating his murder?”

Penbrooke paused before answering. “It wasn’t relevant.”

“Not relevant, or were you afraid of what they might find?” Gabriela asked, her voice low.

Penbrooke straightened in his chair. “I have nothing to hide.”

“Then, why lie about being in the area?”

Penbrooke remained silent.

“Did you have any involvement in Ethan Reyes’s death?” Gabriela asked.

“No,” Penbrooke said forcefully.

“Were you aware of what Ethan Reyes was investigating before his death?”

“I invoke my Fifth Amendment right.”

“Did you take any steps to obstruct Ethan Reyes’s investigation?”

“I invoke my Fifth Amendment right.”

“No further questions, Your Honor.” Gabriela stepped back, her gaze sweeping over the jury, assessing their reactions. She had planted the seeds of doubt, and Penbrooke’s arrogance had worked against him.

Judge Thompson looked over at Laura Mitchell. “Ms. Mitchell, you may cross-examine now.”

Mitchell kept her tone even, nothing like the way Gabriela had pressed him. “Mr. Penbrooke,” she began, her voice steady, “you’ve heard Ms. Sanchez’s insinuations. Let’s clarify a few things. You testified that you were in the ‘general area’ of South Dallas the night Mr. Reyes died. Can you define ‘general area?’”

Penbrooke regained some composure, his tone firm. “It’s a large part of the city. I have business interests there. It’s not uncommon for me to be in that part of town.”

Mitchell nodded as if conceding a point. “So, being in the general area doesn’t necessarily mean you were near the alley where Mr. Reyes was found?”

“Absolutely not,” Penbrooke replied. “It’s a vast area.”

Mitchell paused briefly, allowing the jury to process the context. “South Dallas itself is a sprawling part of the city, including many businesses and residential areas. Just being in the area doesn’t place you at the crime scene.”

“Exactly,” Penbrooke agreed. “It’s a big place.”

Mitchell shifted slightly, leaning forward. “To be precise, Mr. Penbrooke, can you tell the jury exactly where you were in South Dallas that night? What specific location were you at?”

Penbrooke hesitated just a moment before replying. “I was at a warehouse near the industrial district. One of the properties I manage.”

Mitchell nodded, appearing thoughtful. “And what business brought you to that warehouse that evening?”

"I was meeting with a contractor about some repairs. There had been a break-in a few weeks prior, and I wanted to assess the damage and discuss security upgrades."

Mitchell continued with a calm, almost conversational tone. "And how long were you at that location?"

"About an hour, maybe a little longer."

Mitchell tilted her head slightly. "And did you meet anyone else while you were there, aside from the contractor?"

"No, just him. We went over the repairs, looked at the security footage from the break-in, and discussed a timeline for the work."

Mitchell made a brief note on her pad before continuing. "You testified earlier that you did not immediately disclose this to the police. Can you explain why?"

Penbrooke shifted in his seat, his tone defensive. "I didn't think it was relevant. The police were focused on the alley where Reyes was found. I was blocks away. I didn't see anything or hear anything related to the murder."

Mitchell gave a slight nod of understanding. "So, your reluctance to disclose your presence in South Dallas was not an attempt to hide anything, but rather because you genuinely didn't think it mattered?"

"Yes," Penbrooke replied, his tone firm. "I didn't think being at one of my properties would be important."

Mitchell maintained eye contact, reinforcing Penbrooke's rational explanation. "And earlier, Ms. Sanchez suggested that your presence in South Dallas that night was somehow incriminating. You did not disclose it to the police because it didn't seem relevant at the time, is that correct?"

"Yes," Penbrooke said, more confident now. "I was nowhere near the alley where he was found."

Mitchell moved on, keeping her voice steady. "Regarding the financial transactions Ms. Sanchez questioned, you testified they were legal business practices. Can you explain why these practices, such as the use of shell companies and offshore accounts, are not inherently suspicious?"

Penbrooke responded confidently, "These are standard operating procedures for international transactions. Any large corporation uses them for legitimate business purposes."

Mitchell gave him a reassuring glance. "Ms. Sanchez suggested you were 'afraid of what the police might find.' Were you afraid, Mr. Penbrooke?"

"Of course not. I cooperated fully with the investigation."

Mitchell gave a slight nod. "You also testified that you invoked your Fifth Amendment right when asked about Mr. Reyes's investigation. Could you explain why you did that?"

Penbrooke straightened slightly. "I was advised by my attorney to protect my legal rights. It's a legal precaution to protect myself from unfounded accusations. Invoking the Fifth doesn't mean I'm guilty of anything."

Mitchell maintained her calm demeanor. "As a businessman, you're accustomed to being cautious in legal matters, aren't you?"

Penbrooke agreed, his tone more confident. "Absolutely. It's important to protect myself from baseless allegations."

Mitchell allowed the statement to settle before continuing. "So, when Ms. Sanchez suggested that your presence in South Dallas at that time was significant, you didn't immediately disclose it to the police because it didn't seem relevant. Is that correct?"

"Yes," Penbrooke said firmly. "I was in a large area of the city, not near the alley. I didn't think it mattered."

Mitchell shifted her stance slightly, looking back at the jury. "Ms. Sanchez also implied that your use of offshore accounts and shell companies indicated wrongdoing. But would you say that her questions were framed in a way to make standard business practices appear suspicious?"

Penbrooke didn't hesitate. "Yes. She made routine transactions sound like something illegal."

Mitchell kept her tone composed. "You categorically deny any involvement in Mr. Reyes's death?"

"Yes," he replied without hesitation. "I had no reason to harm him."

Mitchell gave a brief, satisfied nod. "And do you have any reason to want to obstruct justice in the case of Mr. Reyes's death?"

"None whatsoever."

Mitchell glanced at the jury one last time, her voice still calm and measured. "No further questions, Your Honor."

"Ms. Sanchez, are there any more questions you'd like to ask the witness?"

Gabriela thought she had to counter what Mitchell had accomplished. "Yes, Your Honor."

"Mr. Penbrooke," Gabriela began, her voice calm but sharp, "you mentioned a warehouse in the industrial district. Can you provide the exact address of this warehouse?"

Penbrooke hesitated, as if uneasy. "I don't recall the exact address offhand."

"You don't recall?" Gabriela asked, her tone incredulous. "A property you own, visited on the night of a murder, and you don't recall the address?"

"It's one of many properties," Penbrooke said, his voice defensive. "I don't memorize every address."

"But you remember meeting with a contractor?" Gabriela pressed. "And discussing security footage?"

"Yes."

"And the contractor's name?"

"I don't remember."

"You don't remember the address, nor the name of the person you met, on the night of a murder, in the same general area of the murder?" Gabriela asked, her voice incredulous. "Is that your testimony?"

"Yes," Penbrooke said, his jaw tightening.

"And this break-in you mentioned," Gabriela continued. "Was a police report filed?"

"I believe so."

"Do you have a copy of that police report?"

"I don't have it on me."

"You don't have it on you. You don't remember the address of the property, or the name of the contractor, but you remember the break-in?"

"Yes."

"Mr. Penbrooke, you've stated that the use of shell companies and offshore accounts is 'standard operating procedure.' But is it also standard operating procedure to use these accounts to move large sums of money in the weeks surrounding a murder investigation?"

"That's a speculative question," Penbrooke said.

"It's a question about the timing of those transactions," Gabriela countered. "Timing that coincides with Ethan Reyes's death. You've also stated that you 'cooperated fully' with the police investigation. Did you inform them of your presence in South Dallas?"

"Eventually," Penbrooke said, with a defensive tone.

"Eventually, after you were compelled to do by a subpoena?" Gabriela asked. "That's your definition of 'fully cooperating?'"

"I answered their questions," Penbrooke said.

"And you invoked your Fifth Amendment right when asked about Ethan Reyes's investigation. Why?"

"To protect myself from baseless accusations."

"Baseless accusations, or relevant questions about your involvement in a murder investigation?" Gabriela asked, her voice sharp. "No further questions, Your Honor."

"Ms. Mitchell, any questions?"

"...No further questions, Your Honor," Mitchell said, ending her cross-examination. She turned to Penbrooke, a subtle nod passing between them, a silent acknowledgment of their shared strategy.

Judge Thompson surveyed the courtroom, his gaze lingering on the jury. "We'll take a brief recess. Ten minutes. Please remember my instructions."

The courtroom buzzed with activity. Gabriela remained still. Her eyes were fixed on Penbrooke. Something about his demeanor, the way he'd answered Mitchell's questions, didn't sit right. It wasn't just arrogance. It was something he had carefully rehearsed.

When the court reconvened, Judge Thompson addressed Gabriela. "Ms. Sanchez, you may call your next witness."

Gabriela rose. "Your Honor, the defense rests."

Judge Thompson turned to Laura Mitchell. "Ms. Mitchell, does the prosecution have any rebuttal?"

Mitchell stood. "No, Your Honor, the prosecution has no rebuttal at this time."

"Very well," Judge Thompson said, glancing at the clock. "Ladies and gentlemen of the jury, we will conclude today's session. Please return tomorrow morning at 9:00 AM for closing arguments and jury instructions. Do not discuss the case amongst yourselves or with anyone else. The court is adjourned."

As the courtroom emptied, Morrison approached Gabriela, a look in his eyes she couldn't quite decipher. "Ms. Sanchez," he began, his voice low, just above the murmur of the remaining people. "There's something I need to tell you... something I haven't told anyone. It's about last night. I received a text."

Gabriela's grip on her briefcase tightened. "A text? What did it say?"

Morrison shot a look toward the departing jurors, then back to Gabriela, his expression grim. "It was a threat, Ms. Sanchez. They said even if I walk out of here a free man, it is not over. And they mentioned Las Palmas, something only someone close to Reyes's investigation could know."

Chapter Twenty-Eight

"Threatened? What kind of things did they mention, Mr. Morrison?" Her voice was low, barely audible above the murmur as the last few spectators filed out of the courtroom. The pace of the day in court faded, replaced by a sense that something was wrong.

Morrison's eyes scanned the emptying courtroom, as if searching for someone. He lowered his voice even further. "They... they mentioned the informant at the warehouse. The one who gave you the flash drive. They knew details... details that weren't public." He swallowed hard. "They also mentioned my... my business dealings in Mexico. Specifics. It was like they were reading Reyes's notes."

Gabriela caught the implication immediately. If someone else knew the details of Reyes's investigation and was still threatening Morrison, they weren't just after him. "Did the text say what they wanted?" she asked, pushing aside her initial shock as her lawyer instincts took over.

Morrison nodded grimly. "The message was clear: 'An acquittal is just the beginning. Silence is your only protection.'" He looked directly at Gabriela. "Ms. Sanchez, I think... I think we've stirred up something much bigger than we realized."

Gabriela remained silent, running through the possibilities in her mind. She looked over at Hayes, who was slowly packing their briefcase. She caught his eye and gave a subtle shake of her head. He stopped what he was doing, concern clear on his face.

"We need to talk," Gabriela said quietly to both men. "But not here." The lingering presence of court staff and the possibility of others overhearing made her uneasy.

They gathered their things and walked out of the courtroom, Gabriela still thinking about what Morrison had just told her. The usual post-court debrief felt different, like there was something dangerous lurking. Gabriela insisted they discuss it in the relative privacy of the defense conference room.

That night, Gabriela's mind raced. The threat against Morrison was deeply unsettling. Was it connected to Penbrooke? Or was there another layer to Reyes's investigation that they hadn't uncovered? She tossed and turned, the cryptic message echoing in her thoughts.

The next morning, Gabriela arrived at the courthouse with a renewed sense of urgency. Hayes was already waiting in the courtroom, seated in the gallery. Gabriela's gaze scanned across the rows of spectators, a practiced habit. Then she noticed the Court TV reporter, her eyes locked directly on Gabriela, a professional detachment in her expression as she observed every move. It was a stark reminder that every nuance of this trial was being broadcast to a national audience.

The moment for closing arguments had arrived. She thought for a moment, preparing for the task ahead. This would be her last chance to persuade the jury to keep her client out of prison. She'd been in this position before, and she had prepared for months for this moment in the trial.

The courtroom doors opened, and the jury filed in...

"Please be seated," Judge Thompson said, his voice resonating through the quiet courtroom. "Ladies and gentlemen of the jury, we have now reached the final stage of this trial: closing arguments. This is your opportunity to hear the attorneys summarize the evidence presented and argue their respective positions.

"Ms. Mitchell," Judge Thompson continued, turning towards the prosecution's table, "as the representative of the State, you will present your closing argument first." He paused. "Following Ms. Mitchell, Ms. Sanchez will present the closing argument on behalf of the defense. Because the State bears the burden of proof in this matter, Ms. Mitchell will then have the opportunity to offer a rebuttal to Ms. Sanchez's argument.

"Ms. Mitchell," Judge Thompson concluded, gesturing towards the prosecutor's podium, "you may proceed."

Laura Mitchell rose from her seat, her posture confident and her gaze steady as she approached the jury box. She laid her notes on the podium and looked directly at the jurors.

"Ladies and gentlemen of the jury, for the past several days, we have meticulously presented to you the evidence in this case, a case about accountability, about justice for Ethan Reyes, a man silenced before his time. The defense has attempted to sow seeds of doubt, to divert your attention, and to paint a picture that simply does not align with the irrefutable facts before you. But I stand here today to remind you of those facts, the solid, unwavering pillars upon which the prosecution's case rests.

"Let's begin with the most tangible and damning piece of evidence: the murder weapon. The .357 caliber revolver that ended Ethan Reyes's life was not some anonymous firearm. It was the defendant's gun. Phillip Morrison owned that weapon. The defense has conceded this, yet they ask you to believe it was merely a coincidence, a stroke of extraordinarily bad luck, that his stolen gun appeared at the scene of the crime. They suggest a frame job, a shadowy figure who conveniently stole Mr. Morrison's specific weapon and used it in a way that would undeniably point back to him. But ask yourselves, is that logical? Is that reasonable? Or is it a desperate attempt to explain away an inconvenient truth? The truth is, the defendant had the means to commit this crime, and that means was literally in his possession until very shortly before Mr. Reyes was killed.

“Beyond the weapon itself, we presented video evidence. While perhaps not a crystal-clear image, the footage captured near the alley where Mr. Reyes was found depicts a figure whose stature and build are strikingly consistent with that of the defendant, Phillip Morrison, present in the crucial time frame surrounding the murder. The defense would have you dismiss this, to say it could be anyone. But consider the context, the other pieces of the puzzle falling into place. This video places someone resembling the defendant near the scene when Ethan Reyes met his untimely end. It is another brick in the wall of evidence against Mr. Morrison.

“Furthermore, the forensic evidence speaks volumes. No one disputes that blood belonging to Ethan Reyes was found in the trunk of the defendant’s vehicle. How did the victim’s blood get into the defendant’s trunk? The defense has offered no credible explanation for this damning finding. They have asked you to speculate about shadowy figures and elaborate frame-ups, but they have provided no evidence to counter the stark reality of Mr. Reyes’s blood being present in the personal vehicle of the accused. This is not circumstantial; this is direct evidence linking the defendant to the victim in a significant and incriminating way.

"The timeline of that fateful night also reveals a glaring hole in the defendant's narrative. Mr. Morrison testified that he left his office around 8:10 PM, yet he did not arrive at the charity gala until approximately 9:30 PM. That is a significant hour and twenty minutes of unaccounted-for time. Where was Mr. Morrison during this crucial period? He initially claimed to be making phone calls, then later changed his story to doing paperwork, neither of which was supported by his own phone records. The defense asks you to overlook this significant gap, to believe it was simply filled with mundane activities he cannot now recall due to the stress of these proceedings. But consider the timing. This missing hour directly overlaps with the estimated time of Ethan Reyes's murder. The defendant had the opportunity to commit this crime during this very window of unaccounted-for time.

"Adding to the suspicion surrounding his movements is the circuitous route Mr. Morrison claimed to have taken from his office to the gala. Instead of a direct path, he described a route that took him through areas that, as the evidence showed, were near the alley where Ethan Reyes was last seen. Why the detour, ladies and gentlemen? Why the indirect path to a social event, he claimed, he was eager to attend, even if late? The logical inference is that his route was not about efficiency or convenience, but the opportunity to encounter Ethan Reyes and take damning evidence from him.

"Finally, let us not forget the testimony of Marissa Ortega, the defendant's own executive assistant. She bravely came before you and testified that she saw Mr. Morrison with a handgun in his office the day before Mr. Reyes was murdered. The defendant attempted to downplay this, to suggest it was an antique. But Ms. Ortega was clear in her recollection. This testimony directly contradicts the defendant's claim that the only handgun he owned was the one reported stolen weeks prior. It demonstrates that Mr. Morrison possessed a handgun around the time of the murder, further undermining his credibility and strengthening the link between him and a weapon.

"Ladies and gentlemen, the defense has tried to point fingers elsewhere, to weave tales of elaborate conspiracies. But look at the evidence. The defendant's gun. His presence near the scene. The victim's blood was in the trunk of his car. A crucial hour of unaccounted-for time. A circuitous route near the crime scene. And his possession of a handgun just before the murder. Individually, each piece of evidence is significant. Taken together, they form an undeniable and compelling picture of guilt. The prosecution has presented a case built not on speculation, but on solid, verifiable facts. Do not be swayed by smoke and mirrors. Hold the defendant accountable for his actions. Justice for Ethan Reyes demands nothing less. We urge you to find the defendant, Phillip Morrison, guilty as charged."

When Mitchell concluded her argument, she returned to her seat at the prosecution's table. Judge Thompson then turned his attention to Gabriela.

"Ms. Sanchez," Judge Thompson said, his voice neutral but carrying the importance of the moment, "you may now present your closing argument on behalf of the defendant."

Gabriela rose from the defense table, leaving her notes behind. She walked with a measured pace towards the jury box, her eyes meeting theirs.

"We've listened to testimony, scrutinized evidence, and watched the prosecution weave a tale they desperately want you to believe about my client, Phillip Morrison, being a cold and calculating killer.

"But that story? It's built on sand. It's a desperate attempt to patch together bits and pieces that don't fit, to force a conclusion they can't prove. They're selling you a narrative stitched together with speculation, assumptions, and unanswered questions, hoping you won't look too closely at the gaps in their story. But you are smarter than that. You know better than to accept a story just because it's repeated often enough.

"Now, let's address the gun evidence. It's the centerpiece of the prosecution's case. Yes, the .357 caliber revolver used to kill Ethan

Reyes was registered to Phillip Morrison. No one disputes that. But here's what the prosecution conveniently glossed over: Mr. Morrison reported that the gun was stolen three weeks before the murder. Three weeks. He did the responsible thing. He notified the authorities, documented the theft, and cooperated fully.

"The prosecution wants you to believe it's just a coincidence that the same gun shows up at the crime scene, as if Morrison somehow staged the theft, only to use it in broad daylight when anyone with half a mind would know it could be traced back to him. Does that make sense? No. It's not logical, it's not reasonable, and it's not supported by evidence.

"Let's think about this: if you wanted to frame someone for murder, what would be the easiest way? Steal their gun. Make sure it's the weapon that shows up when the crime is committed. Use their own property to make it look like they pulled the trigger. Somebody wanted Phillip Morrison to take the fall for this crime. Somebody with motive, with opportunity, and with enough cunning to know how the evidence would be interpreted.

"This wasn't a coincidence. It was a calculated move. Whoever took that gun knew exactly what they were doing. They knew that using Mr. Morrison's own weapon would send the investigation straight to him. That's not random. That's a setup, plain and simple.

"Why frame Morrison? Who would do that, and why? We know Ethan Reyes was uncovering financial irregularities. He found offshore accounts, shell companies, and unexplained cash movements all leading to Stephen Penbrooke. The same man who couldn't recall the address of his own warehouse. The same man who went silent when asked where the money led. And the same man who, by no coincidence, was in the general area when Reyes was killed.

"Penbrooke had the most to lose from Ethan Reyes's investigation. He had every reason to want Reyes gone. What better way to deflect attention than to point the finger at someone else? Someone like Phillip Morrison. Steal his gun. Wait for the right moment. Leave the weapon where it would be found. That is a setup, plain and simple.

"But why choose Phillip Morrison? Why frame him? The answer is clear. Morrison made for the perfect distraction. As long as law enforcement stayed focused on him, no one would be looking into Penbrooke's finances. No one would be asking why large sums of money flowed through offshore accounts out of sight and out of reach.

"Blaming Morrison gave Penbrooke exactly what he needed. Time. Time to cover his tracks. Time to slip away while the wrong man faced the consequences.

"And let's not forget Ethan Reyes's investigation posed a direct threat to Penbrooke's business. He had the motive. He had the opportunity. And he had every reason to let someone else take the fall. And one final point on Mr. Penbrooke. He is right-handed.

"They paraded witnesses before you, pointing out minor inconsistencies, as if the human mind works like a tape recorder. Haven't we all, at times, gotten our memories a little mixed up? Especially when pressed, scrutinized, and grilled by people determined to find fault. The prosecution wants you to believe that these natural human frailties somehow equal guilt. That's not justice. That's grasping at straws.

"Now, let's talk about Mr. Morrison's alibi. The prosecution has tried to poke holes in it, focusing on a missing hour and suggesting it was filled with sinister deeds. But let's be clear: Mr. Morrison testified he was en route to the charity gala after a late business meeting. And his wife, Elizabeth, stood before you and corroborated that he was expected at the gala that evening, albeit arriving late. They were planning to attend together, a fact that underscores his intention to be present at a public event. The prosecution has focused on what they don't know about that hour, asking you to fill that void with suspicion. But I ask you, ladies and gentlemen, is it the defense's burden to account for every minute of a person's day when they are not directly implicated in a crime? The prosecution must prove its case. They must show you, with concrete evidence, that Mr. Morrison was not where he said he was and that he used that time to commit murder. They have failed to do that. They have offered speculation, but speculation is not evidence.

"Remember how he walked in here with that air of superiority, like he thought he could just charm his way through this?

"But let me ask you something plain and simple about Mr. Penbrooke: if you have nothing to hide, why act like you just stepped barefoot onto the Central Expressway in August? That kind of heat makes you jumpy, doesn't it?

"That's how Mr. Penbrooke seemed up there on that stand. He couldn't even recall the address of his own warehouse. Does that sound credible to you?

"And the contractor he supposedly met that night? He couldn't remember his name. Come on now. Don't you think that's just a little too convenient?

"South Dallas is big. Yet he just so happened to be in the 'general area' where Ethan Reyes was found dead? What a coincidence. Or is it more than that?

"My grandmother used to say that if you see one mouse, there are a dozen more hiding in the walls. One shaky alibi? Maybe. Two or three things that don't add up with Mr. Penbrooke? Now, we've got something worth examining.

"He can't clearly explain his whereabouts. He can't recall key details from that night. And he clammed up tighter than a drum when asked about the very investigation that threatened his own business.

"Does that sound like a man with nothing to hide? Or does it sound like someone whose story is falling apart piece by piece?

"Don't let the prosecution's laser focus on Mr. Morrison blind you to the very real questions surrounding Stephen Penbrooke. He is the loose thread in this case, the prosecution hopes you won't pull.

"Ladies and gentlemen, the prosecution wants you to focus all your attention on Phillip Morrison while they try to brush aside Stephen Penbrooke's inconsistencies and suspicious behavior. They hope that you'll forget about the convenient memory lapses, the vague whereabouts, and the man who seemed a little too slick for his own good. They want you to look one way, while the real questions in this case are staring you right in the face.

"Ask yourselves, why would a man who has everything to lose, with resources, lawyers, and powerful friends, choose to walk into an alley and murder a journalist himself? Why would he bring his own gun? Why would he ever leave blood in the trunk of his car? Why would he take that kind of risk when there are ten easier ways to silence a critic? He didn't. Someone wanted you to believe he did, and they did it well.

"And here's the crux of it: Our justice system is designed to protect the innocent. It demands that the prosecution prove guilt beyond a reasonable doubt. Not a little doubt, not a hunch, but proof so solid that it leaves no other reasonable explanation. That's what you pledged to uphold. And that's why we're here.

"We are here, and your duty is to make sure that nobody gets convicted based on stories, guesses, and distractions. They have not met their burden. I ask you to return a verdict of not guilty. Thank you."

Gabriela was exhausted. For the last two months, she had worked on Morrison's case seven days a week, taking no time off for dinner out or golf. Her only outside activity had been Mass on Saturday evening or early Sunday morning. Despite the adrenaline still coursing through her veins, the strain of the trial settled heavily on her shoulders as she returned to the defense table. She glanced at Morrison, whose face was a mask of anxiety. Hayes gave her a small, encouraging nod.

In her rebuttal, Ms. Mitchell addressed the defense's arguments, reiterating the key pieces of evidence against Phillip Morrison. She emphasized the ownership of the murder weapon, the video footage placing someone of his stature near the scene, the presence of Ethan

Reyes's blood in Morrison's car trunk, and the significant unaccounted-for time in his alibi. Mitchell argued that the defense's theories of a frame-up were unsubstantiated and urged the jury to focus on the concrete evidence directly linking Morrison to the crime.

Following Mitchell's rebuttal, Judge Thompson then addressed the jury with his instructions.

Judge Thompson carefully and deliberately instructed the jury on the relevant laws pertaining to the case, including the definition of murder, the burden of proof resting solely with the prosecution, the requirement of proof beyond a reasonable doubt, and the importance of considering all the evidence presented. He explained the role of circumstantial evidence and the need to weigh the credibility of each witness. He cautioned them against speculation or allowing personal biases to influence their decision. Finally, he explained the process of jury deliberation and the requirement of reaching a unanimous verdict.

As Judge Thompson finished his instructions, he turned to the jury.

"Ladies and gentlemen, you will now retire to the jury room to begin your deliberations. Please select a foreperson and begin your discussions. The bailiff will escort you."

The jury filed out of the courtroom, their faces unreadable. Gabriela watched them go, uneasy about what they might decide. Despite the arguments she had presented, the prosecution's case had been strong.

Later, as Gabriela stood to leave, the threats Morrison had mentioned replayed in her mind. Was he telling the truth? The details he cited about the informant and his Mexican dealings were certainly concerning. But why now, after the evidence was presented? Was it a last-ditch effort to sway her, or was there a genuine danger? The timing felt odd. If there was a real threat connected to Reyes's investigation, wouldn't it have surfaced earlier?

A part of her wondered if Morrison, facing the possibility of a guilty verdict, was grasping at straws, trying to create a narrative that would somehow exonerate him even if the jury found him guilty. Yet, the specific details he mentioned gave her pause. She couldn't dismiss it entirely, but she couldn't fully understand it either. The trial was essentially over; the jury held their fate in their hands. What could these threats accomplish now? Gabriela left the courthouse, unsettled. Morrison's words kept running through her mind, undercutting the satisfaction she usually had after closing arguments.

Chapter Twenty-Nine

Gabriela leaned against the wooden table, arms crossed, her gaze fixed on the door. Hayes leaned back in his chair, eyes closed, the only sign of the coiled spring within him was the rhythmic press of his thumb against his index finger.

Morrison sat hunched in the corner, his head buried in his hands, a posture he'd adopted for most of the past three days. Elizabeth sat beside him, her hand a constant, slow circle on his back, a steady presence beside him. "They've been out a while," she said, her voice a fragile whisper.

Hayes opened one eye, his practical side showing again. "That's not a bad thing. Means they're taking it seriously."

Gabriela pushed a stray strand of hair behind her ear, the sleepless nights leaving a gritty feeling behind her eyes. "Sometimes the longer they take, the more they question the prosecution's story. They're wrestling with the reasonable doubt."

But even as she spoke the words, a seed of uncertainty worried her. It was only the first day. They could take several more before reaching a verdict. Had she done enough? Should she have pushed harder on Penbrooke's financial records? His hesitation at her question about the offshore accounts made her wonder if she should have pressed him more.

Morrison finally looked up, his eyes bloodshot and unsteady. "But what if they're stuck? What if someone in there thinks I'm guilty? What if they can't agree?"

Hayes shrugged, a weary smile touching his lips. "Then we will do it all over again. Look, I didn't originate this thought, but I'll share it with you. The only door we care about right now is the back one. As long as you walk out with us, that's a win."

Elizabeth's hand stilled on Morrison's back. "But if they don't see it, what happens to us?" The question stayed with her, hung in the air, heavy with unspoken fears of prison sentences and shattered lives.

Gabriela walked over, her voice softer now, tinged with the weariness of the long wait. "I believe they'll see it. They have to. We've given them every reason to doubt the state's case. Reasonable doubt is the highest hurdle they have to clear. We did our job. Now it's up to them." But the conviction in her voice felt thinner than she would have liked.

Hayes looked at Gabriela, a hint of admiration in his tired eyes. "Smartest thing you've said all day," he muttered, the edge in his voice softened by shared exhaustion.

The first night, Gabriela drove back to her home in North Dallas. She was exhausted from the weeks of work, the tension from the trial, and now from waiting for the jury. She barely slept.. In her thoughts, she replayed Mitchell's confident assertions, the jurors' impassive faces, and her own closing arguments echoing in the empty space.

Hayes called twice, his attempts at reassurance sounding hollow even to his own ears. Gabriela knew he was as tightly wound as she was, the bravado of the courtroom long gone. She wanted to believe his stories about long deliberations leading to acquittals, but each story felt like it was missing that one crucial piece that Morrison's case lacked: certainty.

Two hours later, Gabriela found herself back at her small office. The silence there was different, a familiar quiet that offered a temporary respite from the suffocating tension of the courthouse. Lucia, her assistant, looked up with sympathetic eyes. "Anything yet, Gabriela?"

Gabriela shook her head, managing a weak smile. "Just waiting, Lucia. The hardest part."

"Anything I can do?" Lucia asked, her hand hovering near the phone.

"Just keep things running here," Gabriela said. "And maybe make some strong coffee. I have a feeling it's going to be a long day." She tried to focus on some pending paperwork, a stack of less urgent files mocking her with their normalcy. But her mind kept drifting back to the jury room, imagining the hushed deliberations, the clash of opinions, the slow march towards a verdict.

On day two at the courthouse, the morning passed with stale coffee and forced small talk. Hayes tried his best to maintain a semblance of optimism, recounting tales of juries deliberating for days before returning a not-guilty verdict. But the stories felt increasingly hollow, the forced laughter echoing the underlying fear. Morrison remained withdrawn, his hope visibly dwindling with each passing hour. Elizabeth continued to write in her notebook, her expression unreadable.

Late in the afternoon, the bailiff's message sent a jolt of adrenaline through the waiting room: the jury had a question. The clarification they sought about the timeline of the stolen gun report felt like a double-edged sword. It meant they were scrutinizing the evidence, which was good. But it also suggested that at least one juror was grappling with the defense's central argument of a setup. Morrison's face, already pale, seemed to lose all color.

By the end of the second day, the familiar routine of being sent home without a verdict felt less like a reprieve and more like a deepening of the torment. Gabriela's phone buzzed with more messages, but she still couldn't bring herself to engage. The well-meaning encouragement felt like a reminder of the immense pressure she was under.

On the third day, Gabriela, Hayes, and the Morrisons all sat silent in the waiting room. The air conditioner kicked on and off, its hum the only noise. Every cough and whisper amplified the tension in the room.

Morrison sat hunched, his shoulders slumped, the color drained from his face. Elizabeth's hand, once a source of comfort, now lay limp in her lap, her gaze fixed on the floor, a single tear tracing a path down her cheek. Hayes drummed a nervous rhythm on the table, his eyes darting from the clock to the door, to Morrison, and back again, a silent plea etched on his face. He was a bundle of nerves, flipping through his well-worn notes that offered no fresh insight. Gabriela stared blankly at the wall, her thoughts as chaotic as the paint chips. Each passing hour felt like a step closer to an unknown precipice.

Around noon, Morrison finally broke the oppressive silence, his voice barely a whisper. "What if they find me guilty?"

Hayes offered a weak shrug. "Then we will appeal." Do it all over again. But the words lacked conviction.

"Will I be sent to prison while we appeal? I don't know if I can survive in prison," Morrison said, the quiet despair in his voice cutting through the strained atmosphere.

Gabriela reached out and placed a hand on his shoulder, the fabric of his jacket feeling thin and fragile beneath her fingers. "You don't have to think about that right now. We're not there yet." But she had some of the same thoughts.

Elizabeth wiped a tear from the corner of her eye, quickly turning her head so her husband wouldn't see. Gabriela pretended not to notice, her own throat tight with a mixture of sympathy and dread.

Just after three, the door to the waiting room creaked open, and the bailiff entered again. This time, his usual neutral expression was replaced by a gravity that made the air in the room stand still. Serious. Final.

"The jury's reached a verdict."

Chapter Thirty

Gabriela stood at the defense counsel table, every muscle in her body coiled tight. Beside her, at the same table, Phillip Morrison sat hunched forward, his hands folded like a prayer, staring down at the surface.

In the first row of the gallery, directly behind the defense counsel table, sat Elizabeth Morrison, with their children, Andrea and Phillip, Jr.

Across the room, at the prosecution counsel table, Laura Mitchell presented a facade of rigid composure, her jaw clenched, her eyes locked on the jury door. Behind the prosecution table, in the first row of the gallery on that side of the courtroom, sat the family of Ethan Reyes.

The courtroom held an unnerving stillness, as if the very air had thickened, anticipating the pronouncement. Even the reporters, typically a low hum of rustling and whispered speculation, seemed frozen, their pens poised above their notebooks, momentarily suspended. A lone, muffled cough from the gallery punctuated the silence, sending a sharp thrum of adrenaline through Gabriela's veins.

The door creaked open, the sound amplified in the tense quiet. The bailiff stepped inside, offered a curt nod to Judge Thompson, and then held the door ajar as the jury filed in. Twelve faces, solemn and pale, moved in a slow, almost dreamlike procession to their seats. Gabriela's gaze flickered from one juror to the next, a desperate, silent plea for any flicker of understanding, any hint of their decision. Their eyes remained fixed ahead, avoiding all contact.

Judge Thompson adjusted his glasses, his voice cutting through the silence, steady and deep. "Madam Foreperson, has the jury reached a unanimous verdict?"

The woman in the front row, short with silver hair pulled back tight and a perpetually pinched expression, offered a single, decisive nod. "Yes, Your Honor."

"Please hand the verdict form to the bailiff."

The bailiff moved with deliberate slowness across to the jury box, his footsteps echoing softly on the polished floor. He took the folded paper with careful reverence and carried it to the judge. Gabriela's heart hammered against her ribs, each beat a painful, insistent drum. She found herself holding her breath, her lungs burning for air. Her palms slid against the cool, smooth wood of the table.

Judge Thompson unfolded the paper, his brow furrowing slightly as he adjusted his glasses once more, his gaze scanning the words. He handed the paper to the bailiff, who brought it back to the jury foreperson.

Judge Thompson looked out at the gallery. "When the jury foreperson reads the verdict, I expect no outbursts from the gallery."

There was dead silence. Judge Thompson cleared his throat, the brief pause stretching into an eternity. "Will the defendant please rise?" Gabriela and Morrison stood behind the counsel table.

"Madam Foreperson, please read the jury's verdict."

"In the matter of the State of Texas versus Phillip Morrison, on the charge of murder in the first degree, the jury finds the defendant…"

The silence in the courtroom intensified, pressing down like a physical weight. Gabriela's vision swam for a moment. Elizabeth gasped softly, her hand flying to her mouth. Phillip Morrison, standing beside Gabriela, remained still, his gaze fixed on the table in front of him.

"…Not guilty."

For a long, suspended moment, nothing moved. The words hung in the air, fragile and unbelievable. Then, a more audible gasp escaped Elizabeth, tears welling and then spilling down her cheeks. A shudder ran through Morrison, and his shoulders visibly relaxed as he exhaled. The sound seemed to carry with it the weight of the pressure he had finally released.

Hayes's hand slapped the table, a soft, almost involuntary sound, and a shaky breath that might have been a laugh escaped his lips. "Hell of a ride," he murmured, his eyes suddenly bright as he scrubbed at them with the back of his hand.

Mitchell's face tightened, the muscles in her jaw bunching. Her lips thinned into a hard, bitter line. She leaned back in her chair, her gaze already distant, perhaps anticipating the inevitable gauntlet of microphones and flashing cameras that awaited him outside. As the verdict was read, a flicker of something unreadable crossed Mitchell's face before settling back into its hardened composure.

The air in the courtroom, still and expectant, hit Gabriela with a wave of relief so intense her knees nearly buckled. Months of relentless preparation for this high-stakes trial, a pressure cooker of seven-day weeks and laser focus, suddenly eased after the verdict. Yet beneath the elation, a discordant note struck her. She glanced at Morrison, who had turned to embrace a weeping Elizabeth, his hand moving gently across her back. His fingers tapped a faint rhythm, almost imperceptible but achingly familiar. It was the same pattern he had traced on the conference table when recounting the night of the murder.

Her mind, sharp despite exhaustion, retraced those moments. Marissa had said Morrison seemed oddly calm after learning Reyes planned to publish an exposé about him. He was equally composed when discussing the stolen gun, steady in his claim that he had been framed. And always, that tapping. She had dismissed it as nerves, a tic under pressure. Now, watching him, she was not sure. The rhythm had never wavered. It did not look like stress. It looked rehearsed.

And the blood… Reyes's blood in Morrison's trunk. That had been the prosecution's hammer blow, the seemingly irrefutable link. But if Morrison was the murderer and he left Reyes in the alley, how did his blood get into Morrison's car? Unless… unless the blood got there inadvertently, some other way, a detail they had all overlooked. The questions swirled, a disquieting counterpoint to the courtroom's celebratory atmosphere. And then there were the threats… those anonymous calls, the feeling of being watched. Had they stopped with the verdict? Or was the danger still lurking, a consequence of digging too deep into the secrets of a powerful man, regardless of the trial's outcome?

Hayes leaned closer, his voice low and laced with triumph. "Relax, Gabriela. We did it."

She offered a weak nod, her gaze still fixed on Morrison, who was now speaking softly to Elizabeth, his expression almost serene. The nagging feeling persisted, a tiny seed of doubt taking root in the fertile ground of her lawyer's intuition. Had they truly achieved justice? Or had something vital been overlooked?

As Judge Thompson thanked and dismissed the visibly drained jury, Morrison turned to Gabriela, his eyes brimming with gratitude. "You saved my life," he whispered, his voice thick with emotion.

Gabriela managed a smile, though it felt brittle and unconvincing even to herself. "You were innocent, Mr. Morrison. The truth came out."

Morrison's gaze drifted past her, his face softening with a strange, almost detached quality. "Yeah," he murmured, his voice barely audible, as if speaking to himself. "Truth."

As the courtroom began to empty, Chuck Green appeared at the back, his eyes finding hers. He offered a small, relieved smile, but Gabriela found herself unable to fully reciprocate. Her gaze flickered back to Morrison, who was now surrounded by his family, his hand still, almost unconsciously, tapping that same rhythmic pattern against Elizabeth's arm. A sudden chill traced its way down Gabriela's spine.

Just then, Hayes caught her eye and subtly gestured towards the side door. He waited until the immediate crush of well-wishers around Morrison had thinned slightly before pulling Gabriela a few steps aside, his expression serious, his eyebrows raised in a way that conveyed more than words.

"Gabriela," he said quietly, his voice low and urgent. "Remember when Morrison testified about the antique Colt revolver that Marissa Ortega might have seen?"

Gabriela nodded, the image of Morrison on the stand flashing through her mind.

"After his testimony," Hayes continued, his gaze flicking towards Morrison and then back to Gabriela, "I took photos. Photos of that antique Colt, and photos of the .357 caliber revolver that was the actual murder weapon. I showed them to Marissa."

Gabriela's breath hitched. "And?"

Hayes's eyebrows lifted even higher, a knowing look in his eyes. "She pointed straight to the .38, Gabriela. No hesitation."

A cold knot formed in Gabriela's stomach, a sensation far more unsettling than the tension of the verdict. "But… the Dallas police… they never…"

Hayes's expression hardened, a hint of cynicism creeping into his voice. "No, they didn't. Funny, isn't it?" His gaze flickered back to Morrison, lingering for a moment before returning to Gabriela. The unspoken implication was that Morrison, with his considerable resources, might have ensured certain avenues of investigation remained unexplored.

"Oh, and one other thing I discovered."

"What's that?"

"Morrison played baseball at A&M."

"Okay."

"He was a switch hitter and had a higher batting average right-handed than left-handed."

Gabriela didn't respond right away. She was trying to remember whether Morrison had held his drink in his right hand or left hand when she first visited him at his mansion.

Her gaze locked on Hayes, but her focus had already shifted inward. The corner of her jaw tensed as if she were biting down on a thought. She crossed one arm over her waist, her fingers drumming once against the opposite elbow, slow and deliberate. When she finally spoke, her voice was steady, but her eyes had narrowed with the precision of someone rearranging puzzle pieces in real time.

"Any other pieces of news for me?"

"No, I think that's enough now that it's over."

"I still believe Morrison did not commit the murder."

"And why is that?" Hayes asked.

Gabriela looked at Hayes as her thoughts picked apart everything he had just said. "That doesn't add up," she said quietly, her voice measured. "Why would a man like Morrison, a billionaire with a public reputation and a legal team watching his every move, throw it all away to kill a reporter in an alley?"

She didn't wait for Hayes to answer.

"And if he did," she went on, "and left the body behind, why was the only trace of blood found in his trunk? Not on his clothes. Not on his hands. Not even a smear in the back seat."

She turned fully toward Hayes now. "He got to the gala minutes later, looking composed, surrounded by people, without anyone noticing anything unusual. No blood. No urgency. Nothing."

Her arms crossed. She looked briefly toward Morrison. "Whatever you've uncovered doesn't prove Morrison pulled the trigger."

Outside, the reporters swarmed, a hungry pack descending on the victorious defendant. Cameras flashed relentlessly, microphones thrust forward like accusing fingers. Hayes, ever the seasoned professional, stepped into the fray, deflecting questions and managing the chaos with practiced ease. Gabriela stayed back, the noise and the flashing lights feeling suddenly overwhelming. She needed a moment to process the whirlwind of the verdict and the disturbing new information from Hayes. Among the throng of journalists, she recognized the familiar face of a Court TV reporter, her camera operator already broadcasting live. Gabriela offered a brief, professional nod towards the camera, a tacit acknowledgment of the national attention this case had drawn.

Gabriela looked over at Phillip Morrison. His hand was still, almost unconsciously, tapping that same rhythmic pattern against Elizabeth's arm. A deeper chill settled over Gabriela.

The relief of the verdict felt tainted, overshadowed by the sense that the truth remained elusive, perhaps deliberately obscured. Had justice truly been served? The blood in the trunk… it was a puzzle that didn't fit the narrative of Morrison as the obvious killer, leaving the body in the alley. It suggested either a far more complex scenario or a deliberate act of framing. The trial might be over, but was she safe? Was her family safe?

* * *

Made in the USA
Monee, IL
10 November 2026

98003b20-c6a0-4d78-94c9-ec1a4887cf2bR01